The Social Body

The Social Body

Habit, Identity and Desire

Nick Crossley

SAGE Publications
London • Thousand Oaks • New Delhi

This book is written in memory of my Dad, Tony
Crossley (1943–1998), and for my Mum, Dot,
who has been so brave in bearing his loss.
It is dedicated to my wife, Michele.

SAGE Publications Ltd
6 Bonhill Street
London EC2A 4PU

SAGE Publications Inc
2455 Teller Road
Thousand Oaks, California 91320

SAGE Publications India Pvt Ltd
32, M-Block Market
Greater Kailash - I
New Delhi 110 048

British Library Cataloguing in Publication data

A catalogue record for this book is
available from the British Library

ISBN 0 7619 6639 0
ISBN 0 7619 6640 4 (pbk)

Library of Congress catalog card record available

Typeset by SIVA Math Setters, Chennai, India
Printed and bound in Great Britain by Athenaeum Press,
Gateshead

CONTENTS

Acknowledgements   *vi*

1   Introduction   1

2   Mind–Body Dualism: Investigating Descartes' Ghost   8

3   All in the Brain? A Popular False Start   22

4   Beyond Dualism: Exorcising Descartes' Ghost   38

5   Meaning, Action and Desire: A Preliminary Sketch
    of Embodied Agency   62

6   Habitus, Capital and Field: Embodiment
    in Bourdieu's Theory of Practice   91

7   Habit, Incorporation and the Corporeal Schema   120

8   Reflexive Embodiment: Being, Having and Difference   140

Afterword: Embodied Agency and the Theory of Practice   161

Bibliography   *163*

Index   *168*

ACKNOWLEDGEMENTS

This book was written as an attempt to pull together the conclusions of a strand of thought I first began spinning in the early months of 1990. I had just discovered Merleau-Ponty and was beginning to reflect upon what I believed was the considerable significance of his ideas for the social sciences. In the ten years that have followed a lot of water has flowed under the bridge, and quite a lot of hot air too. I have had many fruitful discussions with colleagues and friends. In particular I would like to thank Simon Williams and Anne Witz for their encouragement and the various thoughts they have led me towards.

This ten year stretch has had many happy moments, but some sad ones too. A number of people close to me died during this time; my nan, Doris; my nan-in-law, Irene; my granddad, Billy; my best mate from school, Rob; and most particularly my dad, Tony. There are few sharper reminders of human embodment than death. If death reminds us of our embodiment, however, then our bodies remind us of that form of life after death that we, as social creatures, enjoy. Others live on within our bodies, not just as memories but in the form of the habits which they put there and the voice of conscience. I would like to thank my dad and my granddad, in particular, for teaching me both to argue and to enjoy it; to go out on a limb, sometimes just for the fun of it; and to have a sufficient sense of humour to avoid pomposity. They would have had much to disagree with in this book, on principle, and I can only hope that my attempts to anticipate and answer their most likely criticisms have made the book better than it might otherwise have been. If the book reads clearly, as I hope it does, they should take some credit for that too; not only because their laughter at verbosity has allowed me to avoid this particular vice, but also because their eagerness to listen, to talk and to reason has taught me that human intelligence and reason need not come in clichéd academic packages.

Finally, thank you to my wife, Michele, who has spent the last eight years debating and discussing the issues of this book with me and who has still refused to give in. The taste of many good bottles of wine has been improved by our discussions and our discussions, no doubt, by the wine.

I would like to say 'blame all these people' for the faults which remain with the finished text, but the self-deprecating obligations of academic culture do not permit such heresies, so I will shoulder that particular burden on my own.

Nick Crossley

1

INTRODUCTION

'The body' has been a major issue within sociology over the last 15 years; longer if we look beyond such seminal texts as Bryan Turner's (1984) *Body and Society* to the sources and debates which he and other early pioneers picked up upon. During this time a great range of studies have been conducted and a similarly large range of issues tackled. In spite of all this work and the many fascinating insights generated by it, however, certain stubborn problems remain. In particular it is my view that sociology, having raised the issue of mind–body dualism, has not found a satisfactory solution to that philosophical puzzle. Indeed, I believe that we remain unclear even on its nature. This is not an isolated problem, however. Dualism is a major hurdle if we aim to embody sociology. It lies at the very root of questions of embodiment and has considerable implications for our attempts to theorise such central issues as agency, identity and the nature of social practice. Failure to resolve it has ramifications for all else that we seek to achieve within the domain of embodied sociology.

In this book I try to open up this stubborn philosophical problem, drawing out its sociological significance. And, with an eye on both philosophy and sociology, I pull together a range of discrete but overlapping bodies of work which both point to a solution and, in doing so, allow us to develop the basis for a properly embodied sociology. The result of this intellectual labour is far from comprehensive even if, on occasion, my canvas has been broader than would be ideal. There are many issues, theories and problems which I have excluded from discussion. If the reward for this restraint is a clearer picture of the problems we face and the possibilities we have for resolving those problems, however, then it is surely worth it. Moreover, we will find that tackling the problem of dualism raises more than enough issues to tackle in a book-length study.

In this first chapter of the book I outline the themes and problems I will address and identify where, in the text, the reader can expect to encounter them. I begin with the general issue of dualism.

Dualism

Dualism is a major issue for sociologists of the body. Many key works flag it up as a problem, and its resolution sometimes appears to be the very *raison d'etre* of sociological interest in the body. Bryan Turner, for example, writes that 'much of sociology is still Cartesian in implicitly accepting a rigid mind/body dichotomy in a period when contemporary philosophy has largely abandoned the distinction as invalid' (Turner 1984: 2) and 'the traditional mind–body dichotomy and the neglect of human embodiment are major theoretical and practical problems in the social sciences' (Turner 1992: 32). Similarly Chris Shilling, albeit with some equivocation, notes that 'sociology has followed a longstanding tradition in philosophy by accepting a mind–body dichotomy...' (Shilling 1993: 8–9). Finally, more recently, Simon Williams and Gillian Bendelow have argued that 'The separation of mind from body,' along with a number of other dualisms, has exerted a great and problematic influence on the traditions of western thought, sociology included (Williams and Bendelow 1998: 1). There is something paradoxical about this sociological interest in dualism. Though 'the body' has not been a central concept in any sociological perspective, neither has 'the mind'. Sociologists have been concerned rather with 'agents', 'practices', 'behaviour', 'action' and 'actors', all of which suggest a unified structure which is both mindful and embodied. Furthermore, some of the more persuasive philosophical attempts to resolve dualism have focused precisely upon 'action' or 'behaviour', regarding it as a neutral concept, between mind and body, which allows dualism to be overcome (Ryle 1949, Merleau-Ponty 1965). Viewed in this light we might argue that traditional sociology had no problem with dualism, even if it had relatively little to say about embodiment, and that it is the concern with 'the body', which is just as much a part of (mind–body) dualism as the mind, that has generated a problem of dualism for our discipline.

Notwithstanding this paradox, our concern with embodiment does put 'the body' onto the sociological agenda and with it the problem of dualism. It is my aim, in the first part of this book, to tackle this problem. I begin, in Chapter 2, with an attempt to clarify both the nature and the problem of dualism in its classical philosophical formulation. I outline the famous argument which Descartes posits in his *Meditations* and then consider both the standard philosophical objections to it and the difficulties which it creates for sociology.

Following this, in Chapter 3, I consider a fairly standard philosophical response to dualism, which is to suggest that the mind is, in fact, the brain. If this is so then the problem of dualism is solved, since the brain is a part of the body and the duality between mind and body therefore disappears. This argument is flawed, however, or at least it creates problems from a sociological point of view. I have no disagreement with the notion that everything we know, do, think and feel involves activity in the brain, but this does not mean that the brain 'is' the mind. And assuming that it does has dire consequences for the social sciences. We need an alternative solution to dualism.

In Chapters 4 and 5 I outline my own preferred solution. My point of departure is Gilbert Ryle's (1949) description of the Cartesian view as the myth of the 'ghost in the machine'. This description has two elements: it describes the mind as a ghost and the body as a machine. Chapters 4 and 5 tackle these two elements respectively. In Chapter 4 I use Ryle's own 'deconstruction' of the language of mind to exorcise the Cartesian ghost. And in Chapter 5 I use Merleau-Ponty's (1962, 1965) work on the human body to critique the notion that it is a machine.

In many respects this takes us back to where sociology started before we become interested in 'the body'; namely, with a social agent. Human beings are neither minds nor, strictly speaking, bodies, in this view, but rather mindful and embodied social agents. We are not quite back where we started, however. The discussion of Ryle and Merleau-Ponty allows me to bring many of the more corporeal aspects of agency into the foreground, such that we do have a more embodied conception of the agent. In particular my discussion draws out and focuses upon the sensuous nature of human perception, emotion and desire, and the corporeal basis of agency, communication and thought.

Habit and Embodied Practice

In challenging dualism, at least in the way I do it, we get far more than we might bargain for. A proper challenge to dualism unsettles many elements in the Cartesian system; most notably it's concept of 'mind', its prioritisation of 'thought' in its definition of the human ego and, with this, the traditional subject/object dichotomy. As we will see in Chapters 4 and 5, we are forced to reject the Cartesian tendency to privilege reflective thought and are presented rather with an image of the human ego as a practical being, physically involved in the world and enjoying practical mastery over it before any reflection can take place. This radically decentres 'the subject'. We learn to see our reflective consciousness and self-consciousness as the tip of an iceberg, founded upon a pre-reflective foundation of perceptual, linguistic and motor behaviours. Moreover, we are forced to think of these behaviours, though purposive, without presupposing a reflective being at the back of them, willing or designing them in any way.

This raises a number of questions and issues. Most notably, however, it requires us to reflect upon what Ryle (1949) calls the dispositional basis of much human activity and what Merleau-Ponty (1962) refers to as 'habit'. Habit has been a much maligned concept within recent social science, not least as a consequence of its appropriation and corruption within psychological behaviourism (Camic 1986). It has a long history of rather more distinguished and sophisticated uses, however, and Merleau-Ponty (1962), along with others in the phenomenological tradition, most notably Husserl (1973, 1989, 1991), who tends to use the term 'habitus' to distinguish his concept from cruder versions, rejoins that more sophisticated train of thought. Habit is a crucial concept for an embodied sociology as it allows us to centre our conception of agency upon practical and embodied human praxis, putting reflective thoughts and projects 'in their place' without dispensing with them or relegating them to an untenable position. For this reason I engage in a detailed examination of the notion in Chapter 7. Before doing this, however, in Chapter 6, I consider the work of the writer who has done most to develop the notion of habit or habitus for socio-logical purposes: Pierre Bourdieu.

My decision to deal with Bourdieu before I consider the phenomeno-logical literature on habit, thus effectively sandwiching him between two chapters on Merleau-Ponty, is twofold. In the first instance Bourdieu weaves the concept of habit into central debates in sociology and ties it into a theory of practice. A discussion of his work therefore draws out the sociological relevance of habit and puts some sociological meat on the bones of the debate on habit before we delve into details. To be fair to Merleau-Ponty, he is by no means oblivious to such sociological concerns. His was a profoundly social philosophy, which drew from sociological work and engaged with the ideas of Mauss, Levi-Strauss, Weber, Marx and Lukács amongst others. Indeed, it is not too fanciful to claim that his work prefigures many central 'structurationist' ideas in sociology. Human beings, Merleau-Ponty argued, are 'in a sort of circuit with the social world' (1964: 123). We become what we are through our 'incorporation' of social structures, such as language, in the form of habit, but our actions, such as speech, are at the same time what gives life to those structures and facilitates their reproduction. In an ideal world, with more space, I would have explored his social theory in more detail (see Crossley 1994, 2001 for some elaboration). In the final instance, however, his ideas only prefigure the more comprehensive and sophisticated reflections upon social practice and structures worked out and explored empirically by Bourdieu. Thus Bourdieu's work is far more appropriate.

My second reason for discussing Bourdieu's theory of habit first is that it raises problems which the phenomenological theory of habit can resolve. There have been many critiques of Bourdieu which are, in my view, unfair and far from the mark. But there are problems with Bourdieu's perspective and we need to address them. The phenomenological work allows us to do this and, at the same time, allows us to elaborate upon and deepen Bourdieu's basic insights.

In addition to the considerable contribution which it makes to our con-ception of agency, the concept of habit is important because it allows us to understand how, as agents, which belong to the social world, and because it provides a key to understanding the 'circuit' referred to in the quotation by Merleau-Ponty above; a 'circuit' equally appreciated by Bourdieu, when he describes the habitus as both a 'structured structure' and a 'structuring structure', and indeed also by Durkheim:

> ... the individual gets from society the best part of himself, all that gives him a distinct character and a special place among other beings, his intellectual and moral culture. [...] the characteristic attributes of human nature come from society. But, on the other hand, society exists and lives only through individuals.

If the idea of society were extinguished in individual minds and the beliefs, traditions and aspirations of the group were no longer felt and shared by the individuals, society would die. (Durkheim 1915: 389)

Individuals must acquire or incorporate the structures and schemas of their society, such as language, in order to become the agents we know them be; but those structures and schemas only exist insofar as they are embodied in the actions of other agents who pre-exist the individual in question. This circle or circuit is one of the most fundamental phenomena that sociology can address, and it rotates precisely around the axis of habit. The circle is possible only because it is the nature of human beings to transform their nature, incorporating the patterns and principles of action they experience in the world around them, absorbing and regulating new forms of know-how and expanding their competence. It is for this same reason, moreover, that human beings are truly 'in' the social world; that is, because that world is 'in' them, or rather, as the ins and the outs smack rather to much of Cartesianism, because their very way of being embodies the structures of the social world. Descartes, as we will see in Chapter 2, is condemned to view the human agent as a onlooker of their society. He must view their relation to their society as that of a thinking subject to an object of thought. This fails to account for the fact that his very process of philosophical meditation is woven within a social fabric of language and shaped by the conventions and procedures of the scientific and philosophical tradition to which he belonged. Descartes is not a on-looker of society. The very gestures which give rise to this thought, his words, prove him wrong, since they are not the gestures of an isolated being but rather the gestures of a group. Descartes cannot speak, cannot think, without betraying his belongingness to the social world; a belong-ingness which runs deeper than choice or reflection, residing ultimately in his animate embodiment, as habit.

This is not to deny the possibility of change or transformation, of course. Human praxis is creative and inventive, and human societies are in a constant process of historical movement. But these transformations are nothing without the power of conservation which prevents them from passing with the fleeting moment. However much history and creativity suggest change they require continuity in equal measure. Events must build upon events, developments upon developments. This is only possible because events and development do not pass away into nowhere; because the sediment within the human body as habits, becoming the ground for the events and developments of the future. These are the issues I explore in Chapters 6 and 7.

Reversibility and Reflexivity

The claim that we 'are' our bodies and that our bodily ways of being are rooted in habit is a constant theme of the book. This argument does not preclude the possibility of reflexivity, however; that is, in this case, the notion that we are aware of our bodies and habits, such that we might experience them as problematic and, in this sense, be said to 'have' them. I am my body but I also have a body, insofar as I can experience my body as an object. Likewise with my habits. This is possible, in part, by virtue of the incorporation of language, a body technique (Mauss 1979) which facilitates the assumption of a reflective posture. More specifically, however, as both Merleau-Ponty (1962) and Mead (1967) argue, the agent exists for herself insofar as she exists for the other and is able to assume the perspective of the other towards herself (Crossley 1996). Mead is particularly interesting on this point as he effectively describes the manner in which, through play, children learn to incorporate the role of the other within their own habitus. I explore this issue at a number of points in the book, but my main discussion of it is in Chapter 8.

The specific theory of reflexivity that I consider suggests that our capacity to turn back upon and inspect ourselves derives from an incorporation of the perspective of others into our habitus. It is an intersubjective theory. This has the consequence, however, that we only become objects for ourselves insofar as we are objects for others and, more specifically, that we come to be aware of ourselves from within general social frameworks and collective representations. This implication is also explored in Chapter 8, with specific reference to the way in which bodily differences are coded within such schemas of representation and classification. Different bodily markers, including genitalia and skin colour, I argue, effectively become tokens of physical capital, opening (or shutting) doors and shaping both life trajectories and, in this way, habits. Social categories penetrate the flesh, manifesting as habitus and hexis.

An exploration of these issues leads us right back in to the aforementioned sociological circle – only this time spinning more quickly. Reflexive projects, I conclude, are shaped by both habits and circumstances, which they, in turn, shape. They emerge within society as a structure of it and are, in effect, society's own way of looking at itself. Moreover, as such, they are always their own blind spot.

Desire

The final theme I address in the book is desire. Following Wrong (1961), and before him Freud (1985), and before him Hobbes (1968), we are accustomed to thinking of desire as somehow essentially in conflict with the normative demands of society; an anti-social biological force. There is much to commend this view. Elias' (1984) work on the *Civilising Process*, for example, offers us good empirical reasons to believe that our current civility, such as it is, is the result of a long historical process of 'taming'. Moreover, we are all familiar with the basic experience of being divided against ourselves, or having to exert discipline and control over ourselves in order to meet shared norms and expectations. Notwithstanding this, it is my contention that we should be wary of assuming that desires are necessarily anti-social and, conversely, of assuming that the emotions and impulses which urge normative transgression originate outside of the social domain. Consider the case of the sportsman who loses control, becoming enraged and disrupting the game: they break the rules, transgress norms and become aggressive. However, they only do so because they are heavily invested in the game, because it means so much to them. Their outburst is anti-social in normative terms, but it is profoundly social in the respect that it stems from their involvement and investment in a wholly arbitrary cultural practice; because signs, symbols and distinctions which mean nothing to the uninitiated mean so much to them. They do not 'burst' for no reason, like a biological or psychological volcano, rather they respond, however inappropriately, to a social situation whose structure they feel intensely within themselves. So it is in the wider social world. Human desires are invested in the games which comprise the social world. They drive us into society with enthusiasm. That is why these games matter to us and it is also why, on occasion, emotions and urges overrun the normative boundaries of those games.

Bourdieu (1998) offers a version of this thesis in some of his more recent work. I have a number of criticisms of his account, however (Chapter 6). In its place, building upon the Hegelian notion, I argue that human desire is primarily a desire for recognition. The desire for recognition drives us into social relations. It is a pro-social desire. But it also tends to drive us into relations of competition and antagonism. This is what we see in the many fields of struggle which comprise the social world.

With this very brief and cursory sketch of the key themes of the book complete, we can turn to Descartes and to the philosophical problem of dualism.

2

MIND–BODY DUALISM: INVESTIGATING DESCARTES' GHOST

> There is no need to conceive of a soul separated from its body maintaining in some ideal milieu a dreamy and solitary existence. The soul is in the world and its life is involved with the life of things...
>
> Durkheim *Individual and Collective Representations*

The aim of this chapter is to clear the way for an embodied sociology through a detailed examination of mind–body dualism. I offer an exposition and critique of the dualist position, as outlined by Descartes (1596–1650), in 1641, in his *Meditations*; or to give them their full title, *Meditations on the first philosophy in which the existence of God and the real distinction between the soul and the body of man are demonstrated* (Descartes 1968). My discussion of this version of dualism reports some, though not all, of the standard philosophical objections to dualism. My key concern, however, is with the sociologically problematic nature of dualism and the significance of the critique of dualism for sociology. A discussion of dualism and its limitations affords an important opportunity to reflect upon the significance of embodiment for sociology and I seek to exploit this opportunity.

Descartes' Ghost

Descartes arrived at dualism in the context of his attempt, in the *Meditations*, to find a point of certainty upon which the newly emerging sciences of his day could build. Aware of the superstition and prejudice which hampered his own thinking and that of his contemporaries, he elected to doubt everything of which he could not be absolutely certain, so as to find a solid foundation for knowledge. However sure he felt of the truth of a particular proposition, he noted, he must be prepared to discard it or at least suspend belief in it if he could find reason to doubt it. What he found impossible to doubt he could then use as an 'Archimedean point' of certainty upon which to build.

The first potential foundation he considers in this context is sense perception. Surely he can be certain of what his senses inform him? This proposition is quickly rejected, however, as he reflects upon the possibility that he may be dreaming or hallucinating. He has, he remembers, had very vivid dreams in the past, which he mistook for reality. Might he not be dreaming now? Indeed, the whole world which appears to him by way of the senses may all just be a dream, like the worlds so realistically simulated in dreams he knows he has had. Perhaps his whole life has just been an elaborate dream! How would he know? Similarly, he is aware of the possibility of hallucinations and of being otherwise deceived by one's senses. Thus he must doubt the evidence of his senses and everything of which they inform him. This includes the existence of the external world and, importantly for our purposes, of his body. His body, too, may simply be the figment of a dream or hallucination. This is not to deny that he can feel his body or perceive it. That *is* undeniable. Descartes is questioning the epistemological status of such experiences, however, and thereby bringing into doubt that of which they otherwise assure him. He sees and feels his body but has seen and felt all manner of chimerical beings in his dreams and hallucinations, such that seeing and feeling can count for nothing, for him, in his quest for certain knowledge and truth.

This doubting of the 'external world' and of his body is followed by a doubting of certain of the truths of logic and reason. These are doubted on the grounds that Descartes could be being deceived by an 'evil demon' who makes the procedures and outcomes of logic and reason seem obvious when, in fact, they are incorrect. How would he know? There are limits to this evil demon argument, however, and here Descartes finds his point of indubitable truth and certainty. Even if he were being deceived by an evil demon, he reasons, that would not and could not cast doubt upon the fact that he is thinking. Even if everything he thinks is wrong he can still be certain that he is thinking. And if he is thinking then he exists, at least as a thinking being. Thus we arrive at the famous Cartesian dictum, *cogito ergo sum* (I think therefore I am):

> There is therefore no doubt that I exist, if he deceives me; let him deceive me as much as he likes, he can never cause me to be nothing, so long as I think I am something. So that, after having thought carefully about it, and having scrupulously examined everything, one must then, in conclusion, take as assured that the proposition: *I am, I exist*, is necessarily true, every time I express it or conceive of it in my mind. (Descartes 1968: 103, *italics* in original)

From this point, drawing upon his (reasoned) belief in the existence of a God that is good and would not deceive him, Descartes begins to challenge his own earlier doubts and to reinstate much of what they had led him to reject. And in the process of doing this he draws a number of conclusions which are central to our concerns here. In particular, he infers from the fact that he was able to doubt the existence of his own body, without thereby calling his existence as a thinking being into question, that his mind and body, or rather his mind and matter more generally, must be different 'substances' and that he must consist, in essence, in the mental substance. If he can imagine himself existing without his body then what he 'really is' must be something other than his body, and he reasons that this something other, given that it thinks, must be his mind. This begs the question of the distinction between mind and body or mind and matter, and Descartes duly offers his own account. The properties of mental and physical substances, he argues, are quite distinct. Matter extends into space; is divisible; and is subject to the laws of physical nature (which eminent thinkers of the day were beginning to discover). Mind, by contrast, does not extend into space; is indivisible; does not obey the aforementioned laws; and more positively, is a thinking substance.

Thus we arrive at the basic dualist position. Human beings are said to be made up of two distinct 'substances', one of which extends into space and obeys the laws of physical determination, whilst the other, a strictly non-spatial and indivisible substance, thinks. Furthermore, Descartes adds that our knowledge of these two substances is fundamentally different in both form and the degree of certainty it is possible to achieve. One's body is, in effect, a part of the external world, he claims. As such it is difficult to know with any degree of certainty. Knowledge of 'external' objects is necessarily mediated by the senses, which are unreliable. Knowledge of one's own mind, by contrast, is not mediated by unreliable senses. It is known from within, immediately and with immediate certainty. The mind thinks and knows that it thinks; it knows, and knows that it knows. It is self-transparent. Thus one's mind is more easily and better known than one's body and, indeed, than anything else.

The mind is clearly elevated over the body in this account. Descartes' capacity to doubt the existence of his body without thereby doubting his own existence *qua* thinking being inevitably implies that his body is a secondary and non-essential aspect of his true nature. The real Descartes is the thinking substance: mind. His body is just one more empirical object in the world. It is important to note the manner in which mind is portrayed here. Descartes' 'mind' is a reflective and contemplative entity whose relationship to the world is rooted in thought and knowledge, and whose knowledge and thought are essentially propositional or predicative in form; that is, they consist in reflective propositions or thoughts *about* the world. The relationship of the mind to anything outside of itself, or indeed to itself, always necessarily takes the form of thought-about it.

Gilbert Ryle (1949), a critic of Descartes who we will encounter later, characterises the Cartesian schema as a whole as the myth of the 'ghost in the machine'. Two points are important regarding this characterisation. Firstly, it draws our attention to the ghostly nature of mind within the Cartesian system; the mind is a substance but it is not physical. It is not 'matter'. Secondly, it draws our attention to the specific conception of the body within Cartesian thought. Leder (1998) describes Descartes' body as a 'corpse' or 'meat', emphasising its sheer physicality and absence of human characteristics. Ryle's depiction is more appropriate for our purposes, however. The body is a machine, akin to a clockwork object or gadget for Descartes, he argues. Its various parts and their means of operating are akin to the springs, levers and pulleys one finds in other physical machines. As I will discuss later, it is necessary to challenge both the myth of the ghost and this myth of the machine if we are to fully overcome dualism.

Descartes' explicit reason for distinguishing mind and body, namely that he can doubt one but not the other, may strike us as both peculiar and weak. Many philosophers have identified a deeper and somewhat more meaningful sub-text to this argument, however. Descartes was writing at a time when the physical sciences, as we know them, were first emerging and taking off at a pace, raising the prospect that the whole of the universe, with everything in it, might be explained in terms of laws of mechanical causation. As an intelligent man he was impressed and persuaded by these developments. Indeed, he contributed to them and his *Meditations* and other writings were intended, as we have said, to remove the pre-judices which might stand in the way of their success. However, he also identified a danger in the process. To explain everything in terms of mechanical causation would necessarily entail a rejection of the notion of human freedom, creativity and the soul. As a religious man he feared this eventuality and its implications. Viewed against this background his attempt to separate mind and body can be read as an attempt to save the self-image of humanity from the advancement of natural science. The body, he could concede, belongs to the world described by science; a world about which Newton, who was born one year after the publication of the *Meditations*, was soon to make considerable claims. But mind is a different matter, or rather 'substance'. It must be studied in a different way and is not subject to the same laws as matter, such that it could never fall within the purview of the physical sciences.

Numerous scientific revolutions and a relative demise of religious worldviews within Western societies have undoubtedly furnished a rather different context for our reception of dualism. We are not con-fronted by the same scientific discourses as Descartes, and neither do we necessarily have the same religious self-image to defend. Nevertheless, the changes are not so profound as to make his fear seem unfounded or absurd. Reductionism and the desire to explain all that is human in terms of insensate and insentient physical processes are as evident now as they have ever been and we, like Descartes, have much to lose if these efforts are worked through to their logical conclusion. It is important to bear this in mind as we take the Cartesian position apart. Descartes' position was, as I will show, wrong; but the problem he was tackling was by no means insignificant and the basic notion of a relatively autonomous human order, irreducible to atomised relations of physical causation, which he sought to defend, is one which many of us still wish to defend today.

Philosophical Problems with Dualism

Having formulated the distinction between mind and body, Descartes himself posited a question that has subsequently been identified as a major problem for dualism; namely, how do mind and body interact? We know that they must interact, if indeed they are separate in the first place, because of their 'mutual involvement' in a wide range of human activities. In relation to perception, for example, we know that 'the body' is involved, in the form of perceptual organs, but we equally know that 'the mind' is involved, as perception is one of the key elements in consciousness. We are conscious of what we see, hear, smell and so on, and that element of consciousness is integral to what is meant by saying that we see, hear and smell. The simplest of experiments, such as covering one's eyes, reveals the interaction between these two elements. When the perceptual organs are blocked we cease to be perceptually conscious of what we otherwise would be. Similarly, we know that all meaningful and intelligent actions must entail 'both' mind and body, since meaning and intelligence are 'mental' but action necessarily entails the body. One cannot write a book, for example, without moving one's body in some way, but if anything is the result of mental processes then a book surely is. The problem is, how is this interaction achieved? This is where dualism falters, philosophically, because no convincing account of interaction has ever been posited, and there is good reason to believe that there never will be a convincing account. Interaction, many believe, is impossible. We can consider two arguments for this (see Carruthers 1986).

Some critics have argued that interaction is literally inconceivable because of the way in which Descartes defines mind and matter. As 'mind' does not occupy space, they argue, it simply could not make any contact with matter, such as would be required for it to have an effect upon matter. Furthermore, as matter necessarily functions according to laws of physical determinism and, by definition, only according to these laws, it cannot be affected by a substance which is itself unaffected by these laws. If 'the body' were to be affected in other ways than by physical causes this would amount to it not obeying the laws of (physical) nature: for example, if 'a' causes 'b' to do 'c' only when 'b' feels like it, and feeling like it is not a physical condition of the same sort as 'a', then 'b' is simply not bound by the laws of physical determinism, as matter is alleged to be. Similarly matter, as a physical substance, can only have effects upon things by way of physical mechanisms and causation. It has no way of acting upon non-physical things. Thus mind could only be affected by matter if it were subject to the laws of physical causation, but it is not, according to Descartes, so it cannot be. Another way of putting this would be to say that Descartes conceives of mind and matter respectively as self-contained but radically different and pre-emptive types of 'system'. We can conceive of interactions within either of these systems but we can only conceive of them as taking place in *one* of these systems and not between the two systems, precisely because both are, by definition, self-contained and thereby preclude the possibility of anything external entering in to them.

Other critics have argued against this, suggesting that there is no necessity for causal accounts to specify mechanisms of causation, nor indeed for them to be physical (Carruthers 1986). If we could find a 'constant conjuncture' between mental and physical events, they argue, then this would be sufficient to establish causation; that is, if mental events of a certain type were always followed by physical events of a certain type we could indeed talk meaningfully of a causal interaction between the two. Having said this, however, it is argued that neuroscience, however limited its knowledge to date, has sufficient knowledge of the brain to know that its network of physical causal pathways are not subject to ghostly interference or 'black holes'. In other words, it is argued that there is no problem, in principle, with the idea of mind–body interactions, but that we know sufficient to say that, in fact, they do not occur.

I find the former of these arguments more convincing than the latter. The latter is flawed on two grounds. Firstly, as I show in Chapter 3, the way in which 'meanings' can have an effect upon our bodies challenges the simple model of physical causation often implied in this argument. There are no black holes in the brain but the notion that everything within the brain can be explained by reference to 'physical stimuli', as such, is problematic. Secondly, to argue that mind–brain interaction is possible in principle but does not happen in fact grossly oversimplifies the way in which facts are differentially construed, not to mention thematised or ignored, according to the conceptual frameworks and technical environments which prevail within the scientific community at any particular point in time. Kuhn's (1970) work in the philosophy of science, for example, challenges the notion that scientific facts, experimental or otherwise, are self-evident. He shows that and how their significance is differentially constituted within specific paradigms. And even Popper (1969, 1972), whose position comes closer to the positivism that this claim about facts rests upon, was unable to avoid the conclusion that the 'facts' revealed in experiments necessarily presuppose certain 'basic statements' which are untested but must be assumed to be true, and which frame the apprehension of facts. Thus we might reasonably postulate that neuroscience has found no 'ghosts in the machine' because, *qua* materialist science, it rests upon the assumption that there are no such ghosts in the first place and, as such, would not and could not recognise a ghost if it saw one. Its paradigmatic framework identifies physical interactions as all that is relevant and all that exists, such that unexplained events, of which there must surely be many, are regarded as 'physical events of which we have yet to find the (physical) cause'.

On the other hand, the argument that notions of mind–body interaction pose irresolvable conceptual problems is persuasive in my view. Critics of this argument, as I have noted, argue that we do not need to understand how interactions between mind and body are possible for us to accept that they happen; all that is required is that we can identify a 'constant conjuncture' between the one and the other. This (empiricist) critique is problematic, in my view, as it presupposes that we could identify a mental act independently of any physical manifestation which might be said to be acting as its agent, and indeed that we could identify the sort of act that it is. To test the effect of mind upon body and vice versa we must be able to view each in an independent and pure state. We cannot do this, however, because we have no way of identifying mental acts other than by way of their embodiment or physical manifestation. Thus, the conditions that the critic specifies for identifying mind–body interactions, in principle, are equally as opaque and mysterious as the notion of such interaction itself, and the issue of inconceivability reasserts itself. We are back to the argument that mind–body interaction is inconceivable. It should be added here that the reason we cannot identify mental substances independently of their embodiment is because the notion of a non-spatial substance is an incoherent one in the first place. There are many aspects of the world which are non-spatial and indivisible; beauty is one and faith is another, but we would not dream of referring to these as 'substances' because substances are necessarily spatial.

Intellectualism

A second line of critique of the dualist position concerns the primacy it affords to reflective and intellectual acts and the predicative or propositional form it attributes to mental life and activity. The key criticism of this position is that reflective and propositional acts necessarily presuppose something other than them, which is never explicated but which, by virtue of being presupposed, entails that they cannot be primordial in the sense that Descartes suggests. This criticism has been posited in relation to the analysis of perception by both Husserl (1973) and Merleau-Ponty (1962). The Cartesian account of perception, they note, suggests that it consists in judgement. What we see is what we judge to be 'there' and we therefore perceive with our minds rather than our eyes:

> If I chance to look out of a window at men passing in the street, I do not fail to say, on seeing them, that I see men [...] and yet, what do I see from this window, other than hats and cloaks, which can cover ghosts or dummies which move only by means of springs? But I judge them to be really men, and thus I understand, by the sole power of judgement which resides in my mind, what I believed I saw with the eyes. (Descartes 1968: 110)

This account is fundamentally flawed, they argue. Descartes' perception of men, referred to in the above quotation, may well be based upon an act of judgement, but what he judges is another, prior perception; namely, a perception of hats and coats. And he cannot claim that his perception of hats and coats is rooted in judgement too unless he can identify a further perception, prior to that, which he has judged. In other words, Descartes' account of perception actually presupposes perception to have occurred. It presupposes that which it purports to explain and is therefore fundamentally flawed. A proper account of perception, whilst it may make reference to judgement, interpretation or other such 'predicative' acts, must first account for the meaningful experiences and perceptions which subtend such acts; experiences and perceptions which cannot be accounted for in the reflective and propositional terms of the Cartesian system.

This is not simply an argument about perception but about the very attempt to define 'the mind' in terms of propositional acts and states. Insofar as we define minds in terms of judgements, interpretations, reflections and so on, conceptualising these acts in predicative terms, we must necessarily presuppose meaningful experiences of states of affairs which are judged, interpreted and so forth; experiences which the intellectualist theory and definition of mind is incapable of explaining.

Another way of approaching this same criticism is posited by Ryle (1949). Because the Cartesian equates mental life with propositional thought, he argues, they necessarily assume that actions are only meaningful or intelligent in virtue of their having being reflected upon or otherwise thought about in a propositional fashion. Walking to the bus stop is meaningful and intelligent, for example, because one has first planned or otherwise thought about doing so. An act must be accompanied by a thought in order to be intelligent or meaningful as thoughts are the source of meaning and intelligence; doing must be accompanied by thinking. This is problematic, however, as thinking and reflecting are acts too and the Cartesian, who wishes to regard them as meaningful and intelligent, must therefore posit prior acts of reflection to account for their meaning and intelligence. Thought, as an action, must be thought about if it is to be deemed thoughtful and reflections must be reflected upon. If the account stopped here this might be acceptable, but it does not. Prior intellectual acts require their own prior intellectual acts to be intelligent and so on *ad infinitum*. Again then, Cartesian or 'intellectualist' accounts are shown to result in infinite regression; each grounding act is itself in need of grounding. Intellectualism is therefore incoherent and unworkable.

It follows from this critique that we need a way of thinking about predicative mental acts which identifies them as (potentially) meaningful and intelligent, without making reference to prior predicative acts which ground them. We will see in Chapter 4 how Ryle does just this, and in Chapter 5 how Merleau-Ponty does it. For the moment, however, suffice it to say that the accounts that each of these philosophers offer suggests that all actions, and not just those we ordinarily deem predicative and mental, can be meaningful, thoughtful or intelligent, without being preceded by intellectual acts of any sort. They challenge the philosophy of mind, narrowly conceived, with a philosophy of action or practice.

Doubting the Body?

As a final point of criticism consider the path which leads Descartes to distinguish body and mind; his method of doubt and, more specifically, his doubting of the existence of his own body. A number of interesting arguments from within the phenomenological tradition have served to call this into question. Husserl (1970), for example, argues that Descartes' doubting of the existence of his body already presupposes the distinction between the two and is rooted, in the final instance, in his appropriation of Galileo's (at that time relatively new and novel) definition of matter. Descartes' reflections are supposed to be a radical and pre-scientific examination of what is given to his mind without prejudice, Husserl notes. The aim of this is to identify indubitable truths upon which to ground science. He falls at the first hurdle, however, because, albeit unwittingly, he incorporates scientific abstractions (that is, the definition of matter) as basic assumptions within his reflections, failing to question or get beneath them as he should. In other words, Descartes is able to doubt the existence of his body because he already assumes it to be distinct from his mind, and he assumes it to be distinct from his mind because he is 'under the influence' of the latest and dominant scientific theories of his day and, in particular, the definition of 'matter' (or 'body') which they advance. This negates any possibility that Descartes' philosophy might ground science, as it already presupposes the arguments of science and any such grounding would therefore be circular. More importantly from our point of view, however, it sets his discussion of mind and body off upon a problematic path. Against Descartes, Husserl's (1970, 1973) own meditations, at least in his later writings, suggest that our most basic experiences are irreducibly embodied, such that any possibility of doubting one's own body and thereby splitting it off from the realm of the mind or experience would be strictly inadmissible.

A very similar criticism to this is expressed in the work of Merleau-Ponty (1962), who adds an important addendum. Our bodies are our way of being in and experiencing the world, Merleau-Ponty argues, but they are not objects of our experience, as such; at least not in the first instance. Or rather, our experience of our bodies is fundamentally different to our experience of objects external to us. This argument is developed over a long stretch in *The Phenomenology of Perception* but we can give two examples of it here. In the first instance, the act of moving my body is quite different to the act of moving an external object. In the latter case somebody (me) acts towards something (the object) in a particular way. But this is not true in the former case. When I move my arm it just moves. Nobody acts towards anything in any way. A similar contrast is apparent with respect to pain. I may say, for example, 'my hand hurts', but in doing so I describe something quite different to when I say 'these glasses hurt'. My hand does not hurt me in the way that the glasses do. Rather I have pain in my hand; my hand is a 'pain infested space'. The point of these observations is that our bodies are not, in the first instance, objects of experience for us, but rather our very means of experiencing; and what we experience is not our bodies but rather something other which they afford us access to and 'intend'.[1] This is not to deny that we can, as it were, turn back upon ourselves and objectify our own bodily form, arriving at an experience of ourselves. We do not escape our embodiment in such cases, however. Rather, to use a clumsy turn of phrase, we have a bodily experience (for example, vision) of our body (for example, as a visual object). Thus, for Merleau-Ponty, our body is not, in the first instance, an object of knowledge or experience which can be variously doubted and affirmed in the manner that Descartes proposes. Descartes' assertion that he finds his body in the world as one more empirical object is wrong, as he would have realised if he had effected a truly radical meditation upon his experience.

Sociological Implications

These philosophical criticisms, particularly the criticism concerning mind–body interaction, can equally be formulated in a sociological manner. Before doing this, however, we should briefly consider the broader sociological implications of assuming a dualist position. The picture is strange to say the least.

In conceptualising 'mind' as an inner 'substance', distinct from the body, Descartes necessarily suggests that mental life is a private state of affairs which exists prior to and independently of the social world. Or rather, he renders the very notion of a social world problematic. Ryle (1949), for example, argues that within a dualistic world:

> ... one person has no direct access of any sort to the events of the inner life of another. He cannot do better than make problematic inferences from the observed behaviour of the other persons body to the states of mind which, by analogy from his own conduct, he supposes to be signalized by that behaviour. [...] Absolute solitude is on this showing the ineluctable destiny of the soul. Only bodies can meet. (Ryle 1949: 16)

Ryle's final sentence, 'Only bodies can meet,' might sound appealing to some sociologists of the body. And there is a sense in which it is true. We can only meet and interact with others in virtue of our embodiment, as meeting and interacting are sensuous acts, dependent both upon the sensory systems required to perceive others and the sensible qualities that allow one to be perceived – not to mention the motor capacities required for communication. In this sense the very possibility of the social world, rooted as it is in interaction, rests upon our embodiment. Ryle is not referring to embodiment here, however, but rather to 'the body' as Descartes conceptualises it; and this conception is extremely problematic from a sociological point of view. Descartes' 'body' is a physical system: 'meat' (Leder 1998). It could be of no interest to the sociologist. Yet it is the only public and thus potentially social aspect of human life within his theory. Those aspects of human life which are of most concern to the sociologist, that is, the meaningful and intelligent aspects, are deemed to belong to an immaterial 'mind' which, as Ryle argues, is necessarily private and non-social for the Cartesian. Furthermore, they can only be known from 'within', not least because, as a non-spatial substance, mind has no outside. There is thus no sense of an intersubjective world of shared meanings and meaning systems:

> ... mental happenings occur in insulated fields known as 'minds', and there is, apart maybe from telepathy, no direct causal connexion between what happens in one mind and what happens in another. [...] The mind is its own place and in his inner life each of us lives the life of a ghostly Robinson Crusoe. People can see, hear and jolt one another's bodies, but they are irremediably blind and deaf to the workings of one another's minds and inoperative upon them. (Ryle 1949: 15)

'Absolute solitude', as Ryle puts it, is the 'ineluctable destiny of the soul'. The sociologist who buys into dualism therefore faces considerable and insurmountable problems. At a methodological level their attempts to analyse the meanings or reasons behind actions and events cannot be other than, as Ryle puts it, 'problematic inferences'. More fundamentally than this, however, the very notion of a social world itself is undermined as nothing of any meaning or significance can be said to pass or otherwise reside 'between' the isolated psychic monads that the Cartesian theory identifies (Crossley 1996a). Each 'thinking substance' is, of necessity, fully formed prior to and independently of the 'community' of monads that we ordinarily refer to as the social world and to which, we want to say, they belong. They do not belong and cannot belong for the Cartesian as their very mental essence is disconnected from anything which might otherwise be deemed to connect them.

This is an extreme form of individualism and it is compounded by the aforementioned intellectualism of the dualist. By defining the individual in terms of their mind, the mind in terms of predicative thought and the relation of mind to anything outside of it as that of a thinking subject to an object of thought, the Cartesian necessarily paints a picture of human beings as removed from the world; always on on-looker but never a part. They cannot conceive of individuals sharing in a common culture or language, for example. Language could not be other than a series of inherently meaningless bodily movements or inscriptions which individual minds bestow individual meanings upon in (mental) isolation. Communication would be a guessing game as would the learning of language. And our sense that we think 'within' a language would necessarily be false; linguistic formulation could not be anything other than a more or less deliberate translation of fully formed thoughts generated in a mental realm completely independent of language – since words, by definition, are sensible, corporeal things and are thus devoid of thought or meaning for the Cartesian. These implications are problematic, and not only because of their extremity. The last point in particular introduces self-contradictions into the Cartesian system as it challenges the notion that the mind is self-transparent. If (reflective) thought does exist elsewhere than in language then this is not something that we are aware of as thinking beings. Our thoughts occur to us in the form of language. We speak to find out what we think and experience any inability to verbalise a thought as an inability to think it. Thus, if Descartes is right about the distinction of mind and body he is necessarily wrong regarding the self-transparency of mind and vice versa.

These points suffice to raise questions regarding the adequacy of the Cartesian system for conceptualising the process of social integration as integration requires our capacity to communicate and share in basic cultural norms (Crossley 1996a). And we can push this questioning further. Ryle is troubled by the thought that *only* bodies meet in the Cartesian system, I suggest, because it strikes him that a great deal of social life and activity involves public scrutiny and debate about mental matters; so much so that the notion that minds are private and inaccessible from outside, other than by way of guess work, seems wrong. Moral reasoning and related practices, for example, rest upon assessments of intention, remorse and motivation; while punishment, advertising and education appear in some way to act upon minds with the intention of changing of them. Moreover, our everyday interactions involve a constant monitoring of the mental states of others, assessing mood and character. Indeed we are by no means averse, on occasion, to suggest that outsiders may know another's mind better than the individual themselves. These observations are important, firstly, because they suggest that mental lives are very much in the public, social domain, and secondly, because they indicate the importance of this state of affairs for processes of social integration (Crossley 1996a). How could we co-ordinate our activities if, in a strict sense, only bodies meet and the mental life of each and every one of us is a strictly private matter? How could we influence each other, as we must surely do to make the social world spin, if we had no access to each others minds?

A Sociological Critique of Dualism

These peculiarities assume the form of a more solid sociological critique of dualism if we connect them with the aforementioned philosophical critique concerning mind–body interaction. If, as Ryle puts it, 'only bodies can meet', then the various processes of social integration that sociologists concern themselves with, including the co-operative construction of local social orders by way of interaction and negotiation, must of necessity be embodied processes. In itself this statement is perfectly acceptable (see also Crossley 1995b). However, if it were true that the mind is distinct from the body and that interaction between them is impossible, then the social processes we are referring to here would be impossible too. A body that could not be made to express particular intentions or ideas could not possibly negotiate order in a public setting or transmit ideas and culture to the next generation.

Running this argument backwards we arrive at a strong sociological critique of dualism. We know, as sociologists, that social integration is a

normal and necessary feature of all societies.[2] And we know that these
processes are achieved by way of interactions which are at once both
embodied and mindful. Given this we can deduce that mind and body
either interact successfully or they are not distinct in the first place. We
know from what we have discussed already that interaction between
mind and body, as the dualist defines them, is impossible. Thus we are
forced to conclude that mind and body are not distinct substances and
that dualism is wrong.

I have framed this point around the issue of social integration but this is
just a special case of a more general issue concerning social action. Social
action is necessarily both embodied and mindful. It is intelligent, meaningful and often rational; but it also entails 'physical doings'. It entails movement through space and (physical) engagement with other (physical)
beings, whether in the form of a communicative gesture, such as a spoken
utterance, a manual engagement with physical objects, or a combination of
the two. Consequently sociology presupposes the co-ordination of the
mental and physical dimensions of our being. It follows from this that the
failure of the Cartesian to explain mind–body interaction necessarily
prevents them from explaining this most fundamental notion in the sociological toolbox. Cartesianism is therefore quite disastrous from a sociological viewpoint. No sociologist can afford to be a dualist and sociologists
have good reason to believe that nobody else should be either.

One further point we may tease out of this is that the Cartesian distinction between mind and body is unhelpful to sociologists because our
object of study falls somewhere between the two. We are not interested
in bodies, as such, in the narrowly physical sense, but neither are we
interested in minds, at least not in the disembodied and desituated form
that Descartes presents. We are interested in agents, action, practices and
praxes, all of which are necessarily and simultaneously both mindful and
embodied. Descartes just cuts the cake in the wrong way for sociology.

Conclusion

We may conclude from this that sociology and dualism do not mix.
Finding this out is one small step in the battle, of course, as we must now
work out how to avoid dualism. But it is an instructive step from the point
of view of an embodied sociology because it allows us to reflect upon the
interconnectedness of bodily, mental and social life. We have established
that human embodiment is central to the constitution of the social world,
since social interactions are necessarily sensuous, depending on our capacity to both perceive and be perceived. And we have established that
social interaction and integration rest, in many cases, upon the public
availability of 'mental states'; a fact which necessitates their embodiment
(since 'only bodies meet'). In effect this suggests that embodiment and
mindfulness are necessary to and inseparably intertwined within the
social world and must be studied as such.

Notes

1. 'Intention' here is used in the phenomenological sense of the term. We do not experience as bodies, as such, but rather experience the world by way of our bodies. Our bodily experience is an experience 'of' the world or rather whatever we come into contact with therein.

2. This doesn't mean that societies are conflict-free or self-transparent, nor that mutual understanding penetrates much beyond the superficial requirements of getting by and going on. Neither does it mean that what mutual understanding there is occurs without effort or in the absence of relations of power, inequality and various forms of discrimination. All it need imply is that agents manage, by and large, to co-ordinate their activities in public spaces and that languages, traditions, skills and knowledge are more or less successfully passed from one generation to the next, albeit often being modified along the way.

3

ALL IN THE BRAIN? A POPULAR FALSE START

> It is obvious that the condition of the brain affects all the intellectual phenomena and is the immediate cause of some of them (pure sensation). But, on the other hand ... representational life is not inherant in the intrinsic nature of nervous matter, since in part it exists by its own force and has its own particular manner of being [...] the relations of representations are different in nature from those underlying neural elements. It is something quite new which certain characteristics of the cells certainly help to produce but do not suffice to constitute, since it survives them and manifests different properties.
>
> Durkheim *Individual and Collective Representations*

In the next chapter I will begin to sketch out what I believe is the most viable path out of dualism. In this chapter, however, I want to consider a possibility that is popular but flawed. This is the view that the mind is, in effect, the brain. The popularity of this view justifies my consideration of it. It will haunt and nag my attempt to find a better alternative unless I dispense with it now.

There are many versions of this theory. Each is complex, sophisticated and different from the others. I do not have the space to consider these varieties and have therefore focused upon a straw model which suffices to illustrate the overall deficiencies of the approach. I will begin with a brief outline of this model before moving on to consider the various objections, both philosophical and sociological, that I have to it.

My basic claim in this chapter is that, although mind and body are not distinct 'substances', nevertheless we cannot reduce the 'mental' to the 'physical' in the fashion that mind–brain theorising inevitably suggests. My supporting argument is twofold. In the first instance I suggest that physical and mental descriptions belong to two distinct discursive registers which cannot be mapped neatly on to one another. Underlying this, however, is a deeper argument that the mental and social life of human agents is a whole which is greater than the sum of its atomised physical parts. Mind–brain identity theory, to be consistent, requires that complex social actions and interactions be decomposable into third-person processes of physical causation: an interaction of chemicals. They are not. My view of the human agent is wholly materialist but I believe that we need a more complex conception of physical structures and the higher orders of reality that emerge within the physical world than the crude and vulgar materialism that is evident in the mind–brain position. This argument will be elaborated in several of the chapters which follow, but some of the key points are elaborated in this chapter.

Overview of the Model

The mind–brain identity theory, which tends to be associated with theories of biological evolution in its contemporary forms, follows fairly readily from either of the first two philosophical criticisms of dualism that I noted in Chapter 2: namely, the criticisms which suggested that there can be no interaction between mind and body, either because it is impossible in principle or because we know that it does not happen in fact (because we know there are no 'black holes' in the brain). Advocates of this view reason that the impossibility of mind–body interactions, combined with our knowledge that 'both' are simultaneously involved in many areas of human life, must lead us to conclude that the two are, in fact, one. Which one is derived as a matter of fact. As we know that the body exists and that it is bound to the laws of physical causation, they argue, the mind must quite simply be the body, or rather, the brain. The brain in particular is selected because of what we know of its central role in the co-ordination of our conscious experiences and intelligent behaviours.

Anticipating the criticism that this undermines the notion of human agency, some advocates argue, to the contrary, that it is actually a necessary requirement of any theory of agency:

> Do we not expect that the causal chain of bodily events being caused by other bodily events will turn out to be unbroken? Are we not confident that every item of cellular activity will ultimately be causally explicable in terms of some prior physical stimulus? Then it seems likely that the dualist will be left in the absurd position of having to deny that our decisions – construed as non-physical events in a non-physical soul – are ever really causes of our physical movements. (Carruthers 1986: 64)

In other words, if our body can only be moved by physical stimuli then any serious theory of agency had better conceive of decisions as physical events which can function as stimuli for our actions. Furthermore, it is argued that physicalism takes nothing away from what we know of consciousness and can, in fact, offer good evolutionary arguments to bolster the common sense intuition that consciousness plays a determinate role within human agency. The argument is that conscious processes, such as decision making, use up such a high proportion of our total energy consumption that it is inconceivable that they are mere epiphenomena. They must serve a real function and, in doing so, confer an evolutionary advantage, because if they did not conscious beings would have lost out in the struggle for survival to 'unconscious' beings who are capable of exactly the same things as us but do not waste valuable energy sustaining an illusion of conscious agency.

This position does not preclude a notion of culture or learning. Indeed, in some cases the notion of cultural transmission has become quite popular, at least in its sociobiological form. Sociobiologists, aware of vast differences in ways of thinking and acting between cultures, not to mention the survival advantages secured by way of knowledge and innovation, have supplemented their accounts of genes and genetic transmission with an account of culturally constituted and transmitted structures which they call 'memes':

> Examples of memes are tunes, ideas, catch phrases, clothes fashions, ways of making pots or of building arches. (Dawkins 1976: 192)

Memes, it argued, 'leap from brain to brain' by way of imitation:

> Just as genes propagate themselves in the gene pool by leaping from body to body via sperm or eggs, so memes propagate themselves in the meme pool by leaping from brain to brain via a process which, in the broad sense, can be called imitation. If a scientist reads, or hears about, a good idea, he passes it on to his colleagues and students. He mentions it in his articles and his lectures. If the article catches on, it can be said to propagate itself, spreading from brain to brain. [...] When you plant a fertile meme in my mind you literally parasitize my brain, turning it into a vehicle for the meme's propagation in just the way that a virus may parasitize the genetic mechanism of a host cell. (Dawkins 1976: 192)

The broad appeal of the mind–brain identity thesis rests upon the achievements and status of the sciences upon which it draws, in my view. Neuroscience and its cognates have advanced considerably in recent years, as indeed have genetics and evolutionary theory, and it is perhaps to be expected, therefore, that people will look to them as relatively safe options for answering philosophical questions. The emergence of a range of brain imaging techniques, which allow scientists to see that and how particular parts of the brain are activated when human beings do and/or experience specific things is a particularly notable advance, and one most likely to encourage the identity theorist. Such techniques seemingly demonstrate, visibly, that mental activity is, in fact, physical activity. It is beyond my competence to question these scientific advances and I have no reason to want to do so. There is good reason to urge caution in our reception of them (Lewontin 1993, Levins and Lewontin 1985, Rose et al. 1984) but I find them as impressive and exciting as anybody else. I do, however, want to question the notion that brain-identity theory, as a philosophical theory built over the top of this science, resolves the problem of mind–body dualism in an adequate way. Moreover, I believe both that the theory sits unhappily with a sociological perspective on human life, and that sociology can mount a reasoned critique of it.

I have three key criticisms to level against at the mind–brain identity theory. Firstly, I believe that it is unjustifiably reductionist. Secondly, I believe that it is a form of vulgar materialism, which could and should be supplanted by a more sophisticated form. Thirdly, I believe that it clings, in many respects, to the Cartesian framework and, as such, reproduces many of its most problematic aspects. In this chapter I will be outlining a number of arguments which support these claims. I should point out at this stage, however, that my arguments will not be concerned to find another possible candidate for 'the mind' nor to suggest a place where it might be found. Part of the seductiveness of the identity theory, in my opinion, is that we tend to assume, following Descartes, that there is a single space, place or thing called 'the mind' which executes all of our mental process and/or otherwise contains them. This prejudice favours the identity theory as the brain is the main 'thing like' structure that we know of which could fit the bill. There is another route open to us, however, which is to abandon reified notions of 'mind' and 'body' in favour of a notion of mindful and embodied agency. This is, as I see it, the best option both for sociology and more generally, and it is this that I will be exploring later in the book. First, however, we must consider the problems of the brain-identity argument.

Meanings of Mind

I will open my case with a common sense argument, which holds a good deal more water than might ordinarily be assumed. The identity thesis sounds wrong to us, I suggest, because we do not believe that we are talking about brains when we attribute mental states to either ourselves or others. Moreover, because we do not need to know anything about brains, or even that we have them, to talk quite meaningfully and intelligently about mental matters. We might regard a novelist as particularly psychologically astute, for example, but this does not mean that they know a lot about the brain or that they write about brains. Conversely, we might believe that some neuroscientists have a relatively poor grasp on mental life or human psychology, despite having a very good understanding of the workings of the brain. The neuroscientist writes about physical structures and chemical reactions; synapses and neurotransmitters. The novelist, by contrast, writes about feelings, motives, perceptions and beliefs. And that fact that each can write so competently and impressively about their domain, without knowing the first thing about the other domain, suggests that we are dealing with two quite distinct domains. It is important to add here that the novelist and the neuroscientist are not representatives of mind and body respectively. We might be tempted to say that there is very little of mental content in what the neuroscientist writes, but the novelist's description of mental states and processes is far from disembodied. They will convey mental states to us, from the 'inside', by reference to bodily feelings and sensations, and from the 'outside', by reference to embodied gestures, actions and conversations. Theatre and film provide even better examples in this respect as their capacity to convey a sense of 'mind' and mental processes is quite clearly bound to the embodied performances of the actor.

The identity theorist will doubtless respond here that we are getting bogged down in 'folk psychology', an unscientific and uninformed conception of mind which is common in everyday life but will eventually be succeeded by neuroscience. I contest this on two grounds. Firstly, it is important to stress that our common sense objection to identity theory centres upon the meaning of the language we use to describe mental life. We are not denying the role of the brain in mental processes, such that we might be corrected by a demonstration showing conclusively that they are involved. Neither are we arguing the case for dualism or some immaterial conception of mind. We are simply saying that we do not mean 'brain' when we say 'mind', or 'firing up of synapse x' when we say 'puzzled', and that no amount of scientific demonstrations of brain activity could convince us that this is what we do mean.[1] A careful analysis of the discourse of 'folk psychology', we might concede, could potentially reveal to us that we do indeed mean something other than we believe we mean when we use the language of mind. This is not the tactic of the identity theorist, however. They are concerned with brains rather than meanings and they aren't really saying that we mean 'brain' when we say 'mind'. In this respect their response to our criticism just misses the point.

We will return to this issue of the meaning of mental terms in the next chapter. For the moment we must consider our second line of response, which would be to say that brain science can never replace folk psychology because we, as social agents, depend upon it and they, as identity theorists, depend upon it too. We depend upon it because, as I argued in Chapter 2, social interaction and integration depend upon our ability to make sense of the mental life of both ourselves and others, and our way of doing this is folk psychology by definition. If we dispensed with folk psychology we would cease to understand one another and the social world would disintegrate. Moreover, this folk psychology must of necessity exclude any reference to brain states as we have no direct access to the brain in social interaction. Brains, like Descartes' mind, are jammed away somewhere deep in the scull and are completely inaccessible to us. Even if we did catch a glance of another's brain this would not really make any difference as the workings of the brain are alien and unfathomable to us and not remotely mentally revealing. The movement of chemicals in the physical jelly that we call the brain does not strike us as remotely indicative of 'love' or 'rational calculation', for example. This leads to the second part of my argument, which is that brain-identity theory and the neuroscience it is parasitic upon necessarily depend upon folk psychology too, at least insofar as they wish to make claims about 'mental matters'. For the identity theorist to identify a part of the brain as responsible for a particular type of psychological function, say intelligence or anxiety, they have to demonstrate a correlation between brain states and psychological states. They need to show that and how the 'x' region is enlarged in intelligent people and how the 'y' region secretes 'p' when we get anxious. But to do this they have to know what intelligence and anxiety are and they can only know this in the same way that anybody else does; that is, by way of folk psychology or some polished intellectual construct based upon it. Furthermore, in identifying their correlation they necessarily concede, if only tacitly, that mental and neurological phenomena are different. They can only reveal the anxiety mechanism of the brain, to reiterate, by identifying a correlation between brain processes and individuals in anxious states – 'when people are anxious their brain goes like this …' – but this suggests that what we mean by anxiety and what they mean by anxiety is not that the brain 'goes like this'. If it was, we wouldn't need telling about it and their explanations would amount to tautologies. A true substitution of neuroscience for folk psychology would be just what it says. It would be an account of brains, synapses and their various secretions that made no reference to perceptions, imagination, motives, thoughts or feelings. We would, I suggest, find little that we would be prepared to call mental in any such discourse. Thus, the mind–brain identity theory is problematic. It tries to collapse two discursive registers into one when it is clearly unnecessary and inappropriate to do so. The 'mind' is not the brain because we mean something quite different when we use mental and neurological language respectively.

This raises the question of exactly what we do mean when we use mental language and what the essence of the 'mental' consists in. I will deal with this in more detail in the next chapter, where I discuss the work of Gilbert Ryle (1949). For the moment, however, we need to extend our critique. I have couched my argument, so far, in terms of 'meaning'. We do not mean 'physical brain process' when we say 'mental process', I have suggested. This is not simply a matter of meaning in any limited sense, however. Once the gap between the language of mind and that of brain is explored we begin to see that our language of mind maps on to a level or structure of human life which is strictly irreducible to the physical processes mapped by the discourse of neuroscience; that is, that there is a level of organisation of the human organism, *qua* behavioural system, which, though entirely rooted in 'physical structures', nevertheless remains irreducible to them and manifests a structure and dynamics which requires a distinct form of discourse and analysis. This point needs to be unpacked.

The Necessity of Reduction?

To refer to distinct discursive registers in the way I have is not to concede anything to dualism. I am not suggesting that mind and body are separate things or substances but rather that they belong to different ways of mapping human life, neither of which is primary. Making this claim precludes the possibility that we might talk of causal relations between mind and body. One sometimes finds identity theorists trying to advance their position by claiming that physical processes in the brain cause certain mental events and are thus more fundamental than them but this tactic is quite illegitimate. It is common, for example, to hear claims that depression, a mental state, is caused by an over-production of the neuro- transmitter serotonin, a brain state. Strictly speaking such claims cannot be allowed within either identity theory or my critique of it because 'depression' and 'serotonin over-production', from either perspective, are just two different ways of describing the same thing and there can be no relationship, causal or otherwise, between them. It may, of course, tran- spire that certain experiences are better accounted for with reference to one of the two registers or indeed that reference to both levels is neces- sary: for example, an individual's depression/serotonin over-production might better be explained by reference to a specific genetic quirk, by ref- erence to a specific life event or some combination of the two. It would never be appropriate to refer to interactions between body and mind in these cases, however, whether causal or otherwise. The illusion of inter- action is created by the gestalt shift involved when we move from one register to the other. We shift from a human description of depression, for example, to a biological description, and we then posit the one (either one) as a cause of the other.

This same argument holds, moreover, against the efforts of the identity theorists to pull any discussion of human agency or mental processes down to the level of the brain. Consider decision making. Many identity theorists concede, as I noted earlier, that decisions are effective causes of various forms of action. We often act in particular ways, they argue, because we have decided to do so and the decision is, in effect, the cause of the action. They qualify this, however, by arguing that it can only be so because decisions are physical events in the brain which mobilise the motor system and so on. At one level this position is acceptable. We can accept that decisions must have some form of physical correlate, that this is true of actions too and that the two physical events are in all probabil- ity linked. Having said this, however, there is no necessity for us to invoke brain states in an account of decision making and acting. The link between decision and action is perfectly understandable without biologi- cal reduction. Furthermore, a biological description of the brain processes involved is no more adequate, deeper or more explanatory. We learn noth- ing new from it. It is just a description of the same process but from a 'lower' level. Indeed, in many respects it is a less preferable level of des- cription because, if carried through consistently, it destroys the rational intelligibility of the decision-making process by breaking it down and, as a further consequence, proves quite unable to engage with the many important aspects of that process that a sociological analysis might reveal. If we really want to dissect and analyse a decision, I suggest, then we are crucially concerned with such things as the reasons and arguments mobilised and effective within it, the information considered and the frame of reference and typifications employed by the decision maker. We are concerned with the methods of information gathering, calculation and reasoning employed. Was a sacred oracle consulted or an accountant? Why was this assumed and not that? These are the effective 'parts' or 'causes' of the decision, if we wish to speak in such a way, and they can be analysed and investigated sociologically. To reduce such processes or the decisions they found to physical processes in the brain, even if it is possible, would be both unnecessary and unhelpful.

Finally, we cannot reduce the relationship of decision to action to processes of physical causation because decisions typically specify goals for action, leaving the actual process by which such goals are realised, the 'physical mechanics', open. I decide to 'make a cup of tea', for example, not to perform the specific physical movements that are required to achieve that goal: for example, 'I'll take three paces forward, lift my left arm upwards and forwards at a 45 degree angle from the body' and so on. My decision specifies a goal rather than a means for attaining that goal. Furthermore, specifying a goal for myself is in no way a proxy for that determinate physical description since the precise physical details of tea making vary between occasions and I will not generally know what the details will be in advance. Having specified the goal of 'tea making' for myself, what follows is necessarily improvised because I will inevitably face all manner of unexpected contextual conditions and obstacles and may well be diverted by other tasks in the process. I will eventually fulfil the goal specified in my decision but perhaps by an unexpectedly circuitous route, such that it would be absurd to claim that the way I actually behaved, physically, was caused by the act of decision making. Even if I make a plan this still holds true since my plan, typically, will consist of a stepwise chain of small goals which add up to the larger goal, rather than a literal description of the activity which realising my plan will entail. This is problematic from the point of view of those who wish to explain the relationship between decisions and actions in terms of biological causes and effects, because it indicates that the physical effect (that is, what an agent does in physical terms, such as movement of specific limbs in specific ways) of the decision is not actually specified at the level of the decision, such that the manner in which the action follows the decision is not strictly decomposable into a straightforward cause–effect relation, whether physical or otherwise. The action 'chases' the goal but how it does so, precisely and physically, is determined by whatever unpredictable contingencies intervene.

I am not suggesting that any of this takes place without goings-on in the brain. What I am suggesting, however, is that physical descriptions do not help us to understand or explain any of this because the manner in which actions follow decisions, when they do, necessarily entails the specification of purposes or goals which are irreducible to whatever physical means may, in the final instance, be used to achieve them. This does not preclude us from referring to causal relations between decisions and actions *per se*. When an individual formulates a decision linguistically they can be said to act upon themselves in such a way as to bring about certain further actions. Much of the work of G.H. Mead (1967) suggests a model of this sort, for example. Furthermore, as Elster (1989) has argued, individuals may take any number of steps to constrain their own future possibilities for acting and thus ensure that the decision sticks. But these are events which belongs to the 'mental' level of description and which are irreducible to the physical level.

Sociology, Black Holes and Meaning

There are a number of ways in which we can extend this argument. My main concern, in the first instance, is to link it to a sociological critique focused upon the role of meanings within action. This argument is levelled against the notion, discussed in Chapter 2, that we know enough about the brain to know that there are no 'black holes' in it, from where 'mental' causes might issue, and that, as Carruthers (1986) puts it, all cellular activity will, in the final instance, be explained by reference to 'physical stimuli'. I do not believe in black holes in the brain but let us consider a situation which rocks the boat a little. Suppose you receive a letter telling you to hurry home because a close relative has had a terrible accident and is close to death. What happens? You are shocked and upset. Perhaps you cry and shake or tremor. Your heart rate and blood pressure rise and you become confused and temporarily paralysed with worry or anxiety. After a while you may well get in the car and drive to the hospital. In short, a whole series of processes are triggered, at both the level of conscious subjectivity and that of physiology, which the mind–brain identity theorist is going to account for in terms of your brain. Your heart rate increased, they will say, because your brain 'told it to' or otherwise 'made it'. They may even show you brain scans which demonstrate how the disarray you experience is being generated in or by your brain. All of this raises the question, however, of the physical stimulus which is supposed to have triggered this off. Was it a physical stimulus? It was a letter and that is certainly physical in two senses. It is made of paper, which is matter, and it is marked by physical inscriptions caused by a pen. But it was not the physical properties of the letter which caused this dramatic effect upon your system. It was the meaning of the letter, what it 'said'. And though that meaning necessarily had to be embodied, its embodiment was, in certain respects, incidental. It was not the specific markings on the page which caused the effect because the basic message of the letter could have been worded in any of a number of different ways and it would still have had the same effect – providing, and this is an important proviso, it was in a language you understand. Indeed, it need not have been a letter at all. You could have been told by phone, singing telegram, smoke signals, Braille or tom-toms and you would still have reacted in the same way. Of course you would react in the same way, a critic will argue, you are being told the same thing! What's the difference? Everything and nothing is different. In terms of the meaning of the message, nothing is different. But at the level of 'physical stimuli' everything is different. A phone call is not at all like a letter or Braille parchment in physical terms. Each of these media interacts with a different sense organ and must necessarily do so to convey its message. We should add that it is the communication of the message which causes the effect, rather than the real event it reports, as is demonstrated by the fact that you would respond in the same way if, unbeknown to you, the message was entirely untrue.

Thus, though we have not found a 'black hole' in your brain, we have identified a factor, or level of factors, which affect it but which are not strictly reducible to physical stimuli. Meanings are embodied but their effects are not caused by the physical properties of that which embodies them. A phone-call message and e-mail message can, as I have said, mean the same thing and, as a consequence, have the same effect upon your action or physical system, but they are physically very different. Furthermore, though we must refrain from reducing meaning to consciousness, it is evident that the letter was only able to affect you in the way that it did because it had a meaning for you; that is, a meaning of which you were conscious. By this I mean both that you became (consciously) aware of it and were able to make sense of it. Had the letter been written in either medical jargon or Javanese, even it 'meant' the same thing, it would not have the same effect upon you and could not do so until somebody translated it for you. Similarly, as long as it remained unattended to it could not affect you, even if its meaning would be immediately apparent to you.

This example involves language but it need not have done. Not only are there a wide range of symbolic systems that have the capacity to affect human behaviour and experience, as the letter did, but our non-symbolic 'perceptual input' functions in this same meaningful way too. The sight of my bank manager walking towards me in the street sends shivers down my spine because of what she means, not because of some physical property which has a direct effect upon me. I will smile, wave and be happy when I see her next week, when my debts are finally paid, even if objectively she looks exactly the same. What counts is what the stimulus means and its meaning is strictly irreducible to its physical properties, to the point where it seems redundant to continue referring to it as a stimulus at all.

This is not to deny that physical stimuli can have a direct effect on me by virtue of their physical properties, bypassing my conscious awareness altogether. If I accidentally eat the wrong sort of mushrooms my experience will undergo a drastic transformation, even if I am oblivious to what I am eating. But this doesn't take anything away from those 'stimuli' which affect me by virtue of their meaning and, in a sense, serves all the more to illustrate their difference. Misrecognising our exemplary letter would change its effect quite drastically (for example, if I thought it was it was sick joke and failed to take it seriously) in a way that would not hold true if I mistook the magic mushrooms in my full English breakfast for the common supermarket variety.

I regard this example as a sociological response to identity theory because it illustrates the central and irreducible role of social meanings and representations in 'mental life' and social action, thereby confirming and conforming to the model of meaningful action which many sociologists operate with, and illustrating the necessity of the *verstehen* approach to social science which sociologists, following Weber (1978), have pioneered. The physicalism of the identity theorist simply cannot be substituted at this level because it is embodied meanings which have an effect at this level, rather than physical stimuli or anything reducible to them.

This is, in essence, a critique of vulgar materialism but not of materialism *per se*. Meanings, I have argued, are necessarily embodied and necessarily apprehended by way of sensuous praxis, in the form of perception. They emerge within the material world, as a part of it, but they are not simple 'physical stimuli' and require of us that we learn to think in terms other than that of 'stimuli'. Thus, I am suggesting that we work towards a more sophisticated and multidimensional form of materialism, which is complex enough to account for embodied meanings. This is really no more than a host of writers from within the phenomenological, symbolic interactionist and (certain) Marxist traditions within sociology have attempted to do, but the forgetfulness of intellectual culture sometimes demands that we reiterate and reformulate such central points.

Brain or Embodied Social Agent?

The notion of meaning and the examples I have given raise further problems for the identity theory. The meanings which affect us are, in the first instance, perceptual meanings. To be affected by these meanings entails, as I have said, that we are conscious of them, and consciousness is revealed to be, as phenomenologists and others (Searle 1983) have put it, 'intentional'; that is, 'consciousness of' something or other. This has two implications. In the first instance it suggests that we should not seek 'minds' or 'mental life' at a point somewhere behind the scull but should rather attend to our interface with the world. To be conscious is to be open to the world and to live one's life therein. In the second instance, though the objective physical requirements for the construction of this interface include a brain and nervous system, they do not stop at this level. They include 'perceptual organs' whose definition might extend to 'the body' as a whole. Our tactile sense involves the whole of our body surface, for example, and our kinaesthetic and proprioceptive perceptions do not stop at the surface. They entail whole-bodily perceptual behaviours which proactively contribute to the construction of the perceptual experience. Furthermore, as the aforementioned example of the letter illustrates, our reactions to that of which we are conscious are whole-bodily too. Thus, if we want to embody the subject or social agent it had better be the whole body, practically engaged in the world, that we are referring to.

It is no objection to this claim to point to experiments which illustrate that and how specific experiences might be generated through an artificial excitation of the brain which bypasses the usual channels, such that the proverbial 'brain in a vat' might have identical experiences to that of the whole human being. It may well be that one can generate experiences akin to external experiences by direct electrical manipulation but, setting aside the objection that such experiments are an ocean away from even an approximation of creating a totally simulated life, the experiments simply serve to show that the brain is nothing without inputs. And in the usual case those inputs come from a total behavioural involvement in a complex environment.

This critique points to one of a number of ways in which the identity theorist is, in effect, a closet Cartesian. They ignore the broader aspects of human embodiment, focusing only upon what they take to be the mental centre of the body: the brain. Like Descartes they believe that mind must be a substance or thing and they therefore opt for the most likely 'thing' they can find: the brain. They tuck 'the mind' away, safely behind the forehead, much as Descartes does, locking away its secrets in a private space. Even the sociobiologists are guilty in this respect, at least in their discussion of memes. Dawkins (1976), for example, refers to memes as brain parasites which 'leap from brain to brain' by way of imitation, but in his rush to get from brain to brain he misses the rich context of fully embodied social interaction that is involved in this process. A specifically human brain may well be a necessary prerequisite for the learning of language, for example, but so too are the sensory systems that allow one to perceive the language one is to imitate, the vocal apparatus and the capacity for motility which launches it into action and, in truth, the body that derives pleasure from this playful form of interaction. An account of memes which ignores this 'whole body experience' is akin to a theory of natural selection which ignores sex: much less interesting and not half as convincing.

A central consequence which stems from this overly Cartesian framing of identity theory is that it tends to reproduce other problematic aspects of the Cartesian theory, particularly its intellectualist orientation. In some instances this is merely in virtue of omission. Identity theories are concerned that the mind is, in fact, the brain, but they do not stop to question whether the Cartesian conception of mind is coherent in the first place. Their 'brain' therefore becomes everything that the Cartesian mind was and, as such, is highly problematic. Some versions of the identity theory compound this problem, however, through their incorporation of the 'insights' of cognitive science and artificial intelligence. This branch of psychology attempts to model the computational processes which it believes to be involved in many of our most basic psychological functions, usually in the form of rules or computer programmes. These are not deemed conscious processes, but neither are they physical processes. Indeed, one problem with cognitive science is that it is unclear where they fit in (Searle 1991). I do not have the space to examine these theories in

detail. I discuss them briefly later in the book but here it must suffice to
say that they have been shown, quite convincingly, to reproduce the problems of Cartesian intellectualism on a grand scale (Coulter 1983, Evans
1993, Button et al. 1995, Searle 1991).

There is a very strong force at work here. If we assume that the mind
really is a substance or thing, then its identity with the brain does seem to
be a virtually inescapable conclusion, and we are highly likely to be
assuming just this, not least because of the sedimented influence of
Cartesian philosophy upon our culture, both academic and more general.
If we can let go of the notion of mind as a substance or thing, however, a
range of further possibilities emerge which are superior in many respects
to the reductive vulgar materialism of the mind–brain identity theorist.

Vulgar Materialism

Much of what I have argued in this chapter has focused upon a distinction between two distinct discursive registers and their irreducibility; that
of social or mental description and that of physical description. In this
final section I want to elaborate upon this, offering a final critique of the
identity theory. My way into this will be through a brief return to
Descartes who, in my view, identified the necessity of the double register
but failed to theorise it properly.

The body, as Descartes understands it, is lifeless matter. It extends into
space, is divisible and is subject to the laws of the physical universe. But
that is all that defines it. By 'the body', he writes:

> I understand all that can be terminated by some figure; that can be contained in
> some place and fill a space in such a way that any other body is excluded from
> it; that can be perceived, either by touch, sight, hearing, taste or smell; that can
> be moved in many ways, not of itself, but by something foreign to it by which
> it is touched and from which it receives the impulse. (Descartes 1968: 104)

This definition applies as much to a stone or sand particle as to the human
body and it is intended to (see also Leder 1998). If scientists are going to
offer an account of the laws governing the physical world then their definition of 'physical' must focus upon the lowest common denominators of
that world and those alone. However, this way of framing the issue,
which reduces the human body to the status of an object in the most
extreme way, inevitably leaves a considerable subjective residue to be
accounted for, not least that of the philosopher or scientist who posits the
existence of this body. If the body really is as Descartes describes then the
Cartesian, as a sentient and intelligent being, is certainly not a body. As
Descartes himself puts it:

> I am not this assemblage of limbs called the human body; I am not a thin and
> penetrating air spread through all these members ... (Descartes 1968: 105)

The Cartesian posits an external perspective on 'the body', which breaks
it down into its constituent parts and lowest common denominators.

Their's is a body seen from the outside but never seeing or otherwise sensing or engaging with that outside. Thus, in the quotation above we find Descartes describing bodies in terms of their perceptible qualities, how they can be seen or touched, but never in terms of their sensuousness; their capacity and tendency to see and touch and so on. This definition is problematic because it presupposes elements which it cannot explain. A description of perceptible qualities necessarily presupposes the sensuousness required to perceive them; and Descartes can define bodies externally, describing his perspective on them, only to the extent that he presupposes a being whose perspective this is. Who or what sees and touches? If the body simply is matter as he defines it, however, it follows that Descartes can only account for this perspective and sensuousness by looking elsewhere than the body. If the body is simply a being which one can have a perspective on and which cannot have a perspective of its own, then he is forced towards dualism in order to explain how and why a perspective on the body is possible in the first place.

This is a deeply entrenched problem, related, as we noted with reference to Husserl (1970) in Chapter 2, to the way in which we define 'matter'. Matter is defined in such a way as to necessitate some 'addition' to it for a full account of even our experience of it. Dualism was Descartes' way out of the problem, but it is not the only one. Merleau-Ponty (1962, 1965) and Husserl (1989), provide another. I will discuss Merleau-Ponty's work in greater detail later in this book. For the moment it must suffice to note that both he and Husserl argue that the complex biological organisation and activity of some organisms is such that they achieve an irreducible 'reversibility'; they are visible but also see, tangible but also touch, in space but also spatially oriented. The body has two sides; sensible and sentient. There is a body-object and a body-subject. And neither side can be reduced to the other, though both, in a sense, realise the other: matter cannot be defined by its sensible properties without there being the sentience required to perceive it as such but equally there cannot be sentience without a perceptible world:

> ... the Body is originally constituted in a double way: first it is a physical thing, *matter*; it has extension, in which are included its real properties, its colour, smoothness, hardness, warmth, and whatever other material qualities of that kind there are. Secondly, I find on it, and I sense 'on' and 'in' it: warmth on the back of my hand, coldness in the feet, sensations of touch in the finger tips. I sense, extended over large Bodily areas, the push and pull of my clothes. Moving my fingers I have motion sensations ... (Husserl 1989: 153)

The problem with brain-identity theory is that it fails to take this reversibility seriously. It is a theory of the third-person Cartesian body. It does not, and I would say cannot, engage with the lived or subjective body; that is, the meaningful, 'mental' aspect of bodily life. Consider Carruthers' aforementioned rhetorical question: 'Are we not confident that every item of cellular activity will ultimately be causally explicable in terms of some prior physical stimulus?' (1986: 64). We have already suggested that the manner in which the meaning of events impacts upon us may call this notion into question but setting this aside, even if we agree, we can say with equal confidence that an analysis of physical stimuli and their causal effects will only ever lead to a greater understanding of cellular activity, never breaking out of the confines of the 'physical' frame of reference so as to elucidate the nature of sensuous, conscious human agency. Reducing mental life down to the level of physical causes means sticking at that level, with no hope of graduating, other than by way of an inexplicable shift of frame of reference, to the level of conscious, sensuous experience. In a sense this is akin to the problem of mind–body interaction discussed in relation to Descartes' dualism (Chapter 2). The identity theorist is no more likely to get from brain to mind than the Cartesian, and for the same reason: viz. 'the brain', as defined within physicalist discourse, belongs to a self-contained domain of physical systems which cannot admit of anything other than such systems. This argument lends weight to my aforementioned reluctance to reduce mind to brain because it suggests that something quite considerable is lost in that process of reduction.

This argument does not entail that we abandon materialism, broadly defined. It does, however, entail that we abandon the vulgar materialism which reduces all that exists to 'matter', narrowly defined in terms of its sense perceptible properties, and which reduces all of human experience to the objective properties and processes of the physical matter of the brain. We need to recognise that some physical structures, the human body in particular, have, as Merleau-Ponty (1968a) puts it, 'another side'; that they do not simply extend into space, whereupon they are perceptible from the outside, but are equally sensuous beings which feel and perceive from the 'inside out'. Furthermore, we must recognise that this sensuousness, *qua* conscious experience, entails qualities which require qualitatively different types of analysis to those offered by neuroscience. No amount of chemical analysis will tell us what it is like to see, feel, desire and so on, and for this reason such analyses can never tell us why we act as we do.

Conclusion: Mindful Embodiment and the Social World

In sociology and the social sciences more generally we are concerned to explain various forms of human activity and action. To this end we often employ, either tacitly or explicitly, a psychological language; that is, a language of motives, meanings, reasons, purposes and so on. Descartes, to his credit, recognised that this way of thinking about human life was irreconcilable with the new definitions of matter and the physical world which were beginning to emerge when he was writing. Consequently he posited the existence of a mind, distinct from this physical realm, in which all of these more human qualities might be deemed to exist. This solution, as we saw in Chapter 2, turns out to be sociologically as well as philosophically problematic. The response of the mind–brain identity theorist is to reduce everything down to the physical level; that is, to chemical interactions in the brain. They actually preserve many of the key problems of Descartes account whilst also failing to preserve his central insight: namely that there is far more to human life and our being-in-the-world than a conception of inert physical matter and its various atomised causal relations could ever hope to capture. They miss the point, grasped by Descartes, that the world is meaningful for human beings; that these meanings shape and occasion action; and that meanings are strictly irre-ducible to atomised physical causes.

I have already hinted in this chapter that a more satisfactory solution may be to accept that mental life is, in effect, an emergent structure, aris-ing out of the physical world but strictly irreducible to it. In the following chapters I will begin to map out the case for this argument. I will begin with a discussion of the work of Gilbert Ryle (1949). This will allow me to elaborate upon the arguments, raised in this chapter, regarding the meanings of our various mental concepts. Following this, in Chapter 5, I will be considering the model of embodied agency developed in the work of Merleau-Ponty (1962, 1965). In Merleau-Ponty's work we will find a powerful and persuasive model of the human agent as a whole which is greater than the sum of its physical parts; one which resonates very strongly with the issues of meaning and purpose that we have raised in this chapter.

Note

1. This argument is complicated, slightly, by the fact that neuroscientific language has now entered the vernacular – albeit to serve 'folk psychological' purposes.

4

BEYOND DUALISM: EXORCISING DESCARTES' GHOST

> ... 'inside' and 'outside' with respect to human action are mere metaphors. When we talk of something inside us, we do not mean a real physical inside that could be reached directly through an orifice in the body as an alternative to the mere indirect access we have via a person's expression.
>
> Joas *The Creativity of Action*

Having discussed the problems of both Cartesian dualism and the vulgar materialism of the mind–brain identity theory, I want to turn in this chapter to a study which sets us on the way to a non-dualistic sociology: Gilbert Ryle's (1949) *The Concept of Mind*. The title of this work may sound oddly out of place in a book on embodiment. Nothing could be further from the truth, however. We will never overcome dualism if we think only in terms of the body or bodies because bodies are just as much part of dualism as minds are. To overcome dualism we must reconceptualise both mind and body. Ryle is invaluable in this respect because his analysis of 'mind', or rather of the concept of mind, offers a reconceptualisation of mental life which is explicitly non-dualist. He exorcises Descartes' ghost persuasively and powerfully. This opens the door for a serious reconsideration of the body too, though, as I argue towards the end of the chapter, Ryle's arguments do not go far enough to allow us to complete this complementary stage of our analysis. This does not diminish the significance of Ryle's position, however. His work represents a crucial and positive turning point in the argument of this book.

Ryle's analyses allow us break with the dualist tendency of seeing 'mind' as a distinct 'thing', separate from the body and from social contexts. He relocates mental life at the level of embodied and contextualised social actions. It is important to note, however, that his critique of Descartes extends beyond the basic issue of mind and matter. Two points are particularly important here. Firstly, as I noted in Chapter 2, he is concerned to challenge the primacy which the Cartesian affords to reflective and propositional forms in their account of mind. We have already seen why he deems this problematic but we will see, in this chapter, how he constructs an alternative to it. Secondly, Ryle challenges the notion of mental transparency that the Cartesian advocates. The Cartesian supposes that we gain self-knowledge by way of an inward glance, as if our mental life were a possible object of experience for us; an 'inner theatre' which we can watch and learn from. Basic phenomenological reflection suggests that this is not so, however. We do not experience our mental life as such. We have experiences of the world around us and any self-psychological insights we might achieve are rooted either upon an indirect inference from these experiences or upon a reflection upon our embodied activities in the world. We will see how Ryle develops this argument at a number of points in the chapter.

Ryle's style of philosophising is conceptually focused. He seeks to consider what we mean by such concepts as 'understanding', 'will', 'consciousness' and so on. Consequently much of this chapter will be structured around separate discussions of his analyses of these concepts. Specifically I will examine, in this order, his analyses of 'emotion', 'consciousness', 'understanding', 'will' and 'the I'. Before I do this, however, it is crucial that we understand where, in Ryle's view, Descartes goes wrong.

Dualism as a Category Error

Ryle (1949) argues that the historical root of Cartesian dualism has three central elements: Galileo's definition of physical matter, the mechanistic worldview which accompanied it, and the optimistic belief that the whole of the universe would be explained within this 'system'. Descartes was greatly impressed by the work of Galileo, Ryle notes, but as a God-fearing man also somewhat worried about its consequences. It left no room for the soul and spiritual or indeed moral life. Consequently, he added 'mind' to Galileo's inventory of the 'stuff of the world' as a way of making space for the spiritual dimension. The way he did this, however, very much remained within Galileo's mould. He posited 'mind' as another 'substance' akin to matter. This was his fatal error.

In positing the existence of mind as a distinct 'substance' Descartes commits what Ryle calls a 'category error'. This is an error which arises when we treat phenomena of one logical type as if they were of another. For example, if a bomber pilot reports back to base that she can see tanks, weapon factories and army barracks but has not yet eyeballed the enemy war machine, she is committing a category error because she is treating 'war machine' as if it were the same type of thing as a tank or barracks. She has failed to realise that a war machine simply is tanks + barracks + factories + platoons and so on. It is not an additional machine of the same sort as them but rather a collective name for all of them together, as they are respectively articulated and co-ordinated. Similarly we might be perplexed by a man who claimed to have three brothers: 'Paul, John and me'. We would want to insist that he has two brothers, Paul and John, or else that he is one of three brothers, but not that he has three brothers. And we might question his ability to use the word 'brother'. It is just such a muddle that Descartes gets into according to Ryle. He assumes that 'mental' language, as it is distinct from the language of matter, refers to a thing much like matter but distinct from it; a different substance. But this is not so. Just because we have a separate language of mind, that does not mean that there must be a distinct object, 'the mind', corresponding to it, any more than there must be a war machine in addition to the tanks and missiles the pilot can enumerate.

Integral to this notion of category errors, at least for our purposes, is the doubling up that it entails. Our man with three brothers, for example, counts himself twice in his reckoning. He is both the I who has three brothers and one of the brothers. And our bomber pilot, in looking for a war machine additional to the tanks and so forth which she has spotted, does much the same. She has seen the enemy war machine, in the form of tanks and platoons, but she does not realise that she has seen it and so is looking for it, a second time over, somewhere else. Cartesian dualism, for Ryle, is just such a victim of doubling up. The Cartesian, he argues, identifies 'traces' of 'mental phenomena' in human behaviour and sensation, but their conception of the body will not allow them to believe that these behaviours and sensations really are the substance of mental life so, much like the bomber pilot, they start looking somewhere else. Indeed, they invent a whole new realm of reality where it 'must' be, even if we cannot see it. Thus, when they witness intelligent behaviour they believe that they are seeing two things: intelligence and behaviour. Their conception of the bodily life to which behaviour belongs will not let them accept that these two bits are aspects of a single phenomena. They cannot accept that 'intelligence' may just be a property of certain types of behaviour, with no other deeper centre or cause. The thrust of Ryle's argument is that they should accept just this.

This critique of doubling up is one which the mind–brain identity theorists could accept to a degree. Ryle does not accept their solution either, however. This 'solution', which collapses 'mind' back into 'the body' in a crudely objectivist and biological fashion, may remove the tendency towards doubling up, but it does great violence to our phenomenological sense of mental life and the meaning of mental concepts in the process (see Chapter 3). Ryle's method, in contrast, is to consider the meaning of mental concepts as we actually use them in everyday life, coupled with a phenomenological reflection upon the possible meanings of such terms. The solution to dualism which this suggests is, to use a phrase from contemporary social theory, 'action-theoretical'. Mental life is embodied for Ryle, but this entails a conception of the body as a sensuous and active being, always already involved in a context. Insofar as mental concepts have a referent, therefore, it is embodied action-in-context. Having said this, if we analyse the use of mental concepts in context we find that they do not always strictly have a referent at all (see below). Words, as Austin (1971) argues, 'do things' and this means doing things in addition to referring.

Moreover, if the same term, for example, 'thinking', has different uses in different contexts, then it also has different meanings and we must be careful not to conflate these or otherwise become confused by them. While he challenges dualism then, and posits a clearly embodied conception of the human agent, Ryle does not directly seek to locate 'mental phenomena' in the body or even in action. He is more concerned with the manner in which mental concepts are used by embodied agents in specific contexts of actions: that is, with their occasions of use and their social and phenomenological contexts. Notwithstanding this, what emerges out of this analysis, in my view, is an embryonic conception of the embodied actor and I will be attempting to draw this conception into the foreground in my exposition. There is much here that requires unpacking. I will begin by considering the notion of language as action.

Language in Context

Like Austin (1971), the later Wittgenstein (1953) and a number of important sociologists, including Mead (1967) and Mills (1974), Ryle maintains that the meaning of words or concepts is derived not from their representational relationship to things which they name but rather from their use or function within social interaction. We make a great deal of use of 'mental' concepts in our everyday lives, he observes, but close examination of our use of those concepts reveals that they make no reference to 'mental states', as such, and serve a quite different purpose. When I say 'that hurts', for example, I am not describing or naming anything. Rather I am exclaiming. My words are the linguistic equivalent of 'ouch!', which clearly expresses something but does not describe or refer to anything. Furthermore, by saying 'that hurts' I may be instructing or requesting that an individual who is causing me discomfort in some way stop whatever it is that they are doing. 'That hurts', in this context, is effectively a request; it means 'stop it'. The same point applies to a wide range of uses of mentalistic terms. When I say 'I think that Man. Utd will win on Saturday', for example, I am not describing any process of thought going on in my head. 'Think', in this context, does not describe or refer to a process of thought. It serves simply to qualify my assertion about the outcome of the game. I am offering my assertion as an opinion rather than a fact and I am owning that opinion as my own: I think Utd will win but that is just my opinion and there may be other views. I may have given no thought, as such, to the outcome of the game, but even if I had my use of 'I think' would not be a reference to or description of that process. If I was in a more confrontational mood I might say that I 'know' they will win, thereby strengthening my claim, making it bolder and suggesting that it is more than mere opinion. That would not mean that something different, or indeed anything at all, was going on in my head, however. I do not have to 'look inside my head', as it were, to see whether I know or I think.

Not only could I not do this but it would be superfluous anyway since, to reiterate, I am not describing any sort of 'mental content'.

It is integral to this argument that a great deal of 'mind talk' serves a social function. For example, when I say 'I am sorry' for turning up late to a meeting I am not describing any inner process or feeling of sorrow but am rather 'doing an apology' and thus repairing the moral damage and potential offence caused by my contravention of the norm of punctuality. I have broken the contract I entered into with another person about meeting at a specific time and need now to indicate to them that this was not a deliberate snub or show of power on my behalf. I reconfirm the equality of our relationship and the mutual recognition it entails through a culturally appropriate ritual of apology. Saying sorry may not be enough, of course. Having breached the social norm of punctuality, other ways of apologising or 'acting sorry' may be expected from the individual. Nevertheless, this does not alter the fact that the meaning of mental concepts derives from their function within social interaction rather than a substantial reference, 'inner worldly' or otherwise.

It is a failure to grasp this basic fact about mentalistic language, Ryle argues, which leads the Cartesian into the aforementioned 'doubling up' upon which dualism is based. Because they assume that such phrases as 'I think' are descriptions, they are forced to search out the referent being described and they therefore posit the existence of an inner mental realm. By challenging their assumption regarding the meanings of mental concepts, therefore, we actually challenge the basis of dualism itself.

A critic may respond to this by arguing that, irrespective of the social function of mental words, individuals do experience such things as feelings. An individual may say 'sorry' as a way of excusing deviant behaviour, the critic could argue, but that individual may *feel* sorry too; or perhaps rather they may *feel* guilty or shameful. In response to this possible criticism we must note, firstly, that Ryle does not deny the existence of bodily feelings or pangs, such as we might associate with guilt, and secondly, that there is no reason why, as a critic of dualism, he should. He intends to show that there is no 'mind' distinct from the human body but that does not preclude the possibility of embodied feelings and sensations; that is, of sensuous embodiment. Having said that, we must be careful how we think about such sensations and their relationship to mental concepts according to Ryle. To unpick his views on this matter in more detail we can consider his ideas on emotion and consciousness respectively (see also Crossley 1998, 2000a).

Emotion

We tend to think of emotions as feelings and we think of feelings as inner occurrences. This is because the language by which we refer to emotions is predominantly a language of 'feeling': that is, we claim to 'feel' happy, sad, jealous, angry and so on. When we ascribe emotional feelings to ourselves we do not describe those feelings, according to Ryle, however, rather, we attribute a cause or meaning to them. When I feel nervous, for example, I may experience any of a number of bodily sensations, including a feeling in the pit of my stomach, a racing heartbeat, nausea, shortness of breath and so forth. Saying 'I feel nervous', whether to myself or other people, does not describe any or all of these feelings, however. It attributes a cause or reason to them which, in itself, need be neither physical or mental and will, in all likelihood, identify a social situation which occasions the feeling (for example, an impending exam). To say 'I feel nervous' or to otherwise recognise oneself as nervous is to attribute whatever weird bodily pangs one is experiencing to a specific set of circumstances. There is nothing 'inner worldly' about emotion concepts in this respect and emotion-ascription is not a matter of introspection. I may experience particular bodily feelings but in calling those feelings emotion (for example, fear) I look to events in the 'outside' world which occasion or cause them. Furthermore, in doing this I draw upon common sense understandings of the meaning of my present context. I make sense of the strange feeling in my stomach by reference to an impending exam, drawing off the notion, taken for granted within my culture, that exams are a source of anxiety and stress.

We can advance this argument on a number of grounds. Firstly, there is nothing specific about the bodily sensations that are entailed in emotional states. The same bodily feelings may be involved in very different emotional states or different states altogether (for example, exercising, being ill, exhaustion or drunkenness). What is determinate is the situation which occasions such feelings and the attribution which we consequently make. Weird tummy feelings and loose bowls constitute nervousness when and only when they are occasioned by an impending exam or some such things. If they occur after a wild night out they may mean something very different. Secondly, no feeling or configuration of feelings is necessary to an emotional state. We generally concede that different people experience or manifest particular emotions in different ways. And even the same individual may manifest their emotion differently between occasions. The notion of emotion as feeling is misleading then.

Ryle's insistence upon the nature of emotion concepts is not rooted simply in the desire to challenge dualism and the Cartesian image of the 'inner world'. It is rooted in sound observations about the nature of language. Emotion concepts belong to natural languages, he observes, and natural languages must be learned. To be learned, however, languages must function in public ways, in accordance with public and intersubjectively verifiable criteria. How could we ever teach an individual to use the concept of 'jealousy', for example, if the meaning of that concept referred to a private state? And how could we have ever learned to use it? As teachers of language we could not point our jealousy out to our pupils and say 'this is jealousy', because they would not know what we were talking about if the emotion was private. And by the same token we would never learn what others meant by 'jealous' if the meaning of the term was inextricably linked to a private inner feeling they were experiencing. What the concept 'jealous' does, in fact, is to render a specific manifestation of sensation and/or behaviour intelligible by identifying it as a particular type of response to a particular type of situation, and we are able to learn and teach this concept because the response, the occasioning situation and the socio-logic of their relationship are all inter-subjective and public phenomena. To be jealous is to respond to a certain sort of situation in a certain sort of way and we learn what jealousy is because others tend to say 'don't be so jealous!' if and when we act in this way. For this same reason, sensations must have some relation to explicit behaviours which sometimes accompany them and, as such, mark them out. Wittgenstein's (1953) famous analysis of 'pain' provides an instructive example of this. The sensation of pain is quite clearly different from the various behaviours which often accompany it, Wittgenstein argues. The sensation caused by dropping a hammer on one's foot, for example, is quite different in kind from hopping and dancing around the room with one's injured foot clasped firmly in hand. On the other hand, because the sensation is strictly private, we could never have a word for it and it could never enter our public language, unless it was also sometimes accompanied by such behaviours. Pain behaviour gives pain a public form, allowing it to enter into social intercourse and therefore language. We can teach a child to say 'I am in pain', for example, because we can spot its gestures of pain as they emerge in response to recognisable occasioning circumstances. It also follows from this that the word 'pain' does not describe the sensation in any respect. Indeed, as was briefly mentioned above, Wittgenstein (1953) suggests that the language of pain is, for the most part, an exclamatory language game which substitutes for our more basic or natural pain behaviours. When I say, 'I am in pain', Wittgenstein argues, I am not describing anything. Rather, I am exclaiming or otherwise expressing my pain. The 'grammar' of my utterance is more akin to a 'youch' than to statements of the kind 'the cat is on the mat'. Indeed, part and parcel of learning to use the word 'pain' has been learning to substitute the words 'I am in pain', in at least some circumstances, for a more natural response. 'I am in pain' is a socialised, some might say 'civilised', version of 'aghhh!'.

Having said this, 'the emotions' cover a much broader range of phenomena than is suggested by the notion of 'feeling', according to Ryle. They encompass phenomena which might not actually involve bodily sensations at all. Emotions are heterogenous and we must be clear to adequately account for their variety. He identifies three further applications of emotion talk whose relation to bodily pangs is, at best, inconsistent. Firstly, there are what he calls 'inclinations', amongst which he includes character traits such as vanity, melancholy and introversion. These are straightforward dispositions (see below), he claims. They entail a tendency to respond to situations of a certain sort with actions of a certain sort, or else perhaps to perform actions in a specific way. These dispositions may entail a proneness to particular feelings; an introvert, for example, will be prone to certain bodily sensations in certain sorts of situation. But this is not necessary, as is evidenced by the fact that the person may not be aware of their 'inclination'. Ryle selects the vain person as his example of this. Vanity does not entail specific bodily sensations, he notes, and the vain person may, very often, be the last person to know about their vanity. Vanity is a pattern of behaviour which the vain person may be quite unaware of. Secondly, Ryle discusses 'moods', like being bad tempered. These are not dispositions, as they are sporadic. Anybody can be in a bad mood sometimes even if some are more disposed to moodiness than others. Indeed, moods, by definition, signal a change of behaviour. As with dispositions these may entail bodily pangs but, again, they equally entail behaviours and may be more apparent from the 'outside' than to the person who is in the mood. It may not be obvious to a jealous person that they are being jealous, for example. They may attribute their vindictiveness towards another as an act of moral righteousness, if they are aware of it at all. They are too busy being jealous, that is, behaving and perceiving in a jealous way, to notice that they are being jealous. Thirdly, Ryle refers to 'agitations'. These are disturbances in one's flow of behaviour. A person who cannot decide between two equally desirable options may be temporarily paralysed, for example, as might a person whose expectations regarding their current situation are not born out. Anxiety is commonly 'experienced' in such situations and this may well entail bodily pangs of the sort we have already discussed (for example, increased heart rate, sickness). It will also tend to involve involuntary behavioural responses too, such as stuttering, tremors and 'response alternation'; that is, first doing or saying this, then doing or saying that, but never quite fully doing or saying anything. As with 'feelings', however, what makes us refer to anxiety is not the specific behaviours or feelings because they are not specific but rather the situation which occasions them.

The important point to grasp in all of these cases is that emotion concepts *do not refer to inner or ghostly mental states, nor even to the various bodily sensations they may entail.* They render specific configurations of sensation, behaviour and disposition intelligible by linking them to a context which has seemingly occasioned them. Emotions are embodied for Ryle; they entail some combination of sensation, behaviour and disposition. But emotion is not defined by these bodily states or activities, as such. The function of emotion language is to render such states and activities intelligible by locating them within the contexts which occasion them and to which they constitute a purposive response. Emotion thus entails an articulation of bodily activity and worldly social context. It is not the property of an agent but of an agent-in-the-world. Ryle makes a very similar case with respect to consciousness.

Consciousness and Perception

Within the Cartesian schema 'consciousness' is understood as a thing or substance. There are physical substances and there are mental substances. The body exists as a thing and the conscious mind exists as a separate thing. This argument is based on a misunderstanding or misuse of the term 'consciousness' according to Ryle. Human beings are conscious, he argues. They enjoy consciousness of various things. But this does not mean that consciousness is a substance, any more than the fact that some human beings are tall makes 'tallness' a substance. Consciousness is a property of the relationship which embodied human beings enjoy to their world. It is rooted in perception which, in turn, is rooted in sensation. It is not a 'thing' in its own right. To pursue this notion we must return to Ryle's analysis of sensations.

Three clear points emerge out of this analysis. Firstly, sensations are physically rooted experiences, for Ryle. Insofar as consciousness consists in perceptual sensations, therefore, it is a property of 'the body' rather than of a separate mind or mental substance. 'The body' in question here is quite clearly not the lifeless corpse or mechanical machine of the Cartesian, however. It is a sensuous being which precisely feels and perceives; a 'lived' body. Secondly, Ryle argues that sensations are never 'neat', by which he means that they seem always to refer us to something else. This is particularly evident in relation to perception, where one's sensation refers one to the object of one's perception. I may have visual sensations of the wall before me, for example. This is also true of less differentiated sensations, however. Our pains generally strike us as being of a particular type, such as 'a stabbing pain' or a 'burning pain', for example, and thus they seem, albeit indirectly and metaphorically, to refer to the type of activity that would produce that sort of pain: for example, a stabbing pain is the sort of experience one would experience if being prodded or stabbed with something. Thirdly, Ryle argues that we do not perceive or observe our sensations. Rather, we have them and, by this means, perceive or observe something else. I do not see my sensation of the car, for example; I have the sensation and see the car. Similarly I do not hear my sensation of the barking of the dog or smell my sensation of the flower. In both cases I have the sensation and hear and smell the dog and flower respectively.

Though he does not explicitly draw the comparison, what Ryle argues here is very much akin to the phenomenological notion of the *intentionality* of consciousness. Consciousness, the phenomenologists argue, is always 'consciousness of' something other than it. It always 'intends' objects. The importance of this 'intentional' definition of perceptual consciousness is that it challenges the Cartesian notion of the 'inner theatre of the mind' and constitutes a first important step towards a critique of introspection. The Cartesian paints a picture in which consciousness is an inner space in which things happen; a furnished space to which the individual alone has access. What Ryle and the phenomenologists are arguing, by contrast, is that consciousness is a relationship to the external world whose 'contents' consist precisely in the contents of that world. I do not look inside myself and find consciousness, perceptions and so on. An inspection of the contents of my consciousness, in effect, amounts to an inspection of the 'furniture' of the world, as that is all that I am conscious of and my consciousness simply is my sensuous relationship to the world. This is not to say that an account of what I percieve may not be psychologically revealing. The fact that I spot one thing on a crowded street and somebody else spots something else may say a great deal about each of us. But any such psychological insights are, of necessity, indirect. I may infer psychological dispositions and preoccupations from my perceptions, or anybody else's for that matter, but I do not have direct access to them – because there is nothing to have direct access to. My dispositions and preoccupations are not 'things'. There is nothing psychological to see within my head, as such, nor indeed in my stream of consciousness.

The same applies, in essence, to imaginary experiences. Much of what belongs to our imagination consists, in fact, in public behaviours. Children's play, theatre, literature and cinema are all examples of this. They are public and embodied manifestations of imagination. Even when people experience private dreams, however, they dream of objects or things from the 'external world', albeit sometimes transformed in fantastical ways. They do not experience an inner world or the workings of their own mind, as such. As I noted with perception, saying this is not to deny the possibility that great psychological advances may be made through the analysis of dreams. They may. But such analysis necessarily proceeds by indirect inference, as when a drawing or story is 'read' with a view to analysing the psychology of its author. Dreams are not transparent pictures of an inner world, conscious or unconscious. They are images and stories of something other than the mind, from which we may make psychological inferences.

Ryle's style of argument here is phenomenological. He is challenging us to reflect upon our conscious experience, whether wakeful or in sleep, and to find anything therein which is not an aspect (real or imagined) of a world which transcends us. And he is expecting that we will fail. Our consciousness is consciousness of things other than itself and any 'inward turn' of our gaze must inevitably find itself back in the one and only 'outer' world therefore. Phenomenology reveals that there is no inner world in any substantive sense. There is also a linguistic argument here, however, which parallels some of the points discussed earlier. To describe the 'contents' of our consciousness we must, of necessity, use language; but languages, as we have said, are public and derive their meaning from their role in intersubjective encounters. Descriptions of consciousness, therefore, must always be descriptions of those aspects of the intersubjective world of which we are conscious. Consciousness, as it is rooted in sensation, is essentially private like any sensation, and as such, even if it did involve other worldly elements there could be no language to describe them.

The 'doubling up' involved in dualism is clearly apparent here. The dualist assumes, from the fact that we perceive the world, that there must be a place where this perception takes place – an inner cinema – and that our perceptions are something which we perceive. Ryle, by contrast, insists that what we perceive is the world and that perceiving, as such, is not a thing which could be perceived. As with emotion, consciousness consists in our embodied relationship to our world.

Understanding

A critic may concede that emotions and consciousness can be accounted for in this way. But, they will respond, what about more obviously cognitive phenomena such as knowing and understanding? Surely Ryle cannot hope to wrestle these away from Descartes? He can, and he does. We can begin our exploration of this more cognitive domain by examining the concept of 'understanding'.

'Understanding' may seem, *prima facie*, to be a good example of a disembodied mental process which occurs 'in the head'. Many psychologists believe just this. This is a mythical view, according to Ryle. To say that we understand something, he argues, is to say that we can do it or do something in relation to it, such as talk meaningfully about it. To understand the game of chess, for example, is to be able to play it and/or talk meaningfully about it to other similarly informed individuals; to be able to criticise and comment. This seems counter-intuitive, Ryle concedes, because our attempts to learn are often accompanied by all manner of sensations, some of which strike us as a 'click of comprehension', and we are inclined to believe that such sensations indicate the existence of an inner process which, in turn, we name with the term 'understanding'. A more thorough reflection suggests that this is not so, however. I would not say that I understand calculus if I cannot do it competently, to the satisfaction of the numerate community, for example, no matter how many clicks and sensations I feel. Indeed, it is very likely that, in the process of learning, I will feel something 'come over me' and say 'Oh I get it,' only to fail at the first hurdle and be forced to concede that I evidently do not 'get it' at all. 'Getting it' is being able to do it, acquiring the skill or competence. Furthermore, I would conclude that I do understand calculus if I am able to do it and apply it appropriately, even if I have never experienced clicks or other sensations whilst doing or learning it. Again there are many examples of this, since I would say that I continue to understand calculus now, long after I originally learned how to do it, even though it has become rather mundane for me and completely devoid of tingles and clicks.

The dualist may concede here that some sort of display of competence is indeed essential to our concept of understanding, but they would insist that this is merely an outward display of an inner process. We expect people to be able to prove that they understand, it might be conceded, and to this end we expect them to do certain things, but proving and actually understanding are two different things. This is precisely where they go wrong in Ryle's view, however. Because they preconceive the body and thus behaviour, following Galileo, as 'dumb matter', they are forced to invent a second site of activity to account for the intelligent and meaningful nature of competent behaviour. The dualist splits off the cognitive and the behavioural because their concept of behaviour is unable to accommodate meaning and intelligence. They are wrong, according to Ryle. The intelligence and meaning entailed in 'understanding' are properties of certain sorts of worldly behaviour. This is born out phenomenologically by the fact that our judgements of understanding, in relation to both self and other, focus precisely upon our behavioural competence and on nothing else. What would it be to understand calculus if one could not do it or talk competently about it? More to the point, what else does understanding calculus involve other than being able to do it and talk competently about it? Nowhere is the category error and doubling up of the dualist more apparent than here.

Simply equating 'understanding' with appropriate or correct behaviour would be problematic, however, according to Ryle. It would leave one vulnerable to the criticism that there are many instances of seemingly appropriate behaviour which we would not deem examples of understanding. If a parrot says '4' immediately after its owner says '2 + 2', for example, we assume that this is the result of either luck or drill, resisting the thought that the parrot really understands addition. It is examples such as this, Ryle argues, which tempt us to imagine that understanding must involve ghostly goings on. If correct behaviour is not sufficient in itself to qualify as understanding we believe that understanding must involve behaviour plus some other (inner) process. He opposes the ghostly theory, however, with a dispositional one. To understand addition, he argues, one must do more than answer a single question over a period of time, 'parrot fashion'. One must be able to correctly tackle any number of addition questions, using the technique with a combination of numbers that one has never encountered before and demonstrating an appreciation of both appropriate and inappropriate occasions of its use. It is because no parrot can do this that we believe parrots don't understand addition. Understanding is therefore a general (embodied) disposition towards correct behaviour which is evidenced in a multitude of situations. It belongs to the domain of the body or perhaps rather embodied praxis.

Does this apply in all cases? Suppose, for example, that two people are watching a game of chess; one understands the game and the other does not. Is the difference between them not something that goes on in their heads? Disposition is still the key in this case, for Ryle. The person who understands the game, he argues, is 'playing it', albeit at one step removed, without touching the board or moving the pieces. And they are doing so because they can; because they are a competent player. They have learned to play the game and also to substitute actual playing for a restrained form in which sub-vocalised stipulations of action (for example, 'move there you idiot!') substitute for actual moves. The lack of understanding of the other is, by the same token, an inability to join in and play in this way. This is not a matter of inner mental processes but rather of embodied dispositions.

This view of understanding is profoundly unfashionable in the present climate, which is dominated by cognitivist and computational models of the mind (Evans 1993). The computational model, whilst usually claiming to remain neutral on the dualism issue, maintains that understanding and related 'mental phenomena', whilst not discoverable by phenomenological means, are nevertheless real unconscious processes. How could such a phenomena as 'doing calculus' not involve mental processes, they ask? Moreover, they argue that it is possible to map such processes by way of computer simulation. If we can make a computer do calculus or play chess, they claim, then we can work out which 'rules' and 'programmes' are involved in the human case (see Fodor 1968). This is wrongheaded. As Searle (1991) argues, there is no reason whatsoever to believe that the ability of computers to perform some of the tasks we are capable of necessitates that we perform those tasks in the same way. Indeed, given that we are organic, rather than metal and plastic, and are non-digital, it is highly unlikely that we 'work' in the same way as computers. Moreover, in the final instance the computational model hits up against the same brick wall as it identifies for the behavioural model:

> … if you ask 'How does a calculator multiply seven times three?', the answer is: 'It adds three to itself seven times.' But if you then ask: 'And how does it add three to itself?', there isn't any computational answer to that; it is done in the hardware. So the answer is, 'It just does it'. And I want to suggest that for a great many absolutely fundamental abilities, such as our ability to see or our ability to learn a language, there may not be any theoretical mental level underlying those abilities: the brain just does them. (Searle 1991: 53)

The point of this argument, in my view, is not that the brain-identity theorists were right after all and that the brain thinks things through.[1] It is simply to say that, to all intents and purposes, there are some things we can 'just do', whether by nature or learning, and that it makes no sense to probe any deeper than this level. We reach a point in our attempts to explain and elucidate where we can go no further without having to abandon the very terms which giving meaning to whatever it is that we seek to explain. And this point is where we should stop. The brain and the language of the brain, as I explained in the previous chapter, is one step too far in my view, since it necessitates a shift from psychological to biological discourse. But there is really no value is positing a hypothetical computational intermediary between brain and behaviour either. If we are forced to concede, even within the computational model, that there are certain things we 'just do' then that model amounts to nothing more than a cumbersome and unnecessary hypothetical detour from proper understanding. It is more parsimonious and sensible to focus our conception of psychological life around the phenomenological-behavioural level that Ryle identifies, accepting that, at this level, there are some things that we can and do 'just do' by virtue of biological constitution and/or learning. Anything 'deeper' is fanciful and unnecessary. Thus, in my view, the embodied competencies to which Ryle refers really are the bottom line on understanding.

Two further critical points can be drawn from this discussion of understanding. In the first instance, contrary to the Cartesian notion that individuals have privileged access to their own mental states and know their own minds in a qualitatively different way to the way others may know them, our example suggests that individuals learn of their own understanding much as one would learn of the understanding of another; that is, by observing the results of their own attempts at whatever it is they wish to understand. Merleau-Ponty, who shares Ryle's view on this matter, puts it in the following way:

> Nothing is changed when the subject is charged with interpreting his reactions himself, which is proper to introspection. When he is asked if he can read the letters inscribed on a panel or distinguish the details of a shape, he will not trust to a vague 'impression of legibility'. He will attempt to read or describe what is presented to him. (Merleau-Ponty 1965: 183)

We don't 'look inwards' when we wish to ascertain whether we understand something, in other words, as there is nothing to see. We have a go and see how we get on. And others too may gauge our understanding in just the same way. Secondly, insofar as it is possible to refer to understanding as correct or incorrect this implies the existence of intersubjective criteria by which our competencies are judged, such that we can argue that understanding is, in these cases, a social phenomenon. It entails conformity to a norm. Mental life is, in this sense, necessarily normative and intersubjective.

Know-how and the Critique of Intellectualism

Ryle's account of 'understanding' forms part of a wider conception of 'know-how' and, as such, forms a part of his critique of the intellectualism of the Cartesian approach. I discussed this critique in Chapter 2, noting that the intellectualist conceptualises mental life in terms of propositional knowledge and that this inevitably ensnares them in infinite regression. They are forced to argue, for example, that thinking must be thought about in order to be thoughtful; that we must think about it before doing it. But this applies equally to thought about thought; that too must be thought about. Plans musts be planned, choices chosen and so on, in an absurd and never ending regression. The only way to avoid this problem, Ryle argues, is to reject the prejudice which makes propositional thought the model for mental life. This does not entail a complete rejection of the notion of propositional knowledge, nor of choice, planning and reflective thought. Ryle would be hard pushed as a philosopher to reject these things as philosophy involves them all. But he argues that we need to move away from the notion that actions can only be deemed 'thoughtful', 'intelligent' or meaningful in virtue of some act of thought which precedes them. This is precisely the path into infinite regression. In place of this he argues that we need to recognise a different kind of knowledge to propositional knowledge, which he terms 'knowledge-how' or 'know-how'. Know-how is a form of embodied competence or skill, an ability to do certain sorts of things in certain sorts of ways, without necessarily requiring the intervention of reflective thought. Indeed, from this perspective reflective thought is itself a form of behaviour which precisely presupposes a degree of competence or know-how, such that competence must be deemed more primordial and basic in terms of human being than reflective forms of activity and knowing. What makes the arguments of a philosopher or anybody else intelligent or thoughtful is not some act which predates the argument, Ryle argues, but rather the way in which the argument itself is 'done', the skill or embodied competence it entails. The brilliance of the philosopher, no less than that of the boxer or gymnast, rests upon an acquired and embodied capacity or skill to do certain sorts of things to certain sorts of standards. And this learned bodily competence is the 'bottom line'. It is not grounded by any reflective considerations, conscious or otherwise, about the processes involved. One just does it.

Intellectual activities and capacities are thus argued to be rooted in practical skills and competencies and a further central tenet of Cartesian thought, that 'the subject' is first and foremost a reflective, thinking being, is challenged. Thinking, Ryle argues, is an embodied activity involving acquired skills and competencies or know-how, and 'the subject', insofar as it remains appropriate to use this term, is therefore first and foremost a skilled and embodied agent, a practical rather than a theoretical being. Moreover, their primary relation to their world consists in practical and skilled engagement, doing in it rather than thinking about it, even if what it is that they are doing at a particular point in time is thinking.

There are many different types of know-how, belonging to different types of activity and different social groups (Nyiri and Smith 1988). Academic pursuits such as philosophy, sociology and science presuppose know-how, as a number of philosophers of science have persuasively argued (Kuhn 1970, Polanyi 1966). But more importantly, for our purposes, our everyday life and activities rest upon shared bodies of traditional know-how. We 'know-how' to operate and utilise the various forms of equipment we encounter in our everyday lives, for example, and do not need to think about how and when to do so. Similarly we know how to play the various 'games' that make up much of the substance of our social life; how to behave properly and make sense of the actions of others. The world is 'ready-to-hand', to use Heidegger's (1962) phrase, in both its physical and its social aspects. We are 'able' to act appropriately within it.

This notion of know-how connects with the broader desire to transcend dualism in three respects. Firstly, it challenges any absolute distinction between 'intellectual' and 'manual' activity; both are forms of competent 'doing' in which agents are skilled to varying degrees. The philosopher's skill at honing in on and attacking the weak points of an opponent's argument is no different, in this respect, from the boxer's skill at finding the weak point in their opponent's defences. In both cases what is involved is a skill or competence born of practice and familiarity 'in the ring' (see also Huizinga 1950: 146–57). Secondly, integral to this, it suggests that embodiment and mindfulness are essential elements of both. Philosophy, *qua* form of thinking, is a 'body technique' (Mauss 1979). It is a particular way of acting and using one's body, particularly one's capacity for speech and writing, which is rooted in a tradition in which one has been trained. Similarly boxing is a 'mind game'. The boxer may have no time for reflective thought but each and every one of their acts embodies an understanding of the game and oozes purpose and strategic competence. Finally, in showing this, Ryle's argument demonstrates that and how 'thought', 'thinking' and their cognates are 'this worldly' activities, belonging within the material world rather than some separate substance or realm. They are bodily activities that we enagage in, *qua* embodied agents, because we have acquired the skill to do so.

Dispositions and Habitus

Both understanding and know-how are, as we have already noted, 'dispositions' for Ryle. But what are dispositions? Ryle formulates his conception of dispositions by way of a sharp contrast with the notion of 'habits' (for other accounts see Crane 1996). This contrast should enable us to appreciate that dispositions are something like habits, but the force of Ryle's argument is actually directed at distinguishing the two. Habits, he argues, are very simple, repetitive and mechanical behaviours. They are acquired by 'drill' and require and admit of no improvisation or intelligence. Dispositions are quite different. Though they are acquired by training or other such experiences, which may entail an element of drill, they consist of flexible and intelligent tendencies which admit of a great deal of improvisation. Like habits they are performed 'without thought' and are not reflected upon or thought about in the course of their execution. But in and of themselves they entail an intelligent and strategic adaptation to contextual exigencies and are purposive. The boxer is disposed to fight, for example, but this entails more than mere technique and fitness. Her disposition consists in her capacity to put these elements together in an on-going situation, making the right moves at the right time and adapting the technique as she goes on. Furthermore, though not thought about, as such, dispositions may be thoughtful. Indeed, to illustrate the point, reflectiveness itself is a disposition.

Described thus we can see that and how understanding and know-how are dispositions, in Ryle's terms, but the concept extends further than either of these notions. Dispositions entail our tendency as well as our capacity to act in particular ways. They entail that we are likely to act in particular ways, given specific circumstances, not simply that we are able to. They are not 'single track' phenomena, however. They are 'multi-track', such that the same disposition might be expressed through a multitude of different types of behaviour. Ryle illustrates this with reference to the disposition of pride:

> When Jane Austen wished to show the specific kind of pride which charac-
> terised the heroine of *Pride and Prejudice*, she had to represent her actions,
> words, thoughts and feelings in a thousand different situations. There is no
> one standard type of action or reaction such that Jane Austen could say 'My
> heroine's kind of pride was just the tendency to do this, whenever a situation of
> that sort arose'. (Ryle 1949: 44)

In other words, like understanding, pride does not consist in a single way of responding to a single question or situation but rather in a range of responses to a range of situations. Dispositions are meaningful, purposive and coherent behavioural tendencies which leave considerable room for improvisation and manifest a considerable flexibility.

The way in which Ryle develops this concept of dispositions, by contrast to habits, is problematic. He adopts a corrupted form of 'habit' and what he means by disposition is, in fact, very similar to what many other philosophers mean by either habit or habitus (Brett 1981, Camic 1986). Indeed, writers such as Bourdieu and Merleau-Ponty tend to use the terms habit or habitus and disposition interchangeably, emphasising that 'habit' is a dispositional concept. Notwithstanding this weakness, however, Ryle's discussion of dispositions is important because it allows us to begin to carve out an intelligible space for discussing human agency, somewhere between the respective excesses of mechanistic forms of behaviourism and intellectualism, or again, between mind and body. Dispositions entail far greater agency than is implied in the behaviourist conception of conditioned reflexes or habits and yet they are habits and thus challenge any over-intellectualised conception of the agent rooted in a notion of propositional mental acts. They are stable, flexible and intelligent behavioural tendencies. Moreover, as specifically behavioural tendencies they allow us to begin to identify the mindful nature of the life of the human body and thereby to think our way beyond rigid and unhelpful dualistic distinctions between mind and body. An additional advantage of the concept of dispositions is that it allows us to ground accounts of action rooted in 'reasons' by reference to a terminal point. Reasons for action are propositional in form and for this reason are subject to the same potential for infinite regression as other propositional acts. For any reason that may persuade an agent to act in a particular way a further reason of why that reason was selected or preferred is always presupposed *ad infinitum*. This holds true whether we attribute reasons to the actions of others or we suppose that they formulate their own reasons for acting before actually doing so. Reference to dispositions breaks this regress, and does so without necessarily precluding the possibility that the reason was indeed an effective element in the process of choice and action. We might say, for example, that an agent chose to act in 'this' way, for 'this' reason, but that 'this' reason was compelling for them because of 'this' disposition. And the disposition would not need to be explained by reference to a further reason or disposition because, in effect, it denotes an aspect of the constitution of the agent. It is the 'just do' bedrock which short-circuits the tendency to infinite regression.

Will and Volition

It might be argued against this account of dispositions that individuals act as they do because of some volition; that is, that their actions are 'voluntary' in a stronger sense than the notion of dispositions allows for. Many philosophers have taken this line and a fair few sociologists too (for example, Kant 1948, 1993, Parsons 1968). Ryle is troubled by 'volition', however. Theorists often talk of will, volition or intention as causes of action, he argues, but this 'doubles' up our action descriptions in the familiar and problematic dualist manner. A voluntary surrender, for example, is perceived to consist in two parts: the act of surrendering and the volitional act of meaning to do so. In accordance with his general critique of dualism, Ryle wants to challenge this in favour of a notion which would suggest that 'voluntary surrender' is a single act, but he must first both criticise the dualist position and explain the utility and appeal it has.

He begins his critique with a phenomenological question. Are we aware of executing any act of will in all of our voluntary actions, he asks, such that I might be aware of willing my fingers to move across the keyboard to type these words and you might be aware of willing your eyes to move across the page, from left to right, so as to read them? Indeed, are we aware of willing things at any time? How would we describe the act of willing? In what does it consist? It is important to note here that Ryle is not referring to the acts of, for example, planning an act, or imagining or desiring a particular goal state. He is enquiring into the existence of an act which might come between planning and action, motivating one's body into action. And he is expecting that we will say 'no', we are not aware of any such thing. From the phenomenological point of view, as we will discuss in more detail in Chapter 7, our body seems to launch into action without any particular instruction from us. If I see a friend across the street I do not need to instruct myself to wave and, in fact, would have no idea how to do so; I just do it or rather, it just happens that I wave. In addition, we are not aware of any independent act of will when we consider the actions of others. All we see of them is their actions. We thus have no evidence to support the notion of will. Phenomenologically it is unfounded.

It is not simply that we have no evidence for the existence of independent acts of volition, however. Like many concepts within the dualist scheme, the notion of will, at least when used to account for voluntary behaviour, collapses into infinite regression. If it is appropriate to ask of any act, was that voluntary or not, Ryle argues, then it must be appropriate to ask it of acts of volition. An agent may have willed to act in a particular way, but did they will to will in that way? And what about willing to will that particular will? This creates a catch twenty-two. If an act of volition is not willed, then how can we really say that that which it wills is willed? And if it is willed, then we are forced to ask if that will is willed too and so on *ad infinitum*:

> So what of volitions themselves? Are they voluntary or involuntary acts of mind? Clearly either answer leads to absurdities. If I cannot help willing to pull the trigger, it would be absurd to describe my pulling it as 'voluntary'. But if my volition to pull the trigger is voluntary, in the sense assumed by the theory, then it must issue from a prior volition and that from another *ad infinitum*. (Ryle 1949: 66)

To further his case Ryle is required to meet the objection that we can and do distinguish voluntary and involuntary actions on a daily basis. How is this possible if what he says is true? His answer is important and interesting. Ordinarily, when we ask if an act was voluntary, he suggests, we mean one of three things:

- Was/is it really an act at all? If I slip on a banana skin, for example, it would be more appropriate to describe this as something which happened to me than as something I have done – an act.
- Was/is the person aware of their action or state? For example, are they aware that it is the local vicar they are inviting to their sex party? If not we would be forced to conclude that they did not 'intend' or 'will' to cause offence.
- Was/is the person to blame?

This last point is the key point and is the one which has the strongest pull for the dualist. As Ryle argues, however, the attribution of blame is not a matter of determining whether or not an ephemeral act of willing took place but rather of asking whether the individual had the necessary know-how and opportunity to have acted otherwise. Only philosophers ask whether all acts are voluntary, he argues, because they have lost a grip on the meaning of 'voluntary'. We do not ask whether morally good or acceptable acts are voluntary in everyday life, only bad and unacceptable acts. And we do this generally by asking whether the individual could realistically be expected to have acted any differently, which is a question about their competence, knowledge and circumstances rather than an ephemeral will.

The Bogey of Mechanism

The reason many academics turn to notions of will, and particularly freedom of the will, Ryle argues, is the fear of determinism or what he calls 'the bogey of mechanism'. He is rejecting the notions of will and 'free will' but he is equally clear to dismiss this bogey of mechanism too. His precise argument against it is not clear, and this is a problem, but I would suggest his account approximates a notion that the atomised physical and mechanical 'parts' which comprise the human agent, form a whole which is greater than and irreducible to the sum of their mechanistic parts:

> The discoveries of the physical sciences no more rule out life, sentience, purpose or intelligence from presence in the world than do the rules of grammar exclude style or logic from prose. Certainly the discoveries of the physical sciences say nothing of life, sentience, or purpose, but nor do the rules of grammar say anything about style or logic. (Ryle 1949: 77)

We have allowed ourselves to become terribly confused by 'mechanism' he argues. Having invented certain machines, we are now seeing them everywhere:

> But in fact there are very few machines in Nature. The only machines that we find are the machines that human beings make, such as clocks, windmills and turbines. There are a very few natural systems which somewhat resemble such machines, namely such things as solar systems. (Ryle 1949: 79)

More to the point, we have allowed ourselves to think of ourselves as machines. But we are wrong:

> Men are not machines, not even ghost ridden machines. They are men – a tautology which is sometimes worth remembering. (Ryle 1949: 79)

The few pages which Ryle devotes to this matter in *The Concept of Mind* and elsewhere (Ryle 1969) are far from adequate to establish the case that he wants to make – a case with which I wholeheartedly agree. We will have to do more in the later chapters of this book to establish the case he wishes to make more firmly and with more evidence and argument. Notwithstanding this, however, they are crucial to a proper understanding of Ryle's argument. He is not simply attempting to exorcise the ghost from the machine, as in psychological behaviourism. He is challenging the machine metaphor too. His diagnosis of the mind–body problem, as I noted in the beginning of this chapter, identifies Descartes' appropriation of the work of Galileo as the root of the problem. If the body is sheer matter, a substance which extends into space and obeys the laws of mechanical causation, then how can we account for sensuous and purposive human agency if not by reference to a mind which is distinct from it? Consequently, his challenge to the dominant philosophical model of mind must equally entail a critique of the dominant philosophical-scientific conception of the body. The myth of the ghost in the machine can only be exposed as a myth if the bogey of mechanism is exposed as a bogey, and Ryle's philosophy of mind must therefore also necessarily be a philosophy of the body. The shame, as I have begun to hint already, is that he does not develop this more but we must bear it in mind as we read Ryle. If he seems to be taking from our conception of mind much of what we hold dear with respect to ourselves it is not in order to dump them but rather to resituate them at the level of embodied agency.

Silence, Introspection and the Systematically Elusive 'I'

Ryle's critique effectively denies the existence of a substantive 'inner world'. This will be extremely counter-intuitive to some, particularly given the emphasis upon the 'inner self' in our therapeutic culture (Rose 1989). Ryle goes some way to addressing this counter-intuitiveness, however. We tend to be misled on these matters, he suggests, because we are accustomed to keeping our thoughts to ourselves or otherwise theorising our own possibilities for action in silence. This encourages us to believe that our mental world is essentially private and other-worldly. What we fail to recognise here, however, is that our silent theorising takes exactly the same linguistic form as if it were done 'out loud'. And there is a reason for this; namely, that it is based upon 'external' speech. Thought, at least of the reflective variety, assumes a linguistic form and must necessarily do so. As such it presupposes a learning process. We learn to think reflectively. And we learn to do so, in the first instance, 'out loud'. This is necessary because thinking can only be taught if the thoughts of both teacher and pupil are mutually accessible. Having learned to speak out loud, however, we then learn to do so quietly: that is, to sub-vocalise. Quiet thinking isn't just an acquisition of individual history, however. It is an acquisition of collective history, as the example of silent reading illustrates:

> It was not until the Middle Ages that people learned to read without reading aloud. Similarly a boy has to learn to read aloud before he learns to read under his breath, and to prattle aloud before he prattles to himself. (Ryle 1949: 28)

Similarly with feinting and deceit. Our capacity to mislead others by what we variously say and do sometimes encourages us to believe that this is because of some disconnection between what we think, inside, and what we publicly do. Ryle, by contrast, argues that these are simply more complex forms of behaviour that we acquire on the basis of more simple and honest behaviours. Having learned to behave in a particular way and observed the sorts of response our behaviour elicits, we may then learn to use those same behaviours to achieve rather different ends. Lying, as Wittgenstein (1953) puts it, is a language game which must be learned like any other.

This point is further strengthened by Ryle's critique of introspection. Although human agents may deceive and hide facts about themselves, he argues, they have no special or privileged form of access to their own mental states of the sort Descartes suggests. We learn about ourselves in a way that could potentially be equally accessible to others, if we did not tend to defensively close them off. We have already touched upon this with respect to 'understanding' but another example of this would be that we learn of our own intentions by way of their verbal formulation. We learn as children to substitute verbalisation for immediate motor action, in at least certain instances, and then to substitute sub-vocalisation for audible speech. My anger at another person would be perfectly apparent to them if they could hear what I am muttering under my breath, and even more so if I had never learned to substitute verbal abuse for physical redress. But my only real access to this anger myself is this sub-vocalised substitute of what would otherwise have been an overt public behaviour. Thus my psychological life is kept relatively private, in fact, but in principle it need not be and, indeed, it only is, in fact, because I was taught as a child, in an intersubjective context, to make it so. My parents were direct witness to my psychological life as a child because all there was of it was plain to see, but they taught me that it is polite and/or in my best interests to keep certain aspects of it to myself (see also Elias 1984, Crossley 1996a).

Ryle pursues this critique further by arguing that 'introspection' is, in effect, retrospection. What we sometimes believe is a look inwards, he argues, is in fact a look backwards, at our history and what we have variously done and been involved in. This might be a long term matter, when we reflect upon our life as a whole, and it may be short term matter, when we reflect upon the events of a moment ago. Always, however, it is a backwards rather than an inwards glance. This point clearly connects with his arguments, discussed earlier, regarding consciousness and intentionality. There is nothing to see 'inside' a human scull or body but physical bits and a reflection upon human psychological life is therefore always a reflection upon our involvement in and belonging to the world. Psychological self-assessment is based upon inferences from behaviour. At a further level, however, Ryle is also criticising the Cartesian notion that human beings have an immediate knowledge or awareness of their self, different in kind from the knowledge we each have of others. Human beings learn about their self in the same way as they learn about others; that is, through observation of behaviour. And as a consequence they may be mistaken about themselves just as they are sometimes mistaken about others.

This may sound narrow and restrictive but I would suggest that it accords very well with our notion that we can learn about ourselves by trying out new things and, indeed, with the practice of taking off on a long trip as a means of 'finding oneself'. If we had some immediate access to an inner world, as Descartes suggests, it would be impossible to learn anything new about oneself as all that there is would be laid bare. What these popular notions suggest, by contrast, is that putting ourselves in unfamiliar situations or trying out new activities makes us act in unfamiliar ways which may be revealing to us. This is just what Ryle is saying.

The potential for misunderstanding with respect to this issue is exacerbated, according to Ryle, by what he calls the 'systematic elusiveness of the I'. Many philosophers, he observes, have noted that the act of self-inspection presupposes an 'I' who performs that inspection but always seems to elude the empirical description of self thereby arrived at. No matter how intensely I interrogate myself, the philosopher argues, the interrogative 'I' seems always to escape interrogation and thus to belong, in principle, beyond its empirical domain. Some, including both Kant (1933) and Husserl (1991), interpret this as evidence of a 'transcendental' ego, somehow removed from the world of ordinary empirical being and therefore distinct from the empirical ego – such as is investigated in social science. Ryle, as we might have come to expect by now, has a more mundane explanation. There is nothing mysterious about the elusive 'I', he argues. It simply reflects the fact that our attempts at self-examination or inspection always, of necessity, exclude our one current activity from consideration, that is, the process of inspection:

> To try, for example, to describe what one has just done, or is now doing, is to comment upon a step which is not *per accidens*, one of commenting. But the operation which is the commenting is not, and cannot be, the step on which that commentary is being made. Nor can an act of ridiculing be its own butt. A higher order action cannot be the action upon which it is performed. So my commentary upon my performances must always be silent about one performance, namely itself, and this performance can be the target only of another performance. Self-commentary, self-ridicule and self-admonition are logically condemned to eternal penultimacy. Yet nothing that is left out of any commentary or admonition is privileged thereby to escape comment or admonition for ever. On the contrary, it may be the target of the very next comment or rebuke. (Ryle 1949: 186)

We can inspect our lives, in other words, but we cannot simultaneously inspect our inspection. Like the proverbial dog who chases his tail we will never catch up with ourselves. And all that we would find if we did is that which is known to us anyway. We can, of course, inspect our own inspections, but this would require a further act of inspection, which would itself be excluded and so on. Thus there is no substantive distinction between an empirical and a transcendental ego nor, indeed, any transcendental ego. Rather we are singular (empirical) egos who never quite catch up with ourselves in our effort to know and understand ourselves. We will see in Chapter 8 how Mead (1967) manages to develop a basic insight similar to this into a very persuasive theory of self and identity.

From Ryle to Sociology

I cannot think of a better way to describe Ryle's account than 'exorcism'. He drives the ghost out of the Cartesian machine. The Cartesian mind, a substance distinct from the body, is a myth, he reveals. Our mental life consists rather in situated behaviour and sensation. This is an invaluable preparatory step but from the point of view of sociology it is only a preparatory step. It clears the ground conceptually, removing myths and muddles that might otherwise stand in our way, but it does not yet afford us an adequate theory of embodied human agency or action. Moreover, though Ryle's antipathy to the 'bogey of mechanism' is only too clear, he cannot offer us the argument we need to refute this particular obstacle to our thinking. His exorcism of the Cartesian ghost is equally a direct challenge to the 'machine' it is alleged to haunt but he is less successful in this second part of his challenge. To push this point further consider this passage from another of his major studies, *Dilemmas*:

> Where there is life there is purposiveness, and where there is sentient, mobile and, especially conscious and intellectual life there are progressively higher and higher levels or types of purposiveness. The biologist, the zoologist and the psychologist must conduct their inquiries as if they were vitalists, even though they feel intellectual obligations to pay lip-service to mechanism. (Ryle 1969: 125–6)

What we have learned from *The Concept of Mind*, I suggest, is that we should not understand these purposive, conscious and intellectual aspects of human life in terms of a realm distinct from that of body and world; that is, in terms of an immaterial mind. We have yet to consider the evidence which will free us of our 'obligations to pay lip service to mechanism'. And we have yet to build the framework which will allow us to study and analyse human life in the purposive terms that Ryle suggests. To do this we need to leave the philosophical questions of the meaning of mental concepts to consider the more social scientific questions of the actual nature of human behaviour and experience. We will not make this transition all in one go, however. Our next step will be to consider the work of a philosopher who allowed his work to cross over more fully into the domain of the social sciences and who, in consequence, was able to challenge the machine myth head on and to reveal, in rich phenomenological detail, the embodied basis of human social agency.

Note

1. But Searle is too sympathetic to the mind–brain argument in my view, even if that is not what he means in this passage.

5

MEANING, ACTION AND DESIRE: A PRELIMINARY SKETCH OF EMBODIED AGENCY

> Men are not machines, not even ghost ridden machines. They are men –
> a tautology which is sometimes worth remembering.
>
> Ryle *The Concept of Mind*

In Chapter 4 I examined Gilbert Ryle's (1949) critique of dualism. This critique, I argued, is persuasive as far as it goes, but it does not go far enough. In particular Ryle fails to adequately address the 'machine myth'. In this chapter I consider the work of a philosopher who takes the next step: Merleau-Ponty (1962, 1965, 1968). Merleau-Ponty's work is in broad agreement with that of Ryle, despite coming out of a very different philosophical tradition (Merleau-Ponty 1992: 59–72). Like Ryle, he challenges the dualist view of the mind as an 'inner theatre' or ghostly substance and seeks to show that mental life consists in embodied and contextualised actions. The dualist is wrong to seek out ephemeral mental processes behind this realm of embodied activity, he maintains. Again like Ryle, he is equally concerned to eschew the 'intellectualist' orientations of the Cartesian approach and to reveal, in contrast, that the human manner of being-in-the-world is, in the first instance, practical and pre-reflective. The intellectual and reflective 'faculties' are secondary acquisitions and structures, he argues, and are, in any case, rooted in practical and pre-reflective habits and skills. What is more important about Merleau-Ponty's argument from the point of view of this book, however, is that he advances and fully establishes the critique of what Ryle calls the 'bogey of mechanism': the 'machine myth'. There is no ephemeral mind distinct from the domain of embodied human behaviour, Merleau-Ponty argues, but neither should behaviour be understood in the 'springs and pulleys' language of mechanism. More to the point, he seeks to actually demonstrate this through a detailed critique of the most sustained attempt to develop the mechanistic approach within the social sciences: psychological behaviourism. It is this critique of the mechanistic model that will concern me most in this chapter.

The exposition of Merleau-Ponty that I offer here is incomplete in at least two respects. Firstly, I am not going to repeat those of his arguments which overlap with the work of Ryle. This chapter must therefore be read in conjunction with the previous one if its full sense is to be grasped. I am beginning here where I left off in the previous chapter and am assuming all that was established in that chapter. Secondly, I have also bracketed out a number of issues which I will deal with in more depth later in the book. In particular, though I refer to them in this chapter, I have deferred a full examination of the concepts of 'habit' and 'corporeal schema' until Chapter 7. For this reason the present chapter is a partial sketch. I hope that it will be read with this in mind.

I begin my account with a brief recap regarding the 'machine myth' and a note on both its incorporation within behaviourist psychology and its contemporary salience. This is followed by an exposition of Merleau-Ponty's critique of the machine myth, which leads me into an account of perception, action and their interrelationship. This, in turn, is followed by a discussion of language. My discussion of perception and language covers the 'cognitive dimension' of Merleau-Ponty's account but he is insistent that our cognitive life does not exist in independence of an affective structure. Indeed, for him, cognition and emotions are mutually penetrating aspects of a common structure. My final task, therefore, is to elucidate this emotional dimension and to explore its roots in human desire.

The Machine Myth

I have referred on numerous occasions within this book to the 'machine myth' which belongs to the more general myth of the 'ghost in the machine' within the dualist schema. The Cartesian, I have argued, is not just guilty of disembodying mental or subjective life, banishing it to a ghostly realm, but equally of reducing the body, conceptually, to the level of a corpse or machine. The body of the dualist belongs to Newton's clockwork universe. It is animated by relations of physical causation and is thereby divorced from the world of meaning, purpose and agency.

It is primarily because of his mechanical conception of the body, as I have said, that Descartes opts for dualism. Dualism is a way of rescuing some element of human meaning and freedom from the clockwork universe of pulleys, levers and forces. Not everybody has been persuaded of the need for such escape attempts, however. In particular, early versions of behaviourist psychology and physiology sought to capitalise upon the clockwork model and to derive a theory of psychology from it. They generally shared the view, expressed in part by Ryle (1949), that the mental domain consists in behaviour, or at least can be regarded to for methodological purposes, but they had no similar reservations about 'the bogey of mechanism'. On the contrary, they believed that human behaviour could be analysed and understood precisely in terms of physical mechanisms. Reflex actions, such as the familiar knee-jerk reflex, where the lower part of a bent leg can be made to 'jump' when tapped just below the knee (on the patella tendon), provided their lead in here. Such reflexes seemed to indicate the presence of basic physical cause-effect pathways within the human organism, linking a particular form of physical stimulus to a very specific mechanical response ('the reflex arc'). Human behaviour, so it seemed, is caused by an external physical stimulus in much the same way that the behaviour of molecules or other physical things within the universe is caused. The task for the behaviourists, who enjoyed dominance within the social scientific field for much of the first half of the twentieth century, was to extend this basic model of reflexes or stimulus-response pathways to cover more complex forms of behaviour, and to show that and how new reflexes could be formed on the basis of older ones – given that some reflexes were quite obviously learned. Pavlov's (1911) infamous dog experiments are one central example of this attempt. He 'classically conditioned' a group of dogs to salivate whenever a bell was rung. This was achieved by ringing the bell whenever the dogs were about to be fed, thereby forming an association within their neurological system between the ringing of the bell and their normal physiological response to food: that is, salivation. A basic reflex response, in other words, was linked to a new conditioned stimulus, by way of an association and substitution with the natural stimulus which would ordinarily cause that response.

It is important to be clear about what is involved in this conception. The behaviourist's notion of stimulus-response pathways, which was intended to explain human behaviour as much as that of any other animal, involves no reference to meaning, purpose or consciousness. It is entirely a matter of mechanically caused responses. Indeed, the true behaviourists believed that stimulus and response were quite literally linked by physical pathways in the neurological apparatus. Thus Pavlov's dogs were not said to 'hear' the aforementioned bell, or at least it was deemed irrelevant whether or not they did. The bell was conceived as a physical force, a vibration, which acted upon the eardrum of the dog, sending signals which provoked the requisite physical response. And that response was regarded as automatic in much the same way that a thermostat responds automatically to changes in temperature. Reflex responses are not purposive movements or replies to particular situations. They are fixed patterns of movement which might be described in just the same way as the movement of a lever in a clockwork contraption. The relationship between stimulus and response is a straightforward case of physical causation.

Put in these extreme terms, behaviourism sounds absurd. It is easy to see why no social scientists today would accept it, at least not in its extreme form. The legacy of behaviourism and its machine-like conception of the human body still lurks within our culture, however, and also within social science. It is evident, for example, that much work within biology and the disciplines which draw from it, such as medicine, still conceive of the body in this atomised and mechanistic way, even if they do not attempt to extend that model to an understanding of behaviour (see Leder 1998). But even those perspectives within social science which have pulled away from behaviourism have not established a new conception of body, at least not to any degree of sophistication, such that one must wonder whether their path beyond it is not, in the final instance, the same as Descartes'. Hermeneutic and cognitive approaches to social analysis emphasise meaning, purpose and reason in human action in a way which is quite alien to the behaviourist model, but their failure to challenge the behaviourist model of the body and, indeed, their general avoidance of questions of embodiment more generally, suggests that, like Descartes, they have achieved a more credible conception of human agency only by splitting the questions of meaning, purpose and reason off from the body, and leaving the body, in a tacit form of dualism, to those biological disciplines which will continue to treat it as a machine. A post-dualistic sociology requires a different solution. We must tackle the mechanistic conception of body and behaviour, as posited within behaviourism, head on.

To this end we can turn to Merleau-Ponty. Drawing upon a range of psychological and biological studies, as well as philosophical writings, Merleau-Ponty (1962, 1965) mounts a powerful critique of behaviourism and suggests a far more persuasive alternative. Though composed entirely of physical 'bits' whose interrelations manifest a mechanical relation, he argues, the human organism, and indeed animal organisms too, when conceived in interaction with their immediate surrounding, constitute a whole which is greater than the sum of their specific parts. More specifically he suggests that the interaction of organism and environment is best understood in terms of the concepts of meaning and purpose, and he maintains that whatever direct influence the environment exerts upon the organism cannot be understood, for the most part, independently of a consideration of the manner in which that environment exists, subjectively, for the organism. This is not a matter of a 'subject' or 'ego' in the philosophical sense, less still of an immaterial mind, but rather of the properties of a decentred behavioural 'system' or 'structure'. There is a great deal to unpack in this claim. I will begin by focusing on Merleau-Ponty's basic critique of behaviourism.

Merleau-Ponty's Critique of Behaviourism

Merleau-Ponty's main criticism of behaviourism is that it is not supported by the scientific evidence. The physiological basis of behaviourism turned out to be largely mythical. There are no 'reflex pathways' in the nervous system, at least not as the behaviourists envisaged them (Goldstein 2000). Furthermore, even the most basic of reflex actions are difficult to isolate in the laboratory, and outside of the laboratory the quest is hopeless (Merleau-Ponty 1965, Goldstein 2000, Buytendijk 1974). By the same token the concepts of 'meaning', 'purpose' and 'subjective perception' prove more parsimonious as ways of accounting for observed behaviours than those of the behaviourist and must therefore be deemed more scientific and preferable. I will briefly consider the findings of the studies which show this, focusing first upon studies of 'stimuli', then upon studies of 'responses'.

Stimuli

Relatively simple experiments reveal that animals can be trained to look for food from the 'lighter coloured' or 'taller' of two containers, such that the same container might be approached on one occasion, when it is the lighter of two, but not on another, when it is the darker (Merleau-Ponty 1965). This is significant as it refutes the notion that any objective property of the stimulus has a causal effect on the behaviour of the organism and reveals, rather, a process of subjective perceptual discrimination and an orientation to meaning. 'Lighter' and 'taller' are not properties of objects but rather aspects of subjective perceptual discrimination and comparison. Indeed, using visual illusions it has been shown that animals will search in containers which only appear taller but are not in fact. Furthermore, when an animal takes relative lightness or tallness as a cue for where to look for food it indicates that its behaviour is oriented to principles or rules (for example, 'always look in the tallest container') and that perceived objects or aspects of such objects are therefore meaningful for it (for example, tallness means 'a likely place for food'), however rudimentary that meaning may be. Stimuli do not act upon the organism, object upon object, but rather have a sensuous, perceptual meaning for it, to which it responds. This may seem somewhat obvious to us, as sentient beings who are only too aware that our world exists 'for' us as a meaningful percept, but it is important because it takes the behaviourists on at their own game and beats them. It is by no means obvious that or how an animal could be trained to search for food in the lighter of two containers from the purely physical and atomistic standpoint that the behaviourist assumes. Indeed, in a strict sense, such behaviour ought to be impossible.

Merleau-Ponty pushes the case further. The effect of any given stimulus, he observes, varies according to its situation in time and space. Experimental studies show that a stimulus 'x' will generate a different response if preceded by events 'a' and 'b', and situated in an environment 'c', than if the environment or antecedent events are otherwise (see also Goldstein 2000). Furthermore, the effect of juxtaposing 'x' with 'a', 'b' and 'c' can in no way be reduced to the simple sum of whatever individual effects may be ascribed to those conditions – indeed the very notion of individual or isolated effects of particular conditions or stimuli is rendered deeply problematic. As with the earlier example, this confounds the behaviourist. The same stimulus ought to produce the same response from their point of view. Invoking Popper (1969), we can argue that these findings offer good reason to reject their position as it provides ample falsification of what one would predict about stimulus-response relations from the atomised and physicalist position they advocate. These studies are still very much consistent with Merleau-Ponty's argument regarding meaningful perception, however, as he can argue that the meaning of any subjectively perceived object, and thus the behaviour it calls forth, is affected by the spatio-temporal background or context against which it is perceived, such that one would precisely expect the variations that the studies reveal. The meaning of a sign or stimuli, as a diverse range of writers from gestalt psychology through to structuralism have suggested, is constituted by its relationship to other elements in a spatio-temporal gestalt whole.

At an experiential level, our perception of music reveals the temporal structuration of perceptual meaning most clearly. We hear any one note within the context of a sequence of notes and the manner in which it strikes us depends upon the sequence. A note only sounds 'wrong', for example, if it does not fit the melodic sequence in which it appears; how we hear the note depends upon what precedes it and may be modified by what follows it. The comparable effect of spatial context is illustrated in Figure 5.1. The pupils in the eyes are identical to the dots on the dice, but what we see and thus the manner in which we are affected by them is quite different because of their context. In the eyes the dots become pupils which look at us; on the dice they form the top line of a bigger configuration of dots which signify the number five. Meaning is shaped by context.

This applies equally to relationships between the senses, as Merleau-Ponty (1971) illustrates with reference to cinema. The (visual) meaning of what we see on the screen is profoundly affected by the background music, he argues. A visual image of a swimmer playing in the sea might be beautiful and relaxing if accompanied by gentle piano music, for example, but the slightest hint of the music from the *Jaws* film will completely change its sense; the ease and innocence of the swimmer becomes almost painful to watch. In everyday life this communication between the senses is even greater as all five senses come into play, each modifying the meanings of what appears to the others.

These examples all turn upon the fact that physically identical stimuli may trigger very different responses if they mean something different. We can approach this same point from the other way around, however, by reflecting upon the manner in which physically very different stimuli generate the same responses if they mean the same thing. A gun shot, whistle, wave or shout of 'Go!' will each affect the behaviour of runners at the start of a race in the same way, for example, despite their physical dissimilarity, because they mean the same thing when presented in that particular context. This example concerns deliberate communication by way of arbitrary signs, of course; but for Merleau-Ponty all perception is communicative of meaning in this way, and all percepts take on a conventionalised meaning as they become a familiar part of our life and acquire a use value for us.

What 'meaning' means in this context is simply that the stimuli is significant for the organism and that its 'effect' upon the organism is

Figure 5.1   *Pupils and dice roll*

irreducible to its physical properties. This does not preclude the possibility that its significance may be biological in form and it certainly does not
necessitate any reflective awareness of or deliberation over meanings.
Significance is practical; that which is meaningful is that which, in some
sense, has a use for the agent. As we will see later, however, meaning in
the human, 'symbolic' environment enjoys considerable autonomy and is
quite arbitrary from a biological point of view.

Response

Similar problems for behaviourism are evident on the response side of
their stimulus-response equation. We know from everyday experience

that a given stimulus often generates 'the same' response across a number of instances, but if we consider what it is that is 'the same' across these instances it is generally the purpose of the response rather than the physical movement it involves. The irritation and tickling which a fly causes by landing on my arm may lead me to swat it in every case, for example, without fail; but the physical movement this entails will vary markedly according to my posture at the time – what I am doing with my hands, and so on. Each action is identical at the level of purpose (I am swatting the fly) whilst it may be completely different at the physical level (for example, any of a variety of karate blows or a swift tennis fore-arm shot with the newspaper). This creates considerable difficulties for the behaviourist as their reflex arc concept dispenses with the notion of purpose, linking determinate physical stimuli to determinate physical movements. From their point of view each and every act of swatting is a completely different act if it entails different movements, and we must postulate the existence of a different and separate reflex arc in each case to explain the behaviour. In effect, given the possible permutations, we would need to assume the existence of hundreds of reflex pathways to explain even the simple act of fly-swatting. Furthermore, there would need to be a separate set of reflex pathways, in each case, from the pro-prioceptive system of the organism, telling it which reaction to select. Whether variability of response can be explained at all in this way, within the atomised frame of reference of the behaviourist, is highly question-able. Even if possible, however, one is forced to conclude that such a con-voluted account would be far from parsimonious when set against a model, such as Merleau-Ponty proposes, which treats the active organ-ism as an irreducible whole whose behaviours are best understand in terms of its purposes.

In addition, the purposive frame of reference is necessary to account for the way in which both humans and other animals will return to an attempt at realising an apparent goal, from a different angle, even when knocked off course by unforeseeable obstacles on a number of occasions. The dog who persists in 'trying to get the ball' from a master who passes it from hand to hand and behind the back is only the most obvious exam-ple of this. Their obstinacy, as much as their inventiveness, demonstrates the purposiveness of their behaviour. They want the ball and the purpose of their action is to get it.

As with 'meaning', what Merleau-Ponty means by 'purpose' may be biologically delineated and need entail no conscious formulation of inten-tion. As with meaning, 'purpose' is a practical matter. The hunting activi-ties of many animals are clearly purposive, for example, and may become quite inventive as animals encounter changes in their environment, but we do not suppose that animals are necessarily aware of what animates them and we would insist that their purposes serve a biological function. As with meaning, however, Merleau-Ponty identifies a flexibility of purpose within the symbolic world of human beings. The goals towards which individuals aim depend upon constructed 'games', he notes, and may only have value within the terms of such games. This is most obvious in literal games, such as amateur sport and board games, where agents may ruthlessly pursue ends and goals which have neither value nor meaning outside of the game itself. The throw of a dice or turn of a card may be an occasion for great anxiety or jubilation despite the fact that their meaning is entirely relative to the game. This point applies equally to the broader games or 'fields' of which the social world is comprised. Even where we act to satisfy basic biological needs this is mediated by complex symbolic economies, such that the relation of our actions to our biological needs is extremely indirect (see also Huizinga 1950). Furthermore, it is by no means obvious that a great many of our actions maintain a link to biological need at all.

The final strand of Merleau-Ponty's critique of behaviourism concerns the observation that organisms seem capable of selecting the stimuli that will affect them. At one level this is a matter of biologically based thresholds and structures of sensitivity. As contemporary 'dialectical biologists' argue, every species, strictly speaking, lives in a different environment, even when they occupy the same geographical location, because their biological constitution makes them sensitive to and thus aware of different things (Levins and Lewontin 1985, Lewontin 1993). Even such obviously physical stimuli as viruses or bacteria have no uniform effect across all species, such that one must conclude that they figure quite differently in the 'worlds' of such species. Over and above this, however, Merleau-Ponty notes how organisms actively select aspects of their environment to be affected by, ignoring others. They appear proactive in both perception and action, not simply reactive. This introduces a circularity into organism-environment interactions which confounds the linear-causal thinking of the behaviourist:

> When the eye and ear follow an animal in flight, it is impossible to say 'which started first' in the exchange of stimuli and responses. Since all the movements of the organism are always conditioned by external influences, one can, if one wishes, readily treat behaviour as an effect of milieu. But in the same way, since all the stimulations which the organism receives have in turn been possible only by its preceding movements which have culminated in exposing the receptor organ to external influences, one could say that the behaviour is the first cause of all the stimulations. (Merleau-Ponty 1965: 13)

The behaviour of the organism, in other words, is affected by what it perceives in its environment, but what it perceives is, in turn, affected by its behaviour, not least its perceptual behaviour. We can advance this point further through a closer consideration of Merleau-Ponty's theorisation of perception (see also Crossley 1994: 8–14, 1996a: 24–31).

The Phenomenology of Perception

I noted Merleau-Ponty's hostility towards intellectualist accounts of perception in Chapter 2. Perception cannot be a matter of judgement, as Descartes believes, I noted, because judgement presupposes already meaningful percepts which are judged. Descartes' judgement that the hats and coats he saw were people precisely presupposed the meaningful perception of hats and coats. Ambiguous images, such as those shown in Figure 5.2 and 5.3, provide some further ammunition for this critique. There are two possible images that can be seen in Figure 5.2, depending upon which aspects are foregrounded. One may see an old woman or a young woman. Similarly, Figure 5.3 can be see either as a cube from the side or as a cube from above. One cannot move between these alternatives by way of an act of thought or judgement, however, as is evidenced by the difficulty one may experience in finding a particular image, even when one knows it to be 'there'. One must interrogate the image from a position of blindness, as it were, seeking out the image with one's eyes and awaiting the moment at which one's focus 'hooks on' to it. Perception is thus revealed as an *embodied activity* and the subject of perception, the subject who sees the image, is revealed to be an effect of the process of perception rather than its cause. Perception both predates and gives rise to the perceptual subject. However, ambiguous images equally challenge empiricist and naively realist conceptions of perception, which suggests that it is the effect of a determinate object. The effort taken to find the image refutes the claim to straightforward determination, as does the fact that one can derive two different images from the same 'stimulus'. The 'object' no less than the 'subject' of perception is revealed as an outcome of the perceptual process and perception is revealed to be an active process in which the organism interrogates its worldly surround, guided by both biological sensitivities and behavioural-perceptual schemas, thereby creating for itself a subjective 'milieu' or 'lifeworld': 'The gaze', Merleau-Ponty argues, 'gets more or less from things according the way in which it questions them, ranges over or dwells on them' (1962: 153). Moreover, it is events as experienced within this subjectively meaningful lifeworld which trigger and shape our other behaviours. We respond to the world as we perceive it.

It is important to be clear about Merleau-Ponty's argument here. He is not questioning the existence of either perceiving subjects or perceived objects but he is decentring both by showing each to be derivative upon a prior interaction between body and environment. And in doing so he is revealing, contra Descartes, that our primordial way of being-in-the-world, whilst active, nevertheless predates and predetermines the subject/object dichotomy. In effect both subjects and (epistemic) objects are effects of behaviour or praxis for Merleau-Ponty. Prior to consciousness our bodies plunge forward blindly into an unknown environment in an attempt to make basic perceptual sense of that environment, seeking out a

Figure 5.2   *Old or young woman?*

point of stable equilibrium. To the extent to which they succeed, a
perceptual subject is born – though note that this is still a far cry from the
Cartesian cogito.

This account begs an important question; namely, how does the gaze fix
upon objects? What guides and shapes its interrogations such that it is
able to 'settle' upon specific gestalts? Merleau-Ponty concedes that there
may be an innate aspect here but much of his work points to the role of
acquired habitual schemas of perception which, in turn, are valued for
their practical significance. We learn to perceive and discriminate in ways
which are useful for the business of practically getting along and surviv-
ing in our immediate physical and social environment. The process of
learning to read illustrates the learned nature of perception most clearly.
The pages of a written text, if in a language we understand, strike us as
immediately meaningful. And yet we know that this manifestation of
visual meaning rests upon our acquisition, in childhood, of both the habitual schemas that allow us to see clustered marks on a page as utterances

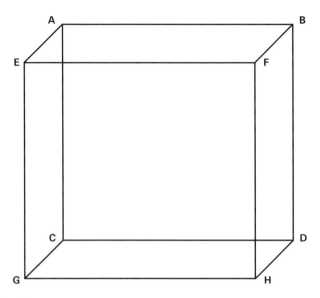

Figure 5.3 *Cube*

of our own language and to understand them, and the habit of scanning the page from left to right, top to bottom and so on. So it is with other perceptual habits. Schematic and interrogative habits must be acquired if we are to 'read' the world through perception.

I will discuss the conception of habit referred to here in detail in Chapter 7. Suffice it to say for present purposes, however, that this usage, contrary to that of the behaviourists, suggests an acquired and flexible competence or skill rather than a fixed reflex action. Moreover, echoing Mauss' (1979) account of 'body techniques', it emphasises the bodily nature of habit. As Merleau-Ponty says of colour discrimination:

> To learn to see colours is to acquire a new way of seeing, *a new use of one's own body*: it is to *recast the body image*. Whether a system of motor or perceptual powers, our body is not an object for an 'I think', it is a grouping of lived through meanings which moves towards its equilibrium. (Merleau-Ponty 1962: 153, my emphasis)

Perception *qua* habit is a 'body technique', an acquired use of the body.

Perception is not only embodied because 'behavioural', however. It is integral to Merleau-Ponty's account that the perceptual consciousness which perceptual behaviours give rise to is embodied too. Consciousness is, in effect, constituted out of a meaningfully ordered configuration of sensations. Perceptual consciousness is a sensuous relationship to the world, effected through embodied interactions with it and the habituated schemas such as interactions manifest. This is an important point because it challenges the Cartesian definition of 'the body', which reduces it to its perceptible qualities, by revealing that the body has another side. The body is not merely composed of perceptible qualities; it perceives. It is not merely seen but sees; is not merely touchable but touches; cannot simply be heard but hears and so on. Against the physical corpse of Descartes, Merleau-Ponty (1968a) juxtaposes animate, sensuous and 'reversible' 'flesh'. The flesh of the human body belongs to the flesh of the world, he argues, we are 'of' the world. But ours is a reversible flesh, not only sensible but also sentient or sensuous.

In addition, the meanings and purposes to which Merleau-Ponty refers in his critique of behaviourism are embodied too. Cartesian thought inclines us to think of 'meanings' in particular as 'ideal' realities, but this is not Merleau-Ponty's view. To speak of perceptual meanings, for him, is to identify the manner in which specific sensuous patterns emerge within our perceptual field which, in turn, acquire a use or function in the organisation of our conduct which is strictly irreducible to a relationship of mechanical causation. In this respect, 'meaning', with 'purpose', is a structure of the natural world, albeit a higher level structure than those normally subsumed within this category.

Perception and Symbolic Behaviour

Perceptual behaviour, to reiterate my earlier point, is intimately bound in to all other of our behaviours. How we act depends upon what we perceive and vice versa. This is demonstrated for Merleau-Ponty, in part, by the psychological experiments of Stratton (1896, 1897). These experiments involved a subject wearing spectacles, over a period of days, which inverted their visual input. At first, Stratton found, the world appeared upside down and motor action was extremely difficult. This persisted over a number of days. After five days, however, when motor co-ordination had, through practice, been restored, the visual field seemed ordered and, to further prove the point, disorientation and disorder only returned when the glasses were removed. The sense of the visual field, in other words, was shown to be dependent upon its co-ordination with motor activity and vice versa. Things only appear 'upside down' or 'right way up' relative to their capacity to successfully aid the co-ordination of action.

This notion of mutual interdependence is illustrated and deepened when, in *The Structure of Behaviour*, Merleau-Ponty reflects upon perception and action in a game of football. I want to pause to consider this discussion in detail because it allows us to pull out a number of important aspects of his approach. For sake of clarity I have divided his comments into three passages which I will address in turn:

> For the player in action the football field is not an 'object', that is, the ideal term which can give rise to an indefinite multiplicity of perspectival views and remain equivalent under its apparent transformations. It is pervaded with lines of force (the 'yard lines'; those which demarcate the 'penalty area') and articulated in sectors (for example, the 'openings' between adversaries) which call for

a certain mode of action and which initiate and guide the action as if the player were unaware of it. (Merleau-Ponty 1965: 168)

A number of points need to be drawn out of this passage. Firstly, Merleau-Ponty alludes to what we might call perceptual 'attitudes'; the footballer's gaze is not contemplative but rather practical and engaged. It is not the detached gaze of a reflective ego but a situated perspective from within, which involves the player in the game. Anticipating the work of Gibson (1979), who was influenced by him,[2] Merleau-Ponty notes that the player's gaze identifies 'affordances' or opportunities for and constraints upon action rather than objects. Furthermore, in contrast to the grounds-man, whose gaze might equally well be practical, it is the specific activity of playing football which shapes the way in which the player's gaze interrogates the pitch and thus what she sees. She sees 'openings' and 'feels' the force of the yard lines. It is important to add here that these openings are only openings for her; partly in virtue of her location on the field but more particularly because she has the competence or know-how, as Ryle (1949) might put it, to take advantage of them. An agent who lacked competence at football would not see 'openings' because, for that agent, they would not be openings. There is a strong sense here in which perception, though shaped by specific perceptual schemas or habits, is equally a function of action and both the broader social competencies it entails and the 'interests' it gives rise to. Perception is never disinterested, but rather always shaped by the interests arising out of the stream of practical activity in which it takes shape (on this see also Husserl 1973 and Schutz 1970).

Secondly, Merleau-Ponty describes the way in which the practical significations and affordances in the players visual field motivate and guide action. The player does not simply see an opportunity for action. She is mobilised into action by this sight, without the mediation of reflective-verbal thought. The coming into view of an opportunity, the sight of an open goal, sparks her into action before she has had the chance to think. Whilst her action is purposive, intelligent and oriented towards a subjectively meaningful state of affairs in her milieu, it takes shape without the intervention of reflective thought and is thus in no respect reducible to a thinking subject or ego. There is an artful synthesis of perception, competence and action which occurs before any act of conscious or reflective thought has taken place. It is important to emphasise here both that the action arises out of what the agent perceives, rather than what may, from the point of view of a detached spectator or social scientist, be 'there', and that it follows perception in a pre-reflective and unmediated manner. Sport is a particularly useful illustration for this latter point as it is usually sufficiently fast moving to rule out reflective mediation.

Finally, note that this whole context of action and therefore all of the meanings and purposes which arise within it are cultural and historical constructions. The footballer will avoid letting the ball over the line as if her life depended upon it, but this 'as if' belies everything because her life does not depend upon it and, assuming she is an amateur, neither does

anything else – at least not outside of the arbitrarily constructed world
of the football community. No one could doubt the agency of the player
or the urgency which invests her every move. If she is good then she is
spontaneous. She is tactical and strategic 'in her bones', without having to
give the matter thought. And yet the sense of everything she sees and
does derives from the game, a contingent historical construction which is
one amongst hundreds and which means nothing to many. An agent not
familiar with football would be baffled by her actions and would fail to
see what she sees.

   This final point connects with my aforementioned remarks concerning
the 'symbolic' nature of the human world. There is a continuum within
the animal kingdom, Merleau-Ponty argues, which even members of the
same species may move up or down between occasions, as to the degree
of autonomy that one's milieu and behaviour can achieve relative to the
givens of the physical world. Some behaviours, of some animals, are
'syncretic'; a fixed stimulus is more or less capable of triggering a fixed
range of purposive action patterns. Others are at an 'amovable' stage,
where means–end patterns of behaviour seem to kick in and animals
become capable of discriminating in their environment according to
principle; animals may be trained, as noted above, for example, to search
for food in the lighter coloured of two containers, even if that means
searching now in what was an empty container at one's last feed. At the
human, 'symbolic' level, however, there is further autonomy still. The
human world is a 'virtual reality' in which the meaning of any object
derives from the symbolic system of which it is a part. This is what we
see in the football example. The player finds the game a 'natural environment' and acts as if she were instinctively attuned to it, but it is a virtual
reality of human construction, a symbolic domain. The goal posts, yard
lines, penalty area, teams and so on have no natural meaning or physical
effect. They are historical constructions which only affect the player
because they have meaning for her, and which only have meaning within
the context of the game. They only affect the player because she, by playing the game, has incorporated the schemas, skills and know-how which
dispose her to read and play the game and thus to be affected in the way
that she is. We will return to this point later. Suffice it to say for now,
however, that football is only one amongst a multitude of games and
game like structures which comprise the human symbolic domain. There
are many others and many which are not recognised as games by those
who play them but rather comprise the stuff of the 'real world' (see also
Huizinga 1950).

   Merleau-Ponty continues his football example by describing the relationship of the player to the game:

> The field itself is not given to him, but present as the immanent term of his prac-
> tical intentions; the player becomes one with it and feels the direction of the
> 'goal', for example, just as immediately as the vertical and horizontal planes of
> his own body. It would not be sufficient to say that consciousness inhabits this

milieu. At this moment consciousness is nothing other than the dialectic of milieu and action. (ibid.: 168–9)

This part of the passage reinforces what has already been observed, stressing the extent to which the player's most basic sense of space is merged with that of the (football) field. She feels the direction of the goal and is pulled towards it in much the same way as her feet would be pulled into a stabilising posture were she to loose her balance. Furthermore, her consciousness itself simply is this dialectic of perceived milieu and action. Consciousness is not distinct from the game but rather takes form within it, as a function of it. Finally, he adds that:

> Each manoeuvre undertaken by the player modifies the character of the field and establishes in it new lines of force in which the action in turn unfolds and is accomplished, again altering the phenomenal field. (ibid.: 169)

Here the dialectic turns full circle, or rather, becomes fully dialectical. The action with which the agent responds to her perceived milieu transforms that milieu in at least two respects. Firstly, in kicking the ball up the field the player sparks off actions in all other players, transforming the configuration of play in which she is enmeshed. Secondly, in doing this, she also transforms her own perceptual vantage point, both by putting herself in a different spatial relationship to events on the field and by plunging her gaze ever forward into fresh situations. Having been called forth by a subjectively meaningful milieu, the action transforms it and the aforementioned circularity of perception and action turns once more.

The football example not only provides a good illustration of Merleau-Ponty's view on the relationship between perception and action, but also provides an important illustration of his view of the relationship of human agents to the social world. In *The Phenomenology of Perception*, for example, he argues that:

> It is as false to place ourselves in society as an object amongst objects, as it is to place society in ourselves as an object of thought, and in both cases the mistake lies in treating the social as an object. We must return to the social with which we are in contact by the mere fact of existing, and which we carry about inseparably with us before any objectification. (Merleau-Ponty 1962: 362)

This is exactly what we see in the football example. The game is not a container external to the players, in which they are located and which acts upon them from without. But neither is it 'in their heads' as an object of reflection or contemplation. The game takes place in the space between the players; the relational space of their interactions. Furthermore, though it is wholly dependent upon the ways in which players perceive and act, their perceptions and actions are at the same time shaped by the game and reflect its structure. Their every move and gesture exudes the logic of the game. This touches upon a further important claim which Merleau-Ponty makes with respect to the social world:

For the philosopher, the presence of structure outside us in natural and social systems and within us as a symbolic function points to a way beyond the subject–object correlation which has dominated philosophy from Descartes to Hegel. By showing us that man [sic] is eccentric to himself and that the social finds its centre only in man, structure particularly enables us to understand how we are in a sort of circuit with the socio-historical world. (Merleau-Ponty 1964: 123)

Again the football example illustrates this. The sense and meaning of the player's actions and perceptions is derived from the structure of the game. We can only work out what they are doing by reference to the game: its purpose, rules, conventions and so on. This is the sense in which agents are 'eccentric' to their selves: the meaning of what they do lies within the between world of social structures, not within them as isolated individuals. We might add that in a historical sense every player's actions are a reply to every other player's actions, insofar as they are aware of them, such that each individual action can only be understood within the context of the unfolding of the game. Having said this, contrary to those structuralists who sought to dissolve the agent within structures, and more in line with Durkheim (1915), who viewed the relation of agent to structure as circular, Merleau-Ponty argues that this structure finds its centre in the human agent. What he means by this is that the structure only exists insofar as agents competently enact it and, indeed, insofar as its principles, the skills its requires and the basic disposition towards enacting it are transmitted across generations. We will see in Chapter 7 that Merleau-Ponty believes these basic dispositions take root as habits within the 'corporeal schema' of the agent. For the moment, however, note that the player does not think about the game; that they are 'tuned in' to it in such a way that their every perception and action embodies its structure and logic.

In his brief discussion of this football example, and of Merleau-Ponty's work more generally, Wacquant notes that it anticipates much of the work of Bourdieu (Bourdieu and Wacquant 1992). The latter's definition of *habitus* as a 'feel for the game' and of *illusio* as an unconscious 'belief in the game', in particular, are both captured well by this example. Furthermore, it is interesting that Merleau-Ponty should use this example, given the centrality which the game metaphor was to assume in Bourdieu's sociology (not to mention the work of a great many other sociologists[3]), particularly his concept of 'fields' (see Chapter 6). Merleau-Ponty clearly takes a big step in the sociological direction when he selects this example. Wacquant claims that Merleau-Ponty falls short of the full sociological understanding offered by Bourdieu, however, as his analysis remains focused at the subjective level, failing to draw back and achieve an objective view; that is, he argues that Merleau-Ponty focuses exclusively upon the player's perception of the game, where Bourdieu steps back to look at the game itself and thus to see how it affects the player in ways they may be unaware of. I disagree with this assessment. In this example

Merleau-Ponty limits his focus to the player's perceptual horizon, but elsewhere he seeks to develop a theory of history and society which precisely focuses upon 'the game' rather than the player's perception; or rather, which examines both perception, game and the mutual influences between them (Crossley 1994, 2001). He is acutely concerned with the question of how 'direction' and 'dynamics' emerge in the course of history which do not correspond to the intentions or expectations of social agents, for example, and how these dynamics influence action both from without, by provoking agents to action, and from within, as they sediment in the form of habitual schemas of perception and action. I do not mean to suggest here that Merleau-Ponty achieves the degree of sociological sophistication achieved within the work of Bourdieu (see Crossley 1994: 41–102). But like Bourdieu, he is clear of the need to keep hold of both the subjective and the objective poles of the social world in his examination of them:

> ... the social, like man himself, has two poles or facets: it is significant, capable of being understood from within, and yet at the same time personal intentions within it are generalised, toned down, and tend towards processes, being (as the famous [Marxist] expression has it) mediated by things [that is, forces of production and relations to them]. (Merleau-Ponty 1964: 114)

Moreover, perhaps more than any other philosopher, he allows us to view the subjective and objective as polarities of a united whole. The player does not exist independently of the game nor vice versa. Being-in-the-world means living within a mutlitude of configurations of interdependence and games; and perceiving, thinking and acting in a way which, for the most part, accords with and thus reproduces the symbolic structure of those relations and games. It does not mean that the dynamics of those games are reducible to the agent or their perception, however. To the contrary. It points towards the complexity and irreducibility of historical structures and processes (Crossley 1994).

Speech, Reflection and Dialogue

Merleau-Ponty's account of perception constitutes a powerful praxiological critique of the philosophy of the subject or consciousness. As I have stated, he argues that the perceptual subject, the subject who perceives, is the outcome of a habitually structured interaction between body and environment. This critique is extended further when he considers how a reflective form of subjectivity emerges out of this pre-reflective realm. The reflective subject is, in his view, a function of language, or rather speech. We think reflectively by way of speech, he notes, and this is equally the way in which we become aware of our own thoughts. Speech 'breaks the silence' of the perceptual world, spreading a further layer of significance over it and, at the same time, bringing the subject into relationship with their self. They think and equally hear their own thoughts, such that

they may inspect those thoughts. Their reflectiveness is a relation to and
dialogue with their self made possible by way of speech. But speech itself
cannot, in the final instance, be the result of a reflective act. I may plan what
to say but I can only do so in words and these words themselves cannot
be planned. I cannot think or plan an act of speech without speaking
and thus speech must be regarded, like perception, as an originary,
pre-reflective act which brings the subject and object of speech, the speaking subject, into being. Furthermore, speech is an embodied activity and
language, like perception, is a body technique. To acquire language is to
acquire a new way of using one's body:

> ... a contraction of the throat, a sibilant emission of air between the tongue and
> teeth, a certain way of bringing the body into play suddenly allows itself to
> invested with a figurative significance ... (Merleau-Ponty 1962: 194)

Speech is the body of reflective thought, its 'flesh'. To pursue this further
we must briefly consider Merleau-Ponty's philosophy of language or, as
it is perhaps better regarded, his philosophy of speech and dialogue.

Even in his later writings, which turn to the work of Saussure and
anticipate many of the themes of structuralism, the emphasis of Merleau-
Ponty's examination of language is always upon speech. 'Language' is an
abstraction, he argues. What exists are concrete historical languages and
each of these is a 'moving equilibrium', reproduced and transformed
by way of speech. Languages are the debris or sediments of the past communicative acts of a community, stored within the corporeal schemas of
the contemporary population. They are gestural habits, taken up and
modified by successive generations in the course of their communica-
tions. Furthermore, contrary to the intellectualist tendencies of structuralism and post-structuralism, he argues that linguistic habits are practical.
Saussure, he notes, marvels at the diacritical constitution of meaning; the
fact that each word depends upon every other and thus upon the whole
for its meaning (Merleau-Ponty 1964). But this is a scholastic absurdity. If
meaning was dependent upon the whole then it would be impossible
since the 'totality' of language is, as we have said, a 'moving equilibrium'.
It is never complete or totalised. Moreover, the learning of language and
everyday sense-making would be impossible if Saussure were right, since
no speaker has access to the whole of language and learners must always
begin with a few words. Rather than thinking of words as concepts,
whose meaning is explained by further concepts and so on *ad infinitum*,
Merleau-Ponty argues, we should think of them as tools whose meaning
consists in the effects they achieve and uses to which they are put in concrete interaction contexts. The grasp which the speaking agent has upon
their language is, in the final instance, practical and embodied. We learn
language by learning to do things with words:

> The word has never been inspected, analysed, known and constituted,
> but caught and taken up by a power of speech and, in the last analysis, by a
> motor power given to me along with the first experience I have of my body and
> its perceptual and practical fields. As for the meaning of the word, I learn to use

it as I learn to use a tool, by seeing it used in the context of a certain situation. (Merleau-Ponty 1962: 403)

There are many similarities here with the work of Wittgenstein (1953), Austin (1971) and Searle (1969). Words do things, for Merleau-Ponty. Moreover, like Mead (1967) and also Husserl (1970) and Schutz (1972), he identifies language as a manifestation of our power of conceptual habituation, our power of typification (see Chapter 7). Language affords us a grasp upon the world by condensing and mapping it, subsuming the haecceity of each particular moment of experience within generalised categories. In contrast to these other writers, however, he equally emphasises the affective element of language, describing it as a manner of 'singing the world'. The language of a society or social group, he notes, is an expression of the various emotional attitudes that its members have collectively adopted towards the world, the manner of living it that they have developed. And to learn their language is therefore to enter the collective symbolic milieu of the group. This is not a static matter, however. As I noted earlier, language is a 'moving equilibrium' in which new creative significations perpetually burst forth, smashing aside the debris of past acts of expression before sedimenting into the same themselves.

An essential aspect of this philosophy of speech concerns the relationship of speech to thought. It is common to distinguish speech from thought, Merleau-Ponty notes, and to ponder the relation of the two. Some argue that speech determines language and others vice versa. Against this he argues that the two are inseparably intertwined sides of the same coin. Language is the body of thought and thus its means of real existence. He offers a number of arguments in defence of this claim. We can consider two. Firstly, he notes how certain linguistic disorders, such as aphasia, involve a loss of certain uses of words, particularly forms of categorisation, without a loss of the word itself. A person may be able to say the word as one of a number in a list, for example, but then prove unable to apply it in a context. This illustrates the above mentioned point about words being tools and having uses but it also suggests that speech is not simply a matter of motor action – since the aphasic has no problem saying the word. The aphasic has not lost a word but rather a function. Their ability to say certain things is an inability to think certain things. The intellectualist will take this as evidence of the determination of speech by thought but Merleau-Ponty has a response for them also. If speech presupposed thought, he argues:

> … we could not understand why thought tends towards expression as towards its completion, why the most familiar thing appears indeterminate as long as we have not recalled its name, why the thinking subject himself is in a kind of ignorance of his thoughts so long as he has not formulated them for himself, or even spoken or written them. (Merleau-Ponty 1962: 177)

A number of points are crammed into this relatively brief quotation. On the one hand Merleau-Ponty is appealing to our own experience to confirm that our ability to think something and enjoy the grasp which reflective thought affords us on the world coincides with putting it into words. Even if we have an occasional feeling of a thought we cannot put into words we are forced to conclude that this thought is not fully realised if it fails to achieve linguistic articulation. Aside from the subjective experience, however, Merleau-Ponty is asking why we put our thoughts into words, outside of communicative situations, if language is merely a translation of thought? If I want to plan my day I must talk to myself about it, albeit in silent soliloquy, but this suggests that I cannot think the thought without speaking it. What would be the point of speaking quietly to myself if this were merely matter of translating something fully formed independently of speech? Why would I waste the energy? These points both relate to the accomplishment of thought. Merleau-Ponty adds as a third point, however, that linguistic formulation is necessary for us to become aware of our own thoughts. I must speak, he argues, to find out what it is that I think (Merleau-Ponty 1974). I effectively hear myself thinking and it is by this means that I become aware of my own thoughts:

> Among my movements there are some that go nowhere …: these are the facial movements, many gestures, and especially those strange movements of the throat and mouth that form the cry and the voice. These movements end in sounds and I hear them. […] as Malraux said, I hear myself with my throat. […] This new reversibility and the emergence of the flesh as expression are the point of insertion of speaking and thinking into the world of silence. (Merleau-Ponty 1968a: 144–5)

Indeed, the very process of thinking, whether spoken or written, involves me in a kind of dialogue with myself. My verbalisation raises issues or questions to which I respond, and this calls for a further response and so on until a conclusion or solution is reached. The reflective subject is thus a dialogical subject.

This account overlaps with that of Mead (1967) and the comparison is instructive as Mead adds two vital elements to it. In the first instance he argues that we learn, as children, to substitute verbal formulation for immediate motor action in at least certain cases. We learn to say 'I want' or 'please', for example, instead of simply grabbing. It is this process of substitution, he argues, that makes planning and reflection possible. We formulate our action as a linguistic idea which then makes it possible for us to debate its pros and cons before literally enacting it. And this generates the possibility that we may decide against enactment if the cons are too great, or upon strategic modification of the act to better ensure its success. There is more to this than words, however. To dialogue with oneself and achieve the reflectiveness and self-consciousness this entails, he argues, requires that one can break free of one's own perspective and assume the attitude of another towards oneself. One must genuinely become other to one's self. Such reflexivity is not innate however. One becomes capable of it by acting out the roles of others as a child and thereby incorporating their perspective within one's own corporeal schema. When I dialogue with myself I literally slip into the role of those with whom I would ordinarily consult, playing both my own part and theirs in what becomes a genuinely dialogical situation (see Chapter 8). Later this is modified by playing games and learning to incorporate the perspective not simply of other players but of the game itself: the 'generalised other' as Mead refers to it. The sentiments of the group are literally 'embodied' in the corporeal schema of the agent where they both guide action and become voices in self-dialogues. In this respect, to tie our two points together, the 'cons' an agent may consider in their dialogue could include the normative consideration that an act is wrong or undesirable from the point of view of the other.

The interdependency and intertwining between thought and language is further illustrated, for Merleau-Ponty, by genuinely dyadic communication itself. It is sometimes supposed that listening to or reading the words of another involves us thinking about their words, he notes, but this is false. We may, of course, think about their words but, as in perception, this presupposes a prior phase of grasping the significance of those words. In the first instance we must 'think along with them', as it were, allowing their words to form our thoughts for us. It is in this way that they can make us think things we have never thought before, as, for example, when we enter the magical world of a novel or find ourselves thinking for the first time in the fashion of a new philosophical or scientific school. We are not forced to agree with what they make us think, of course. In Merleau-Ponty's dialogical conception of speech and language, utterances provoke responses, both for speaker and for listener, and neither need agree with what is said. But they cannot disagree if they have not first followed the thought and allowed their self to be possessed by it.

When such sharing of thoughts takes place, an interworld or common ground is formed between the interlocuters. They are 'woven into a single fabric' and the actions of each can be understood only by way of this common whole. An irreducible dynamic kicks in, in which:

> … my words and those of my interlocuter are called forth by the state of the discussion, and they are inserted into a shared operation of which neither of us is the creator. (Merleau-Ponty 1962: 354)

Each thinks through the other and makes the other think. Every action is a reaction or response and is thus shaped by the action (of the other) which precedes it:

> … the objection which my inerlocuter raises to what I say draws from me thoughts which I had no idea I possessed, so that at the same time I lend him thoughts, he reciprocates by making me think too. (ibid.)

Such harmony is only possible, for Merleau-Ponty, when speakers share in a common linguistic heritage and thus move in the same social circles. Moreover, it will be exploited or destroyed if strategic or instrumental aims are allowed to become too prominent within it. Notwithstanding this, the notion of interlocuters being woven into a single fabric highlights a very important aspect of his theory; namely, the intersubjective or dialogical nature of human agency. Our thoughts, feelings and actions do not spring out of a vacuum, he believes, but rather out of the on-going dialogues, interactions and interdependencies that constitute the basis of our lives.

Emotion, Sexuality and Desire

Speech is intimately connected with affect for Merleau-Ponty. Like Mead (1967), he believes that it derives from gestural communication and that gestures derive, in large part, from forms of emotional expression. This is what was meant earlier when speech was described as a way of 'singing the world'. Emotion does receive an independent analysis in his work, however, and this deserves discussion. We can begin with the following claim:

> We must reject the prejudice which makes inner realities out of love, hate or anger, leaving them accessible to one single witness; the person who feels them. Anger, shame, hate and love are not psychic facts hidden at the bottom of another's consciousness: they are types of behaviour or styles of conduct which are visible from the outside. They exist on this face or in those gestures, not hidden behind them. (Merleau-Ponty 1971: 52)

This quotation resonates with Ryle's (1949) view, which we discussed in the previous chapter. Merleau-Ponty conceptualises emotion in terms of behaviour and argues that, as such, emotions are intersubjective. My emotions exist for you because they comprise my embodied manner of acting in and thereby relating to my environment. Elsewhere he adds:

> Faced with an angry or threatening gesture, I have no need, in order to understand it, to recall when I myself used these gestures on my own account. I know very little, from the inside, of the mime of anger so that a decisive factor is missing for any association by resemblance or reasoning by analogy, and what is more, I do not see anger or a threatening attitude as a psychic fact hidden behind the gesture, I read anger in it. The gesture does not make me think of anger, it is anger itself. (Merleau-Ponty 1962: 184)

In other words, we do not need to think about the gesture or compare it with gestures of our own in order to grasp its meaning, as it speaks directly to us and affects us. The word 'read' which Merleau-Ponty uses in this context is particularly appropriate here. When we read a page of text we scarcely notice the physical inscriptions upon the page, unless they are particularly unusual. We are simply absorbed in and affected by the meaning or message of what we read. Our understanding of the words manifests in the reaction it provokes from us. So it is with gesture. The anger of the other does not make me think of anger nor do I notice the specific gestures it entails. Rather it communicates directly and provokes a response from me. Perhaps I am fearful or I laugh or get angry myself. There is something immediate in the communication, in the literal sense of 'unmediated'. This does not mean that the meaning of the gesture lies beyond culture, however: 'I do not even understand the expression of the emotions in primitive [sic] people or in circles too unlike the one in which I mix' (Merleau-Ponty 1962: 184). The gesture of the other moves me as it does because we share collective habits of emotion. We inhere in a common cultural tradition, and different cultures have different forms of emotional behaviour. Or rather, we have different ways of living emotion and being emotional:

> ... the behaviour associated with anger or love is not the same in a Japanese and an Occidental. Or rather, to be more precise, the difference in behaviour corresponds to a difference in the emotions themselves. [...] Feelings and passional conduct are invented like words. (Merleau-Ponty 1962: 189)

As this quotation indicates, the terms 'behaviour' and 'conduct' do not quite capture the full sense of Merleau-Ponty's understanding of affective life. Emotions are ways of being-in-the-world; that is, ways of making sense of and acting in the world. To be in a particular emotional state entails perceiving the world in a particular way; noticing things that one might not usually notice and being affected by what one sees in ways that one might not normally be affected. One's milieu or lifeworld is transformed as are the meanings of all that one encounters therein. And the way in which one acts in the world, comporting oneself towards objects and others, is transformed too. It hardly need be stressed here that these are bodily transformations which operate at the pre-reflective level. A particular emotional state is something that 'comes over' one like sleep. One finds oneself responding in a different way, or perhaps one does not even notice. One may try to put oneself in an emotional state of course, by, for example, acting out that state, just as one may try to bring on sleep by lying curled up in bed; but one must nevertheless wait to be 'taken' by the emotion as one must wait to be taken by sleep.

For the most part Merleau-Ponty seems to agree with the Heideggarian notion that our manner of being-in-the-world is always 'mooded' (Heidegger 1962); that is, that even the most 'cold' or 'neutral' of affective states are nevertheless affective states and that everything we experience and do is therefore charged with an affective sense. At a number of points, however, he seems also to concur with Sartre's (1993) understanding of emotional outbursts as 'magical' transformations of situation which bring new levels of meaning into it. Emotion, for Sartre, is a magical modality of our being-in-the-world which reconfigures our sense of the world and brings new forms of meaning into it, particularly when our view of the world is threatened. Envy, for example, may entail a magical transformation of objects we desire into objects we hate and wish to destroy, whilst laughter diffuses a situation, converting tension to comedy (see also Crossley 1998a). None of this would be possible, however, as both Merleau-Ponty and Sartre note, if emotion were not a constant aspect of our milieu. We cannot come to hate an object in envy if we do not first desire it and we will only celebrate or despair over that which matters to us: that is to say, that to which we always already have an affective tie.

This raises the question of what, indeed, does matter to us. What drives us? What is the nature of our desire? Over and above the basic desires for food and comfort Merleau-Ponty explores the nature of sexual desire. His main argument in this respect, which follows directly from his critique of behaviourism, is that human beings have no fixed sexual instinct. By this he means that there is no 'hardwired' reflex in the human case, as there appears to be in some animals, which links fixed stimuli to a determinate set of behaviours. This is revealed by the great cross cultural and historical diversity that we can identify in human sexual behaviour, not to mention variation between individuals within the same culture and within the same individual across a temporal trajectory (see also Gagnon and Simon 1973). Moreover, sexual arousal is not triggered by definite physical stimuli but rather by the meanings which situations have for us, meanings which are structured, in part, by collective and shared history but which may also bear the hallmarks of an individual history. For this reason there is almost no limit to what may strike us as sexual, but equally no necessity that anything will strike us as sexual (ibid.). Sexuality is a dimension of our being-in-the-world, shaped by all other dimensions in the total context of our social life. To talk of sexuality and meaning in this way, however, is equally to concede that our perceptual and motor life is sexually structured. Though our levels of arousal vary across times and situations, interacting with other aspects of our mood and circumstances, sexuality pervades every aspect of our life, action and perception *qua* sensuous structure of meaning.

Much of what Merleau-Ponty says with respect to sexuality corresponds with Freud's (1973) notion of the 'polymorphous perversity' of our basic sexual state and he acknowledges the debt. Moreover, like Freud, he believes that the current sexual disposition of any given social agent is a function of their sexual history. Certain versions of the Freudian account are equally incompatible with his holistic and purposive view of the human agent, however; particularly those centred upon the notion of the drive. Goldstein (2000), whose work was a major influence on Merleau-Ponty, makes the point most clearly. The notion of a drive is biologically untenable in much the same way as the notion of an isolated reflex, he argues, and for the same reason: namely that there is no room for such an 'autonomous system' in an otherwise integrated whole because nothing can be autonomous or indeed prioritised in this way in a thoroughgoing holism. However central sexuality, or aggression for that matter, might be in human affairs, this is not and could not be in virtue of an autonomous drive within the organism. Sexuality is a function of the whole organism, he notes. When we act sexually our whole being is oriented towards sexual meanings and activities. But this is only so because our sexual tendencies are aspects of and are subordinated to our total pattern of being.

The Desire for Recognition

Over and above this distinctly sexual aspect of desire, following Kojéve's (1969) reading of Hegel, Merleau-Ponty identifies a distinctly human desire: the 'desire for desire' or 'desire to be desired'. The origin of this 'desire for recognition', he argues, lies in our discovery, in childhood, of other consciousness'. It is by recognising that others have a consciousness of the world and a consciousness of us that we develop self-consciousness, but this also ties us up in a relationship of interdependency with the other (see Crossley 1996a). Our awareness of their awareness of us generates a paranoid tension and alienation, an insecurity, which can only be resolved if we win their recognition. We experience our own view of the world as a partial perspective, in need of completion. We must prove ourselves to the other in order to prove ourselves to ourselves.

This 'desire for recognition' is central to the constitution of the social world for Merleau-Ponty, as for many other post-Hegelians, including Mead (1967) and Honneth (1995). Its consequences are by no means straightforward, however. On the one hand it pulls individuals together and encourages conformity. The desire for approval and acknowledge-ment, as Homans (1961) amongst others has argued, is central to the processes of socialisation and social control. It draws the infant into the process and motivates them to achieve and develop. On the other hand, however, the stability which this engenders is threatened by the competi-tive element that desire constitutes. As Mead puts it, our sense of self must be recognised by others and correspond to the image they have of us 'to have the very values we want to have belong to it', but '... there is a demand, a constant demand, to realise one's self in some sort of supe-riority over those around us' (1967: 205). We seek to distinguish and elevate ourselves, or at least keep others from elevating their self above us. This may manifest in grand 'contests' but not it need not necessarily do so:

> We may come back to manners of speech and dress, to a capacity for remem-bering, to this, that and the other thing – but always to things in which we stand out above people. We are careful, of course, not to directly plume ourselves. It would seem childish to intimate that we take satisfaction in showing that we can do something better than others. We take a great deal of pains to cover up such a situation; but actually we are vastly gratified. (ibid.)

Within this competitive context, moreover, seemingly useless objects, which come to signify the desire of the other acquire a high symbolic value. As Kojéve puts it:

> ... an object perfectly useless from the biological point of view (such as a medal or the enemy's flag) can be desired because it is the object of other desires. Such a Desire can only be a human Desire and human reality, as distinguished from animal reality, is created only by action that satisfies such Desires: human history is the history of desired Desires. (Kojéve 1969: 6)

Even as agents struggle for recognition, however, they remain within the boundaries of the symbolic order. As Kojéve's remark suggests, agents struggle for goods and symbolic distinctions whose value is culturally defined and thereby wholly contingent and arbitrary. Moreover, as Kojéve's remark also indicates, these struggles are, in themselves, generative of social and cultural forms. They motivate social interactions and thereby mobilise the potential for change.

Huizinga's (1950) fascinating work on play and the playful or *ludic* element in culture provides an important corroboration to these points and also relates them back to some of our earlier points. Play, he notes, has two basic elements. On the one hand it involves a degree of arbitrariness; elements within the environment take on a particular symbolic value peculiar to the game and actions pursue purposes and obey conventions and rules which have no basis or meaning outside of it. One is reminded here of the 'virtual realities' which Merleau-Ponty (1965) identifies with symbolic behaviour and of his footballer, whose actions and perceptions are formed within the horizon of the game. Indeed, I referred to these symbolic realities specifically as games. On the other hand, play often involves a competitive or *agonistic* element, which corresponds to struggles for recognition. In play we struggle, tussle and compete. Using this definition Huizinga shows how play, and particularly playful contests and jousts, lie at the centre of much of culture; and how they have played an important role in the development of many central cultural activities, including philosophy, science, poetry and politics. He shows how the philosophy of the ancient Greeks, for example, grew out of 'riddle contests' in which orators and thinkers sought to outwit one another in public forums.

Another central reference for this particular point is Bourdieu. His notion of social fields, as I discuss later in the book, trades heavily off the metaphor of games, and his vision of the social world corresponds closely to this notion of arbitrarily bounded contests over symbolic stakes. His 'agents' compete for glory within the fields of science, sport, religion, politics and so on. However, he reintroduces the important Hegelian theme, also emphasised by Merleau-Ponty but neglected by Huizinga, of domination and the various forms of power and violence (both symbolic and physical) which structure the state of play within social games. In some games, he shows, the 'cards are stacked' and the advantage this secures for some may be maintained through force.

Returning to our original theme, then, emotionality is a constant aspect of our milieu on account of the fact that things matter to us. And though things matter to us on account of their use value, they equal matter because they are symbols of the desire of the other. We desire desire.

Conclusion: Merleau-Ponty's Embodied Agent

I stated at the outset of this chapter that my outline of Merleau-Ponty's model of the agent would be both preliminary and a sketch. I reiterate that now. There is much more we need to do to put flesh upon these bones. Before ending this particular chapter, however, it is important to reflect briefly upon its general themes.

In Ryle (1949) we encountered a robust critique of mind–body dualism. There were limits to Ryle's critique, however. He exorcised the ghost from the machine but fell short of a thorough critique of the machine myth. Merleau-Ponty (1962, 1965) takes this next step. Like Ryle he finds the concept of 'behaviour' suggestive for the dissolution of mind–body dualism. In addition, he mounts a powerful and persuasive critique of mechanistic accounts of behaviour, which regard it is a caused reflex response to a fixed stimulus. Behaviour, he shows, is purposive and oriented to meaning. To explain it we must therefore first understand the matrix of meaning in which it is located and the purpose which it serves. In the human case this will involve analysing the symbolically constructed 'virtual realities' in which agents co-participate; the games they play and the goals they chase after.

In the process of doing this, Merleau-Ponty brings many of the more 'bodily' aspects of social agency to light. In particular he explores the nature of perception, as a sensuous apprehension and understanding of the world, and he considers the nature of emotion and desire. Desires and emotions are not switches that we turn on and off, for Merleau-Ponty, nor are they autonomous 'drives' with their own independent logic. Our relations to the world are always already mooded and desirous. For this reason we are never the narrow cognitive beings that some sociological models might suggest but, by the same logic, neither are we the 'desiring machines' which certain other, latter day Hobbesians might suggest. Desire, emotion, cognition and perception are not, strictly speaking, separate parts of our behavioural life but rather integrated and mutually affecting aspects of a single and coherent structure.

To read Merleau-Ponty simply as a critic of the machine myth is to grasp only half of the significance of his work, however. His focus on 'behaviour', which challenges mind–body dualism, is equally an effort to challenge the philosophy of consciousness and, particularly, its intellectualism. Perception, thought and the meanings they involve are not the work of a subject. The subject is an outcome of perceptual and linguistic behaviours, most of which are rooted in habits and acquired schemas. The reflective subject is a product of habituated behaviours which subtend it and make it possible. In this respect Merleau-Ponty clearly decentres the subject. More importantly he posits a truly radical conception of the body. The body is more than an object, for Merleau-Ponty. It acts purposively and both seeks out and replies to meanings within its environment. And yet it is less than a subject; possessing none of the trappings of 'the subject' as conceived within the philosophical tradition. Some commentators designate this 'third term', between object and subject, the 'body-subject'.

The next step of our exposition of Merleau-Ponty will involve an exploration of the concepts of habit and corporeal schema which have been hinted at in this chapter, and a more direct reflection on his conception of choice and human freedom. Before we move onto this examination, however, we must, in the next chapter, take a detour through the work of Bourdieu. This detour, as I will explain at the beginning of the chapter, is necessary both because it situates the concept of habit, sociologically, flagging up its importance, and because we are only able to appreciate the strength and importance of Merleau-Ponty's conception of habit, when we have considered some of the weaknesses in Bourdieu's conception, as it stands.

Notes

1. To see the cube from the top one must pull corners a, b, c, and d to the foreground of one's perceptual field; to see it from the side one must pull e, f, g and h to the foreground.

2. I am grateful to Alan Costall for informing of the direct line of influence between Merleau-Ponty and Gibson.

3. For example, Elias 1978, Huizinga 1950, Mead 1967, Winch 1958, Garfinkel 1967.

6

HABITUS, CAPITAL AND FIELD: EMBODIMENT IN BOURDIEU'S THEORY OF PRACTICE

In Chapter 7 I will be returning to Merleau-Ponty in an effort to explore and elucidate the nature of human habit and the 'corporeal schema'. Before doing this, however, I want to open up the issue of habit by way of a reflection upon the work of Pierre Bourdieu. Bourdieu's theory of practice is, in my view, the most persuasive and interesting approach in contemporary sociology. It combines philosophical sophistication with thorough empirical engagement and application. Its elegance and parsimony is much needed and very refreshing in an era dominated by the monstrous and often ludicrous theoretical constructions of the various postmodernist cults. More specifically, it puts embodiment at centre stage, facilitating a strong sociological grasp upon it, and it is the most obvious way to extend the insights of Merleau-Ponty into the sociological arena. Indeed, though the intellectual genealogy is unclear, it is commonly held that Bourdieu builds upon the work of Merleau-Ponty and presupposes it in much that he argues (Bourdieu and Wacquant 1992, Wacquant 1993, Dreyfus and Rabinow 1993). If Bourdieu offers us a way of extending Merleau-Ponty's work more fully into the sociological domain, however, it is nevertheless also true that Merleau-Ponty, and other phenomenologists, are in a position to repay him in kind by helping him out of a number of the difficulties that his work otherwise incurs, specifically regarding the notion of habit or habitus. Although, as will become clear, I do not share many of the criticisms that have been levelled against Bourdieu, there are problems with his approach, problems which can be resolved through a return to the phenomenological roots of the concept of the habitus. This is why, having examined Bourdieu's work in this chapter, I will return to Merleau-Ponty and the phenomenology of habit in the next. Through a dialogue with phenomenology we can deepen and strengthen Bourdieu's theory of practice without detracting from its central claims in any way.

The chapter begins with an account of Bourdieu's conception of the habitus. Following this I introduce a number of further central concepts, including capital and field, and I discuss the role which desire or libido has come to play in Bourdieu's more recent work. Through the concepts of habitus and desire we get a strong sense of the dialectical process whereby social practices are incorporated within the body only then to be reproduced by way of embodied activity. This is further developed in the next section of the chapter where I consider the concept of 'physical capital' and the implication which this has for our understanding of various forms of body modification. Loic Wacquant's (1995) study of boxing is used to exemplify this point. Finally, in the last two sections of this chapter, I consider a number of criticisms that have been levelled at Bourdieu's work and I offer my own critical assessment.

Bourdieu's Habitus

Bourdieu (1992a) formulates his theory of 'habitus' in the context of a critical engagement with structuralism and social physics, on the one hand, and social phenomenology on the other. Against social physics and structuralism he argues for a notion of competent and active agency. The social physics of the early sociologists, such as Comte, is challenged on the familiar grounds that it fails to recognise the role of active interpretation and decision making in social action. The structuralism of Levi-Strauss is acknowledged to be more sophisticated but its rule-bound conception of practice is deemed problematic on three grounds. In the first instance, Bourdieu contests the explanatory status of rules. The structuralist's 'rules', he notes, are observational codes derived from the study of regularities in social practice. They 'stand for' those regularities in the discourse of the observer. As such they may be instructive but to attempt to use them to explain regularities in practice is circular; the regularity of practice is invoked to account for its regularity. Rules can only be used to explain behaviour if, on the one hand, they are formulated and oriented to by the agent, or, on the other, they enjoy an independent existence and properly 'causal' power. Neither of these preconditions are met by the structuralist's 'unconscious' rules, however, and thus the notion that rules explain action collapses. The rule is an intellectual construct with considerable heuristic value but it only maps regularities in practices. It does not explain them.

This first criticism deals with 'constitutive rules'; that is, rules or regularities which are constitutive of the meaning, intelligibility and identity of specific social practices. Bourdieu's second criticism, by contrast, addresses itself to normative rules; that is, rules which stipulate, for agents, what ought to happen in specific contexts of practice and which, with some effort, they could outline for a researcher in an interview. Parsons' (1951) account of norms in *The Social System* is a good example of a theory which relies upon this type of rule but the structuralism of Levi-Strauss, with its emphasis upon the incest taboo and rules of matrimonial exchange, is an equally good and more relevant example. In his critique of this type of rule-based explanation Bourdieu, using his own fieldwork on kinship structures, points to the somewhat more messy and strategic nature of social life. Structuralist analyses focus upon the official picture of social relations, he notes, but this is often a far cry from the negotiated situation one finds at the ground level. Actors do not simply follow rules. They bend them, working around them so as to maximise their own best advantage.

Finally, rejoining a line of criticism that has emerged out of Wittgensteinian accounts of rule following (for example, Taylor 1993), Bourdieu points to the underdetermination of action by rules and the potential for infinite regress which an account of rule following engenders. Rules must be applied, he notes. More to the point they must be applied appropriately; at the right time, in the right place and in the right way. This raises the question, however, of how we are to explain rule following. Are there rules governing the application of rules? If there are then we are locked into an infinite regression because those second order rules presuppose further rules and so on. If not, however, then rules presuppose another form of explanation of social practice.

What emerges out of this critique is the need for a conception of human action or practice which can account for its regularity, coherence and order without ignoring its strategic nature. This is what the concept of the habitus is designed to achieve. An agent's habitus is an active residue or sediment of their past experiences which functions within their present, shaping their perception, thought and action and thereby shaping social practice in a regular way. It consists in dispositions, schemas, forms of know-how and competence, all of which function below the threshold of consciousness, shaping it in particular ways:

> The schemes of the habitus, the primary forms of classification, owe their specific efficacy to the fact that they function below the level of consciousness and language, beyond the reach of introspective scrutiny or control by the will. (Bourdieu 1984: 466)

These dispositions and forms of competence are acquired in structured social contexts whose pattern, purpose and underlying principles they incorporate as both an inclination and a *modus operandi*. Their acquisition amounts to an incorporation of social structures and practices. A child brought up in an art-loving family, for example, is far more likely, statistically, to develop their own 'love of art' and will acquire the dispositions and know-how proper to 'true' appreciation and criticism (Bourdieu et al. 1990). In this respect habitus are 'structured structures'. Insofar as these incorporated habits dispose the agent to continue with particular forms of practice, in particular ways, however they are equally responsible for the generation of practice. The child who goes on in later life to appreciate and criticise art, on the basis of their childhood learning, for example, actively reproduces the artistic field. In this respect habitus are 'structuring structures'. Or rather, they are structured structuring structures:

> ... systems of durable, transposable dispositions, structured structures predisposed to function as structuring structures, that is, as principles which generate and organise practices and representations that can be objectively adapted to their outcomes without presupposing a conscious aiming at ends or an express mastery of the operations necessary in order to attain them. Objectively 'regulated' and 'regular' without being in any way the product of obedience to rules, they can be collectively orchestrated without being the product of an organising action of a conductor. (Bourdieu 1992a: 53)

> ... the habitus, the product of history, produces individual and collective practices, and hence history, in accordance with the schemas engendered by history. (Bourdieu 1977: 82)

This account is reminiscent of the 'circularity' which Durkheim (1915) refers to in his discussion of the relationship between society and individual (see Chapter 1) and to Merleau-Ponty's notion that we are 'in a sort of circuit with the socio-historical world' (see Chapter 5). Society shapes the individual but, at the same time, depends entirely upon the actions and dispositions of individuals for its own existence. Bourdieu is clear to distance himself from the mechanistic picture sometimes (wrongly) associated with Durkheim. Like Merleau-Ponty, he emphasises the role of both competence and improvisation in his account of habitus. The schemas of the habitus function like an underlying grammar which allows for a multitude of innovative forms of expression, he argues; facilitating action as much as they shape it. Social agents are like players in a game, actively pursuing their ends with skill and competence, but always doing so within the bounds of the game. What this analogy with games also serves to bring out is the strategic element which enters into habitual action and which, as I noted above, Bourdieu has observed in his own fieldwork. Habitus predispose agents to act in particular ways without reducing them to cultural dopes or inhibiting their strategic capacities. Like game-playing skills, the structures of the habitus facilitate the competent pursuit of specified goals. I will return to this point later.

Each individual agent's habitus will be different to some degree, as no two biographies are exactly the same. Notwithstanding this, individual biographies are but strands in a collective history for Bourdieu. The individual belongs to a group or variety of groups, and the individual habitus therefore tends to manifest many group specific characteristics. Indeed, the individual and individual habitus are but variants of their collective root:

> Since the history of the individual is never anything other than a certain specification of the collective history of his class or group, *each individual system of dispositions* may be seen as a *structural variant* of all other group or class habitus, expressing the difference between the trajectories and positions inside or outside the class. 'Personal' style, the particular stamp marking all products of the same habitus, whether practices or works, is never more than a deviation in relation to the style of a period or class ... (Bourdieu 1977: 86)

The emphasis upon compecence, know-how, skill and disposition which we find in this concept resonates with a similar emphasis in those schools of sociology which Bourdieu collectively terms 'social phenomenology'; that is, interactionism, ethnomethodology and Schutz's phenomenology. He is critical of these approaches too. They remain focused upon the interpretative horizon of the agent, he argues, failing to step back from that horizon to locate it in the structural context from which it emerges. Put crudely, this leads to: a failure to identify the differences between the interpretative frameworks of particular groups; a failure to examine the conditions which give rise to particular frameworks and to differences between them; and a failure to identify the relations of power which allow one framework to acquire greater legitimacy and recognition than the others. Like the ethnomethodologists, Bourdieu is interested in 'member's methods'. Unlike them, however, he argues that these methods diverge because there are divergent groups for members to be members of, each of which is formed in and shaped by its relations with other groups and specific material conditions. Furthermore, he argues that the relations between groups are, at least in part, power relations, and that the methods of the powerful have a greater chance of achieving legitimation than those of others.

Distinction provides one very clear example of how Bourdieu (1984) pursues this idea. In this study he identifies differences in the aesthetic dispositions of different social classes. Different classes have different tastes and the formal aesthetic disposition identified by Kant is revealed to be very much specific to the educated middle classes. Bourdieu explains these differences in terms of the respective distances of these classes from the realm of material 'necessity', or at least from specific necessities, and he identifies the relations of symbolic power which effectively place these different aesthetic outlooks in a hierarchical structure, such that they seem to legitimate the inequalities upon which they are founded. Differences which are the effect of class are effectively mis-recognised as natural causes of inequality and thus function to legitimate the very class structure which produces them.

Structuring, Structured Structures – and Practice

Bourdieu's theory of habitus is already a partial theory of practice, and already identifies a central interplay between body and society. The habitus, he argues, is a structured structure; it takes shape by way of the involvement of an agent in a structured domain of practice. But, it is equally a structuring structure. Having been formed it generates practices which accord with its own conditions of generation. The body enters into this picture since the habitus consists of 'incorporated' structures; that is, the structures of the habitus, which function as a hinge between past and present, agency and structure, are bodily structures. Learning a language, for example, as we discussed in Chapter 5, is a matter of acquiring a new use of one's body. Moreover, this is not a use to which 'we' put 'our bodies' but rather a use which subtends our conscious subjectivity and gives rise to 'us' *qua* speaking subjects. We only learn of our thoughts by way of the bodily effort which produces them in linguistic form and simultaneously thereby makes them available to us in the form of expression.

The habitus is only one dimension in the theory of practice, however. Practice, Bourdieu argues, is an outcome not simply of habitus but equally of what he refers to as 'capital' and 'field'. This view is expressed, somewhat schematically, in *Distinction*, in the form of an equation: *[(habitus) (capital)] + field = practice* (Bourdieu 1984: 101). This formulation is problematic in my view. It reads like the social physics that Bourdieu (1992a) is elsewhere so keen to criticise and distance himself from. The meanings and improvisation belonging to habitus and practices are simply deleted and we are asked to regard their relationship as if it were mathematical in form – which it is not. Notwithstanding this, the formula does give us the basic gist of his theory of practice in a relatively clear way. He suggests that practice is the result of various habitual schemas and dispositions (habitus), combined with resources (capital), being activated by certain structured social conditions (field) which they, in turn, belong to and variously reproduce and modify. To push this exposition further we must discuss 'capital', 'field' and some related concepts.

Capital, Class and Domination

By 'capital' Bourdieu means the resources distributed throughout the social body which have an exchange value in one or more of the various 'markets' or 'fields' which, as we shall see, he believes comprise the social world. The most obvious or at least familiar example is economic capital, which entails all income, savings and assets which have a monetary value, defined in terms of that value. Economic capital is a highly rationalised form of capital. It has a precise numerical value and a reified and independent existence, in the form of money, which allows it to be accumulated, stolen, given away and invested. As such it tends to serve as a model against which other forms of capital are compared and conceived. However, Bourdieu is perhaps more renown for introducing, or at least developing, the notion of 'cultural capital'; that is, the exchange value which accumulated forms of culture have within the social world. Cultural capital is potentially much less rationalised than economic capital but in his work on the education system, Bourdieu has pointed to qualifications as one of the more institutionalised forms that this capital can assume. Qualifications, whilst not such a flexible or transferable currency as money, can nevertheless be 'cashed in' for employment offering monetary rewards. Their acquisition is itself, at least to some degree, a conversion of inherited cultural capital from within a family. The education system, Bourdieu argues, bestows value upon the specific dispositions and 'cultural arbitrary' of certain dominant groups, such that the offspring of those groups are afforded a considerable advantage within it. What appears to be a fair competition over qualifications is therefore far from it.

The school, with its ideology of fair competition, effectively 'launders' the advantage of the cultural elite. It rewards, in the name of educational achievement and in the form of qualifications, inherited cultural disposi- tions, simultaneously thereby disguising those dispositions as talent and motivation.

Economic and cultural capital are clearly the two major forms of capital for Bourdieu. Notwithstanding this, however, there are at least two further forms of capital afforded prominence in his work. On the one hand he refers to 'symbolic capital', which broadly amounts to status or recog- nition. This may have an objectified or institutionalised form. Various awards and prizes are measures of symbolic capital, for example. In many instances, however, symbolic capital consists in the manner in which an individual is perceived and has no objectified form as such. Racism, sexism and various forms of stigmatisation are extreme forms of capital deficit in this respect. Finally, Bourdieu refers to 'social capital', by which he means the connections and networks which an agent can call upon in their effort to achieve a specified goal. The 'old boy' networks of the public school and elite university systems, famed for their capacity for 'string pulling', are one very obvious example of this.

Cultural, symbolic and social capital can assume a fairly 'field specific' form, and their value, as such, may be tied to specific social 'worlds'. What counts as valuable in the academic world may be of less value in relation to the theatrical, sporting or artistic worlds, for example, and the 'connections' and status which afford one power in one area of life may not do so in another. Some forms of capital, however, such as economic capital, have a relatively general value on account of the pervasiveness of the field (the economy) to which they belong. The economy impinges on many other social fields, such that economic capital exerts a force within them. Furthermore, Bourdieu is keen to examine both the ways in which agents can transform their various forms of capital into other forms, in relation to other fields, and the ways in which agents vie to establish the dominance of their fields and forms of capital within the broader 'field of power' (Bourdieu 1996) or society more generally. In particular he perceives a conflict in the field of power between those whose dominance is rooted in economic capital and those whose dominance is cultural or educational. Both, he maintains, seek to establish the dominance of that form of capital which secures them their privilege in society. Thus any analysis of capital must investigate both its particularity and its position within the wider social formation.

Capital looms large in another of Bourdieu's central concepts: social class. Class, as he understands it, refers to the respective amounts of the various forms of capital that individuals possess (Bourdieu 1986b). Like Weber (1978) he acknowledges that every individual will have a some- what different 'class situation', on account of slight differences in their levels of capital, but again like Weber he acknowledges degrees of closure and cleavage around and between certain groups which constitutes them precisely as groups. Much of his work is devoted to an analysis of the way in which this closure is effected and the various strategies which agents adopt to both maximise their capital and reproduce, it inter-generationally.

This account of capital and class interweaves with the notion of the habitus in a number of respects. In the first instance, capital, because of its exchange value, is a factor, alongside habitus, shaping an agent's possibilities for action in any given situation. They can only do what they can afford to do. Secondly, and more directly, one's class position, which is defined by one's capital assets, shapes the context within which one's habitus is formed. The experience of working class and middle class children differs, on account of the capital possessed by their families and the opportunities and constraints this generates, and this is then registered corporeally as those experiences sediment in the habitus. Thirdly, forms of capital depend upon recognition or 'misrecognition' for their value. They are valuable to the extent that we agree that they are valuable. Habitus are important in this respect as they simultaneously effect and disguise these agreements. To say that we 'agree' upon the value of paper or plastic money, or indeed qualifications, is to recognise the arbitrary nature of these tokens of value; that they are precisely tokens. And yet we do not actively agree to their value. We assume it and treat the token as if it really had value independent of us; that is, we misrecognise these tokens as valuable. We are able to do this, for Bourdieu, because the 'agreement' is rooted at the level of unconscious habit. Finally, following on from this, Bourdieu suggests that much of the strategic manoeuvring required to reproduce capital and the forms of inequality it entails are sedimented at the level of habitus, such that they often pass unnoticed, both by those who benefit and those who suffer from them. In doing what comes naturally to them, the classes tend to reproduce themselves. And because this happens at the pre-reflective level of the habitus it can be misrecognised as a matter of natural talents and facts of life.

A very similar argument to this is also evident in Bourdieu's theory of political legitimation and domination. At one level this account is focused strongly upon discursive argument and the public sphere. Governments, he argues, are called to account for their actions and expected, within bounds, to explain, defend and announce their intentions to a potentially critical public. The importance he attaches to the public sphere is emphasised by a number of pointed critiques he has made regarding its erosion in recent years. Identifying both the art world and television as possible platforms for public debate and criticism, he has been strongly critical of the role of patronage in the former and commercial interests and 'dumbing down' in the latter (Bourdieu 1998b, Bourdieu and Haacke 1995). In both cases, he argues, the potential for critique is being undermined. At a deeper level, however, Bourdieu is critical of those theories of the polity which focus only upon processes of discursive legitimation. In the first instance, he argues that the range of issues debated in the public sphere is but the tip of an iceberg when compared with the range of unspoken assumptions upon which the legitimacy of the state rests. Moreover, he emphasises the role of the body in this respect. It is a mistake, he argues, to believe that the 'cognitive structures' which support the state are 'forms of consciousness'. They are rather 'dispositions of the body' (1998a: 54). He uses the term 'doxa' to designate this deep seated structure of embodied dispositions. Doxic beliefs are unquestioned beliefs, embodied in actions and feelings but seldom formulated in words. They manifest as sentiments, routines, assertions, aversions and 'calls to order':

> The social world is riddled with calls to order that function as such only for those who are predisposed to heeding them as they awaken deeply buried corporeal dispositions, outside the channels of consciousness and calculation. (Bourdieu 1998a: 54–5)

The picture of the public sphere which this gives rise to, expressed diagramatically in Figure 6.1, is one of a small space of discourse, structured within a much broader range of unspoken assumptions and postures. Bourdieu has pushed this further by arguing both that many citizens are not disposed to engage in political debate in the public sphere and that 'public opinion' is largely an artefact of public opinion polls which persuade agents to sign up to attitudes which often have no bearing on their lifeworld at all. Public opinion can only be said to properly exist, he argues, in the context of social movements whose formation involves the production of views which are then fought over (Bourdieu 1993). For the most part the citizen's habitus disinclines them from political involvement.

On these matters Bourdieu is in agreement with a great many sociologists, most notably Habermas (1988). He does add a distinctive and important dimension, however, when, in *Distinction*, he shows that (embodied) dispositions towards involvement in politics and the public sphere follow the same sort of class distribution as the other forms of lifestyle activity he examines in that book. The habituated disposition towards 'civil privatism' which Habermas (1988) attributes to the population in general, it would seem, is a more differentiated phenomena than Habermas' analysis suggests. Different degrees and forms of political involvement manifest in the habitus of distinct classes and class fractions. In particular the educated middle classes are far more likely than the working class to become involved in political public debate and to articulate views on political matters.

Field

Capital, class and domination constitute a 'vertical' differentiation of society but society is equally differentiated along a 'horizontal' axis, for Bourdieu, into discrete but overlapping social spaces. Functionalist sociology (for example, Parsons 1951), with its account of the division of society into discrete institutions, such as family, law, politics, media,

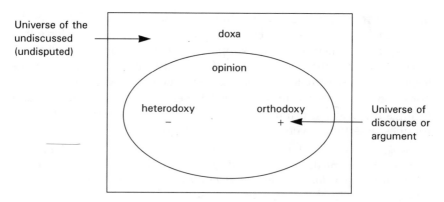

Figure 6.1   *Doxa, Orthodoxy and Heterodoxy (After the fashion of Bourdieu 1977: 168)*

education and so on, approximates this notion. There is no necessity to equate social spaces with institutions, however. Some social spaces are 'pre-institutional' or perhaps sub or transinstitutional. Moreover, functionalism tended to ignore the manner in which horizontal differentiation is diffracted through vertical differentiation and vice versa. Social spaces, such as the family or media, are never constituted independently of the vertical axis of gender and class (or race and disability) differentiation. And vertical differentiations are always expressed in and through multiple 'horizontal' contexts.

The concept of a field is Bourdieu's way of conceptualising these horizontally differentiated social spaces, as they are intersected by vertical differentiation. A field is a distinct social space consisting of interrelated and vertically differentiated positions, a 'network, or configuration of objective relations between positions' (Bourdieu and Wacquant 1992: 97). These positions may be occupied by either agents or institutions but what 'positions' them, as such, is their concentration or possession of specific 'species' of capital and power. They are positions in a specific distribution of capital and power.

At times Bourdieu likens fields to 'markets', a metaphor which captures the centrality of capital exchanges within them and allows us to make sense of the 'invisible hands' or 'forces' which emerge and have effects within them. Another, perhaps more useful metaphor that he uses, however, is that of games. Fields are like games which agents play. Although, in contrast to games, they are not generally recognised as such by those 'play' them:

> ... in the social fields, which are the products of a long, slow process of automomization, and are therefore, so to speak, games 'in themselves' and not 'for themselves', one does not embark upon the game by a conscious act, one is born

into the game, with the game; and the relation of investment, *illusio*, investment, is made more total and unconditional by the fact that it is unaware of what it is. (Bourdieu 1992a: 66)

Distinct social spaces, such as the field of higher education, or science, or hockey or television, are so many games in which players pursue specific goals and ends. This metaphor is more helpful than that of the market or indeed the more literal definitions of field which Bourdieu offers, in my view. It allows us to draw out the sense of the culturally arbitrary shape of fields and their 'stakes'. One is reminded of Merleau-Ponty's (1965) symbolic 'virtual realities', each with their own sense and meaning struc- tures. The scientist, priest or artist, no less than the football player, circumnavigates their 'playground' with due but largely unconscious consideration to concerns and conventions which are quite incomprehen- sible to outsiders. Each field, like a distinct game, has its own norms and logic; a specific 'point' and stakes which players must incorporate within their corporeal schema if they are to play. To liken fields to games is to invite sociologists to explore and discover the unique configuration of norms, stakes, patterns and logic that comprise each one. The sociologist must approach each social field as if approaching a new game for the first time, attempting to discern the point and the sense at work within the hurly burly of practice.

The game metaphor also has the additional advantage that it brings to light the interdependency of capital and field. Fields may consist of spe- cific distributions of capital and/or power, but those forms of capital and power are themselves relative to and dependent upon the game, as surely as checkmate is to chess. The economy, for example, is comprised in large part of varying distributions of economic capital, but economic capital is only capital and only has any value in virtue of the economy; that is, in virtue of the fact that it is recognised as 'currency' within the economy. This is most clearly, if only partially demonstrated by the instant devalu- ation that 'foreign money' undergoes when we return from holiday. In a (national) field where it is not recognised it has no value. Similarly with all other forms of capital. They may have value in one or many fields, but never independently of a field.

This account of fields relates to the concept of the habitus in a number of ways. On one hand we need to combine consideration of a player's dispo- sitions and competence (their habitus), and their resources (capital), with a grasp upon the state of play of the game and their location in it (field), if we are to fully understand and explain their action. Agent's actions are shaped by their habitus, their capital, and by the exigencies and logic of 'the game' as it unfolds. At a deeper level, however, it is because of their habitus and the way in which this shapes their perceptions, motivation and action, that the player is disposed to recognise and play the field in the first place. Or rather, as noted above, field and habitus are locked in a cir- cular relationship. Involvement in a field shapes the habitus which, in turn, shapes the perceptions and actions which reproduce the field.

Desire, Affect and Illusio

Individual agents, as the game metaphor suggests, are bound to social fields by a strong affective grip. The rules and stakes of a specific field might seem worthless and arbitrary to an outsider but players feel their 'weight' with a great emotional intensity. Bourdieu theorises this attachment in terms of 'libido' and its social moulding:

> One of the tasks of sociology is to determine how the social world constitutes the biological libido, an undifferentiated impulse, as a specific social libido. There are in effect as many kinds of libido as there are social fields: the work of socialisation of libido is precisely what transforms impulses into specific interests, socially constituted interests which only exist in relation to a social space in which certain things are important and others don't matter and for socialised agents who are constituted in such as way as to make distinctions corresponding to the objective differences in that space. (Bourdieu 1998a: 78–9)

I disagree. In my view the most fruitful way to develop this line of thought is to reject the notion of an undifferentiated biological impulse and to posit rather a notion of a 'desire for recognition' which can, as Kojéve's (1969) work shows (see Chapter 5), become attached to whatever arbitrary cultural objects come to symbolise it. We desire the rewards and goods at stake in a particular field because those goods have come stand for recognition (the desire of the other) for us. Bourdieu may object to this on the grounds that the Hegelian conception of desire, as least as developed in *The Phenomenology of Spirit*, is a metaphysical and idealist notion which does not sit happily with his own materialist position – hence, I suspect, his reference to biological impulses. I agree. However, writers such as Merleau-Ponty (1962) have found space for a desire for recognition within their more sophisticated materialist framework, recasting it in a more praxiological manner (see Chapter 5). Moreover, Axel Honneth (1995) has identified a 'less metaphysical' conception of the desire for recognition in the earlier work of Hegel (that is, Hegel's Jena writings), one not rooted in the philosophy of consciousness, and has suggested that these notions are developed in a more materialist, indeed evolutionarily grounded form, in the work of G.H. Mead (1967) (see also Joas 1985). Mead posits a materialist version of Hegelian desire, according to Honneth. Thus we can appropriate the 'desire for recognition', within a materialist framework, without buying into the idealism or metaphysics of the Hegelian system.

The notion of a desire for recognition gives us an account of the motivational springs which might give rise to any number of contests for status, privilege and anything else which ultimately represents recognition. This, I suggest, is precisely what fields are; structured spaces of contestation which have emerged within societies to give expression to the desire and need for recognition. Moreover, because the stakes in each field are, in a sense, simply arbitrary tokens of recognition, it is relatively straightforward to comprehend how they emerge and are displaced through time, or indeed, as Bourdieu says, how they are constructed and renegotiated in the course of struggle itself. The stakes in any field are not valued in virtue of their intrinsic worth. They are valued and desired because they represent the desire of the other. As such, they are liable to transformation in the course of the struggles through which they are pursued. This is not to deny that intrinsically worthy outcomes or even 'rules of the game' may be produced in this context (see Sayer 1999), but it suggests a deeper psychosocial dynamic behind such worthy developments.

There are many advantages to formulating the issue in this way. For present purposes, however, it is most important to note that a 'desire for recognition' is far more intelligible and easier to work with than an 'unspecified biological impulse'. The latter sounds more tangible and scientific, less mysterious, but just the reverse is true. A 'desire for recognition' is a specifiable disposition towards acting in particular ways. Its existence, *qua* disposition, may potentially be confirmed or rejected and explored through empirical investigation (see Honneth 1995, Benjamin 1991, Crossley 1996a). Indeed many perspectives in social science, from behaviourism (Watson 1930), through social exchange theory (Homans 1961), to the more exotic varieties of contemporary psychoanalysis (Lacan 1989, Benjamin 1991), all take some form of desire for approval or recognition as a demonstrable fact about the human organism, and all have sought to show, in different ways (often less eloquently than Kojéve), how this desire becomes attached to arbitrary cultural objects and pursuits. An unspecified biological impulse, by contrast, is what? It cannot really be anything if it is unspecified. And for this reason, in contrast to a desire for recognition, it is not clear how it could be harboured or channelled within the meaningful interactions that constitute the socialisation process. I will, therefore, stick with a materialised form of the desire for recognition in my account.

This socially moulded desire forms the basis of what Bourdieu terms the *illusio*; that is, a deep seated 'belief in the game' or 'enchantment' with it. Every social field, he argues, presupposes players who 'grant recognition to the stakes' and 'are not indifferent'. Even in highly competitive and conflict ridden fields there is:

> ... a profound complicity between the adversaries ...; they disagree with one another but they at least agree about the object of disagreement. (Bourdieu 1998a: 78)

They agree and do not even question that 'the game is worth the candle' (1998a: 77). This is not simply a matter of desire, of course. Agents desire the culturally arbitrary stakes of the game, and are 'ready to die' (ibid.) for them, only because the game, which is kept alive by themselves and others, is misrecognised as an independent fact about the world. Players must mistake the value which they invest in the game for a value which it already has independently of them. This presupposes players who have incorporated the game within their corporeal schema, as habitus; who adhere to its rules and distinctions, as doxa; and who consequently make it happen and 'do' it in their every gesture. Nevertheless, desire is integral if we are to conceive this process as 'interested' and to grasp and make sense of the deep affective investments it involves, and the heightened emotional reactions it invokes. Embodiment has a twofold relation to fields in this sense, constituting both the know-how and the impetus required to play.

It will be apparent, I hope, that this account of the struggle for recognition opens the way to a much greater appreciation of the affective component of the social world. I argued in Chapter 5 that emotions are generated in social situations because aspects of those situations matter to people and that they matter, at least to some extent, because of the desires that underlie action. It should be apparent now that these desires very much connect with the social world, even if some of the emotions that they generate are, by a common sense definition, 'anti-social'. Agents who are, in Bourdieu's words, 'ready to die' for social stakes are ready to do many things. We need to get away from the view, Hobbesian and Freudian in equal measures, that the 'unruly emotions' which periodically surface within social contexts are residues of a basic natural state which is denied or repressed by society. Human desires are invested within society and it is the frustration of those desires, and the intensity with which agents become involved in social games, which generate the outbursts which tempt and sometimes lead agents to transgress norms.

Invisible Hands and Field Dynamics

Fields are dependent upon the habits and socially constructed desires of 'flesh and blood actors'; or more precisely upon the forms of relationship and interdependence which such agents generate, on the basis of their dispositions and desires. Having said this, it is important to appreciate that Bourdieu is as much, if not more concerned with the underlying and invisible dynamics within fields; that is, with 'forces' within fields which shape the opportunities and actions of the incumbents of various positions, without those incumbents being necessarily aware of the fact. Here the market, with its 'invisible hands', is perhaps a more fruitful metaphor for fields, though Bourdieu does not share Adam Smith's positive appraisal of such handywork. He is more inclined to suggest, as many have with respect to economic markets, that they 'lend a hand' to some at the expense of others, that 'the cards are stacked' in these games. Furthermore, at least in relation to educational markets, he has emphasised and explored the possibility of crises within fields (Bourdieu 1986a). As in any market, under and over production of capital goods (for example, qualifications) are both possible, as is profit decline, and this can generate structural problems.

Integral to this emphasis on the 'underlying' and 'invisible' dynamics within fields is a critique of interactionist and ethnomethodological sociology. These approaches focus analysis at the level of face-to-face interaction, adopting a view that all there is to be studied in the social world is observable within the details of such interaction (for example, Coulter 1982). Whilst he is clearly influenced and impressed by this strand of sociology, not least because it reveals the embodied work that goes into the production and reproduction of social fields, Bourdieu resists the view that the social world is entirely 'done' *in situ*, suggesting that what is done, *in situ*, very often rests upon its position within broader configurations and patterns of interrelationships which are not evident at the face to face level.

We can illustrate this by way of a brief discussion of the consumption of works of art within museums. The details of the manner in which viewing is done and the spatiality of the gallery constructed through the interactions of participants are clearly of great sociological interest. We may learn a great deal about the meaning of art from listening to and analysing the way in which spectators talk about and constitute their experience. Furthermore, we may wish to examine the bodily nature of this experience; the way in which galleries are physically arranged, for example, and how viewers interact with that physical environment; the nature of the aesthetic gaze and the embodied know-how brought to bear upon the appreciative experience. But to fully grasp the meaning of art in modern societies, at least from a sociological point of view, we would also want to know who visits such galleries and, more to the point, who does not. Is art appreciation a primarily middle class pursuit, as Bourdieu's own early work suggests (Bourdieu et al. 1990)? We can only know this by going beyond the visible details of the gallery and studying the omissions (that is, the non-attenders). We must attend to the invisible aspects of gallery attendance and draw comparisons between the attending publics and the wider population. But we can only do this by standing back from the immediacy of the embodied activities which constitute the gallery experience, to objectify it and set it within a broader comparative framework. Certain of the 'social facts' of art appreciation require statistics, comparison and technical measures of class and social position to bring them to light.

This same critique of interactionism is made with respect to questions of power. Bourdieu criticises those who suggest that power is 'done' *in situ*, or indeed who reduce the power of actions to their immediate conditions of executions, by pointing to the institutionalised relational configurations which support them. His account of symbolic power captures this well (Bourdieu 1992b). He begins this account with reference to Austin's (1971) notion that linguistic utterances 'do things' and that many things are done by way of words. On this point he agrees with many discourse analysts and interactionists who have stressed that parliaments are dissolved, convicts imprisoned and wars started, by way of words. He notes that Austin qualifies this, however, by reference to 'felicity conditions'; that is, specific conditions which must be met if words are to be able to do whatever it is that they do. The prime minister may dissolve parliament by way of a form of words, for example, but one must be a prime minister in order to dissolve parliament in this way. Similarly, whilst a psychiatrist's diagnostic talk may be sufficient to have a patient forcibly incarcerated and perhaps also medicated or subjected to ECT against their will, any diagnosis which the patient may make of the doctor, no matter how astute and potentially scientifically credible, will have no such power because the utterances of the patient are not sanctioned in the same way. The patient's demeanour and diagnosis may be indistinguishable from that of the doctor at the technical and performative level, or even better, but it is still the performance of the doctor which carries the day, or carries the power to carry the day. Only their words generate the 'performative magic' that is psychiatric power. For Bourdieu this indicates that the power of words, 'symbolic power', rests upon relations of interdependence which transcend the immediacy of the 'doing' of the face-to-face encounter. The power of the psychiatrist's words, relative to those of the patient, derive from the vast institutionalised network in which they are involved, which regulates their practice and sanctions their power, and which is itself sanctioned by the state. Moreover, the process of sanctioning is in both cases historically rooted; the psychiatrist is sanctioned because they have passed through a training and the sanctioning of the psychiatric establishment itself by the state is a result of a long and conflict ridden history (Busfield 1986, Porter 1987, Scull 1993). The proper focus for a sociology of psychiatric power, or any other form of power, must be this vast, historically evolving complex or field.

Physical and Embodied Cultural Capital

Bourdieu's theory of practice allows us to maintain a strong sense of the embodiment of social structures without thereby falling back into what, in my view, would be a naively behaviouristic or positivist position. His accounts of the habitus and illusio, for example, illuminate the circular process whereby practices are incorporated within the body, only then to be regenerated through the embodied work and competence of the body. And this allows us to grasp the emotional/libidinal intensity of social processes and practices. On the other hand, the notion of fields allows us to see beyond this ground level of immediate visibility of 'the body', to locate the agent within the broader games in which they are involved, and to explore the various dynamics and forces of those games. Bourdieu introduces a further aspect to this embodied conception of social life through his notion of 'cultural capital'. Cultural capital, he argues, comes in three basic forms; an objectified form, such as the paintings or books one might own; an institutionalised form, by which he means qualifications and other official documents of cultural standing; and an embodied form, by which he means the manifold embodied competencies which carry a cultural value. The perceptual schema which allows one to competently 'read' a painting, discuss a musical work or identify a fine wine would be one example of this, as would the various aspects of one's bodily hexis: that is, one's comportment, accent, manners and all other such visible markers of social standing. This latter form clearly coincides with what Boudieu describes under the rubric of habitus. What the notion 'capital' adds, however, is an attention to the exchange value which specific dispositions have within particular social fields. When an agent's ability to 'read' great works of art or their accent and demeanour suffice to impress others sufficiently that they 'connect' with those others and secure a strategic advantage in the pursuit of their goals, for example, then those specific dispositions function precisely as capital. The notion of exchange has a metaphorical dimension to it here. One cannot 'spend' a posh accent in the way one does money. An accent stays posh even when it has been 'spent' and, as such, it retains its value. The point is, however, that it can be used, consciously or not, to procure other desired ends in a situation on account of its own perceived value or desirability.

Shilling (1991, 1992, 1993) has developed this notion of embodied cultural capital into a notion of physical capital. He pushes the notion of embodied cultural capital beyond its purely cultural dimension to include other aspects of 'the body' which may be objectified and constituted with a specific value within given social fields, so as to function as capital. The various aesthetic qualities of the body provide one example of this, whilst such qualities as fitness, strength, stamina, toughness and so on provide others. Any of these features can have an exchange value in certain fields and, as a consequence, can function as capital. Moreover, insofar as they acquire a value within specific fields, these bodily attributes become desirable to social agents.

This notion of physical capital is very important, in my view, for making sense of the various ways, indirect as well as direct, in which social agents modify or transform and mould their bodies. Much sociological work has suggested that this does happen and the implication of this work, at least, is that people modify their bodies because they desire the outcome. What the notion of physical capital does, is to locate those bodily states that might be deemed desirable within the context of the markets in which they have value. We can begin to see how bodily attributes function as currency, securing further rewards and serving as a valuable resource. Thus, I suggest, we can begin to understand more clearly the motivation for specific forms of body modification. Agents create and mould their bodies in accordance with the fields in which they are involved and the demands of those specific fields.

Wacquant's (1995) work on boxers is an interesting, if somewhat extreme, example in this respect. It focuses upon the various ways in which boxers build a body suited to and valued within their field; a body which is skilled in the ring, combining the rigour and precision of specific technical skills with the improvisation required to make it happen appropriately, but also a body tough and strong enough to take a hammering. He describes, with some pride, for example, the manner in which his own nose ceased to bleed so frequently after he had acquired some sparring experience. And he describes both the general work taken to turn a raw recruit into a potential contender and the more specific work, before each fight, to prepare the boxer for that fight.

In addition to this focus upon the production of physical capital, Wacquant describes the physical dangers, not to mention pain, to which the boxer is exposed and the role of the *illusio* in the rationalisation which the boxer is able to construct in the face of those dangers. In a very obvious sense, of course, the boxer could die in the ring. But short of this the physical damage caused by the constant pounding of the punchbag and the potential for brain damage caused by blows to the head, all make boxing a painful and risky sport. Boxers must live with this, however, and either get over or learn to cope with the fear this inevitably generates. Integral to the way in which they do this is the *illusio* of the field. Wacquant describes a 'non-thetic quasi-organismic commitment (akin in many respects to addiction)' (1995: 88) which simultaneously constitutes the subjective state of the boxer and the objective preconditions of their field:

> The boxers *desire* to fight flows from a *practical belief* [a 'state of the body'] constituted in and by the immediate co-presence of, and mutual understanding between, his (re)socialised lived body and the game.
>
> The boxer wilfully perseveres into this potentially self-destructive trade because, in a very real sense, he is inhabited by the game he inhabits. A veteran middleweight who has rumbled on three continents for over a decade and who reported breaking his hands twice and his foot once, persistent problems with his knuckles (because of calcium deposits forming around them) as well as a punctured ear drum and several facial cuts necessitating stitches, reveals this doxic acceptance made body, of the stakes of pugilism when he fails to find cause for alarm in this string of injuries: 'Sure you do, you think about it, but then you regroup yourself, start thinkin', you can't [give it up], it's *in your blood so much* ...' (Wacquant 1995: 88, *italics* in original)

What is so fascinating and important in this account, I suggest, is the multiple 'levels' of embodiment it entails. At one level the boxing field exists because agents grew up within it or were otherwise lured into it, either as players or spectators, such that they came to 'feel it in their bones' and were disposed to reproduce it by way of continued participation. The structures of the boxing world are embedded in their habitus. They live and breath boxing on a subjective level and objectively reproduce it in practice. The world which shapes the habitus, by being incorporated within the corporeal schema, is then reproduced by that schema and habitus. That is not all, however. The field which is generated in this way, *qua* market, demands a certain sort of body or physical capital for its effective functioning and generates rewards to encourage the shaping of such a body. It requires agile and combative bodies, armed and skilled in the techniques of the game and slimmed down to 'fighting weight'. This, in turn, generates a form of bodily labour upon the body. Agents act upon their bodies, by way of diet and training, to generate the physical capital that will make them a contender and perhaps even a winner. Then there are the fights; physical combat.

These, needless to say, are the focal point of the field and quite necessary to sustaining the excitement and *illusio* which generates it. They are also the final stage of body modification, however, and the boxer must draw upon the *illusio* of the game to cope with the fear and pain which it will personally cause them. There is a familiar Durkheimian circularity here; as the focal point of the field the fight sustains the *illusio*, but at the same time the fighter must draw upon that *illusio* to muster the courage to fight.

What is also very important about this boxing example, however, is that it reveals certain wider, perhaps more invisible dynamics that shape the body. Boxing is a horizontally differentiated field; a world with its own rules, interests and practices. But it is also intersected by various forms of vertical differentiation too. It is notable, for example, as Bourdieu (1978) has pointed out, that boxing, having once been a predominantly middle class sport, particularly in the English public schools, is now primarily a working class sport. And, we might add, a predominantly 'black' sport; or rather a sport more open to blacks than many sports are. It is fairly commonplace to assert, as Wacquant does, that sport is one of the few 'escape routes' open to black youths living in poor areas, and that boxing, in particular, seems to serve this purpose. Furthermore, boxing is a predominantly male sport. Indeed, it is only recently that official female bouts have taken place and each has generated a considerable degree of controversy. I will say more about such forms of differentiation in the final chapter. For the moment, however, suffice it to say that gender functions as a form of status or symbolic capital, ascribed on the basis of biological markers and their place within (embodied) schemas of social classification, and that this form of symbolic capital can be a condition for entry into particular fields, notably the boxing field. Thus, the embodied processes whereby fighting bodies are constructed and contested are themselves cross-cut by vertical differentiations such that the boxing bodies produced are always also class, raced and gendered bodies. Boxers, trainers and spectators may feel, subjectively, that they freely enter into the game, because they want to, but sociological analysis reveals a rather more complex and social picture.

Boxing is, admittedly, an extreme case. Wacquant's basic observations have a much wider application, however. Physical capital is a fact of everyday life and many social fields have some version of it. Even in politics, for example, as Margaret Thatcher's famous voice change and hairdressing regime illustrate, particular types of body are demanded and agents, to be successful, must be prepared to modify themselves. How politicians look, sound and comport themselves plays a crucial role and they cannot ignore this.

Bourdieu's Critics

Bourdieu's work has attracted a great deal of critical appraisal and is rapidly becoming one of the most influential perspectives in contemporary sociology. It has also met with certain criticisms, however. I will deal with two such criticisms in this chapter. Both, I will argue, fail to stand up to scrutiny. But each contains a kernel of truth with which we must deal. The first criticism is posited by Alexander (1995). He argues that the habitus concept constitutes one of two mutually incompatible theories of action which co-exist in Bourdieu's work. The habitus concept, he argues, explains action in terms of inherited cultural traditions. But Bourdieu also seemingly identifies a strategically-rational purpose behind every action: 'For Bourdieu, even the most traditional peasant plays the game of life like the stock market' (ibid.: 150). This second version of agency is problematic in its own right, for Alexander, as it reduces all action to instrumental self-interest, implying that apparently quite altruistic acts are, in fact, highly effective ways of realising one's own selfish ends. In addition, however, it is problematic because it cannot be coherently reconciled with the theory of the habitus:

> There is a theoretical contradiction ... between two different versions of Bourdieu's practical action theory. One stresses the role of nonrational action and objectively constructed habitus, the other the role of rational motivation having an objective result. (ibid.: 153)

I have some sympathy with the principle underlying Alexander's sarcastic remark about the stock market. The emphasis which Bourdieu sometimes puts upon the strategic and self-interested nature of action can, as in rational choice theory, become excessive and reach a point where these concepts cease to demarcate or clarify the nature of action in any meaningful way. Alexander's argument regarding contradiction is problematic on a number of grounds, however. Firstly, Bourdieu's conception of the habitus is not centred upon a 'culturally dopey' model of blind adherence to rules, norms and traditions. The habitus forms the practical-social basis for innovative and improvised action. It consists of forms of competence, skill and multi-track dispositions, in Ryle's (1949) sense, rather than fixed and mechanical blueprints for action. Action generated by the habitus is not therefore 'traditional' or 'habitual' action in a narrow sense. I will illustrate this shortly but first we must acknowledge a second point, which is that the strategic rationality of action is always relative to specific fields, for Bourdieu, and the habitus is absolutely necessary in this context *qua* 'feel for' those fields. Our strategic rationality is only possible on the basis of a level of assumed know-how and skill which is constituted by our habitus.

These points are best illustrated with reference to games, such as football, rugby or hockey. The action of players in these games is strategic. They act, for the most part, so as to maximise the game-specific 'capital' (goals) of their team, and their actions are strategically rational. It is also evident, however, that their ways of maximising their interests are highly specific to the game they are playing – one might say highly traditional and arbitrary. What counts as perfect play in rugby, for example, might be stupid in footballing terms and sufficient to get one sent to the dressing room. Thus, when a footballer crosses the ball into the goal mouth of the opposing team and to the foot of their team mate, their action combines strategic and traditional elements in an irreducible and indissociable manner. In addition, as Merleau-Ponty notes (see Chapter 5), the agent's adherence to these 'traditions' and their strategic orientation are both largely pre-reflective. To be a player is to be 'at one' with the field; seeing, thinking and acting in accordance with its structure and form.

The situation is no different when reflective thought and calculation are involved. The competent poker player, for example, is no less situated, pre-reflectively, within the arbitrary traditions of their game than the footballer. Like the footballer their every action is a strategically complex advance towards specific ends, a specific capital, but like the footballer this is all necessarily contained in and constructed through a habitually based pre-understanding of the game they are playing. They think and reflect deeply but not about the rules, nature or purpose of the game. For the duration of the game the player is in it, believing in it totally and experiencing its arbitrary, conventional and narrow limits as the limits of reality and possibility itself.

These examples suggest that Alexander is wrong to view tradition and strategy as incompatible. They are not. He has a further criticism, however. Bourdieu, he argues, is a determinist. Alexander's own argument for this point is far from clear. He is one of a number of writers who has suggested it, however, and a clearer and more elaborate case is made by Jenkins (1982). Jenkins identifies two points at which, he claims, Bourdieu lets determinism back in. His first point focuses upon the notion of the habitus as a structuring but also structured structure. Bourdieu appears to let agency and subjectivity in, he argues, when he defines the (subjective) structures of habitus as generative of objective practices; but then he closes this off immediately by making those subjective structures, in turn, the product of external and objective conditions. Determinism reappears 'in the final instance':

> ... the habitus is the source of 'objective' practices but is itself a set of 'subjective' generative principles, produced by the 'objective' structures which frame social life. In essence, it must be recognised that such a model constitutes no more than another form of determination in the last instance. (Jenkins 1982: 272)

His second point expands upon this by focusing on various references which Bourdieu makes to the 'subjective expectation of objective probabilities'; that is, of the manner in which expectations are shaped by objective life chances in such a way that people seldom expect more than they are actually able to achieve – a highly effective ideological mechanism:

> So far as Bourdieu is concerned , the actors subjective knowledge and expectations can only apprehend the 'objective' world in a limited fashion, up to the point at which misrecognition inhibits the formulation of 'objectively' more accurate propositions concerning that world. The relationship between these modes of knowledge is problematic and contradictory. (ibid.: 273)

Like Alexander's above-mentioned criticism, neither of these criticisms really does justice to Bourdieu's account; at least not if the more recent work is taken into account. The 'last instance' in which Jenkins locates Bourdieu's 'determinism' is clearly his own, for example, not Bourdieu's. It is of course true that every agent is born into a structured world which predates them and to which they must adapt. They must incorporate objective social structures, such as language, before they can become social agents. In this strictly biographical sense objective structures do predate and shape, if not determine, subjective structures, and Bourdieu is right to say so. In a broader historical and ontological sense, however, the relations of objective and subjective structures are, as noted earlier, 'circular'. If Bourdieu explains the subjective structures which generate objective structures in terms of prior objective structures, it is only insofar as he equally accepts that those prior objective structures are themselves generated by subjective structures, and so on. Across generations and through history the circle of subjective and objective structures turns, without any 'final instance', determinate or otherwise.

A similar misreading is evident with respect to the shaping of subjective knowledge and expectations by objective conditions. A number of points need drawing out here as this point touches upon a particularly dense area of Bourdieu's work. In the first instance, the notion that the expectations of dominated social groups reflect their social position and are, in this sense, realistic, does not imply structural determinism. On one level Bourdieu is simply claiming that agents come to expect and predict that which they find themselves repeatedly subject to, that such expectations are often collectively produced and shared, and that they are transmitted and conveyed to offspring who see little evidence to contradict them. The agent is wholly active here in constructing an inductive picture of the world, even if their construction is relatively fatalistic. There is no determinism in any meaningful sense of the word, just pragmatic adaptation and realism. It would be extremely strange if the parents of a working class child were to convey an expectation to their child that she would likely become a leading professional or corporate director. This would involve conveying a sense of a world which they know little about and which nothing in their experience as members of a particular social group could lead them to expect that their child will succeed.

This may not be quite what Jenkins has in mind. He may insist that his concern is with Bourdieu's relative inattention to the possibility of resistance. On this point I would concede that Bourdieu has had more to say about 'reproduction' than about 'transformation', but this is only a matter of emphasis. Bourdieu does and always has made reference to struggle and conflict in his work. He argues, for example, that the various 'unconscious' expectations, assumptions and beliefs, the *doxa*, which hold the *status quo* in place are outcomes of a historical process, and have often been preceded by open conflict:

What appears to us today as self-evident, as beneath consciousness and choice, has quite often been the stake of struggles and instituted only as the result of dogged confrontations between dominant and dominated groups. The major effect of historical evolution is to abolish history by relegating to the past, that is, to the unconscious, the lateral possibles that it eliminated. (Bourdieu 1998a: 56–7)

Legitimation and stability are not inevitable therefore, but are rather the contingent and observable effect of a dying down of struggle and perhaps, in some cases, a forgetting of it from historical memory. Moreover, Bourdieu often makes reference to the possibility of crises, such as 'Mai '68', in which a dissonance emerges between subjective expectations and objective outcomes which, in turn, stimulates the possibility of critique. In such situations, he argues, doxic and embodied assumptions are brought into the sphere of discourse:

The critique which brings the undiscussed into discussion, the unformulated into formulation, has as the condition of its possibility objective crisis, which, in breaking the immediate fit between the subjective structures and the objective structures, destroys self-evidence practically. [...] ... the would-be most radical critique always has the limits that are assigned to it by the objective conditions. (Bourdieu 1977: 169)

Two points are important to note here. Firstly, Bourdieu concedes that subjective expectations/dispositions and objective conditions can slip out of synchronisation. He seems to regard this as a consequence of changes in objective structures, which makes them unable to meet expectations, but we might equally posit that communicative engagements between agents can alter subjective dispositions and expectations to equal effect. Secondly, he perceives the effect of this as a general calling into question of doxic assumptions and beliefs. When the 'fit' between objective structures and subjective expectations is broken the opportunity for critical reflection and debate upon previously unquestioned assumptions is made possible. In this respect, the fit which Bourdieu identifies between objective and subjective structures is a temporal point between the historical struggles which preceded and established it and the future potential crises and movements which might pull it apart and once more open it to debate.

The concepts of crisis and critical discourse also distance Bourdieu from a further criticism that has been levelled against him. Kogler (1997) has argued that Bourdieu's perspective falls into a familiar problem, usually associated with the sociology of knowledge. In identifying the objective conditions which generate the subjectivity of those whom he studies, Kogler argues, Bourdieu is forced either to afford himself an unwarrented epistemological privilege or to cut away the ground from under his own feet. His position is self-defeating. What Bourdieu needs is a more hermeneutic perspective, in Kogler's view, which admits of human reflexivity and which understands sociology as an extension of this basic capacity. This criticism resonates with Jenkins' (1982) paper. The tone and scare quotes in Jenkins' account indicate an uneasiness with the distinction that Bourdieu introduces between the subjective worlds of social actors and his own more objective account. It is beyond the remit of this chapter to discuss the epistemological issues that these criticisms open up but a brief case can be made in Bourdieu's defence.

Whatever epistemological position Bourdieu advocates, there is a pragmatic and perspectival aspect to it. The subjective horizon and knowledge of all social agents is shaped by their practical involvement in a specific part of the social world, in this view, such that all agents, including social scientists, must see the world from 'somewhere'. Nobody enjoys a God's eye view or epistemological privilege. More to the point, as the note regarding critique and crisis indicates, everybody is capable of reflexively elevating assumptions and presuppositions into discourse and reflection. Bourdieu's perspective is 'hermeneutic' in this respect. His argument, however, is that agents are unlikely to adopt a critical-reflexive posture unless prompted by an experience which disturbs their faith in the *status quo*; or unless they are in a position, like an academic sociologist, where they have a financial and symbolic incentive to do so. In his more recent work Bourdieu (1998a) has invoked the phenomenological notion of the 'natural attitude' to add depth to this point. This notion is premised upon the idea that practical action requires a relatively unquestioning and unreflexive attitude towards life, at least by philosophical and sociological standards. Like footballers involved in a game social agents must perceive and treat (misrecognise) the arbitrary framework of social fields as real and natural if they are to play effectively. They cannot afford to reflect upon the arbitrariness of the game or their own role in reproducing it if they want to score goals and win. And it would really be of little value to them, at least in the short-term, if they did. Referees are not known to respond favourably to the charge that a foul is a social construction. However, the academic on-looker, who is not caught up in the game, or rather whose game is different, can afford and is inclined to see things differently. Academics score points for unearthing assumptions. The two different forms of practice, academic and everyday, operate in different ways, according to different constraints. These are not just different points of view, however. The academic perspective, as we have said, involves a reflexive turning back upon the social world, freed from its immediate practical exigencies, so as to illuminate that which usually escapes attention. Moreover, and perhaps more importantly, it involves the use of specialised research methods, from ethnography through interviews to surveys and statistics, which afford the academic a perspective upon the world which is simply not available to the introspection or reflection of the everyday lay agent. Indeed, it is precisely by these means that sociologists take themselves beyond the lay perspective. In these ways the sociological view is a superior and more critical view than the lay view. Having said this, however, sociology is a part of the social world and can be put at the disposal of those whom it studies. This is why critique is worthwhile. Bourdieu does not regard those whom he studies as laboratory rats or insensate social 'molecules' who will be forever alienated from his research and his craft. Sociology, like all other sciences, is a means of liberation for Bourdieu; a means by which social agents can seek to uncover those forces and forms of 'misrecognition' which shape their life, so as to confront and change them. In this respect sociology is a set of practices and technologies which social agents can engage in, in an effort to achieve a more critical view of their world than is available to them by means of mere reflection and armchair theorising. From a practical point of view of carrying on life as normal this critical perspective is no better, in fact it is inferior, to the everyday lay knowledge of the agent, but it does offer a more rigorously worked out analysis which is of great value for those who seek deeper self-understanding or critique and change.

Respecifying the Criticisms

Having defended Bourdieu against his critics I suggest that there are some problems with his account. Three more moderate criticisms can be drawn from the points just discussed. Firstly, I suggest that Bourdieu has not done enough, philosophically speaking, to spell out and establish his 'middle path' between determinism and free will. He claims that the habitus offers us a path between these extremes but it not entirely clear how it does so. This is one reason why the critics can persist in labelling his work deterministic.

Secondly, Bourdieu allows the concept of the habitus, for the most part, to pre-empt his conception of agency (though see below for the exception). Indeed sometimes he substitutes the habitus for the agent. This can be useful for the purposes of scientific explanation, where the concept of the habitus serves to delineate very precisely and economically the underlying dispositions which structure a particular practice. But in the context of a more general theoretical discussion it can both mislead and create problems. It is not habits which act, after all, but rather agents. Similarly, it is not habits which improvise but again agents. Finally, to touch upon Alexander's point, it is not habits which act strategically but agents. I do not mean to deny, in making this claim, that mature social agency is habitual through and through. It is however, we need a more substantive account of the agent or 'creature' of habit if we are to account, for example, for the formation and acquisition of habits. Habits are sedimented effects of action, indeed of repeated actions, and any account of them therefore presupposes an account of action, such that action cannot be reduced to habit in the manner that Bourdieu sometimes suggests. In a sense he recognises this when he deems the habitus a 'structured structure'; habits emerge, he argues, out of an agent's active involvement in a structured field of practice. This begs the question of the agent who engages in a field of practice before they have incorporated its structures, so that they can actually incorporate those structures. How can we explain this pre-habitual action? Furthermore, though Bourdieu is at pains to emphasise that habits facilitate improvisation, he does not take the next and important step of considering that and how the underlying structures or principles of fields of practice mutate over time, and with them the habitus required to produce them. The social world is not the perfect circle described earlier. It changes. And as a consequence of this we must recognise the potential for creativity and forms of innovation in practice, which generate a transformation of habits. Fields of practice are, as Merleau-Ponty (see Chapter 5) says of both language and the traditions of painting, a 'moving equilibrium'. They are subject to 'coherent deformations' which modify and transform their structure. This is possible because some actions deform and thereby transcend their own habitual root, modifying that root and, on occasion, giving rise to new habits. Just as habits generate practices, so too creative and innovative praxes generate and modify habits. The circle of social life, in which practices generate habits which generate practices, is an evolving circle. And the impetus for evolution within it derives from the creative and innovative potential of action itself.

None of this happens randomly or *ex nihilo*. The flux of both fields and the material conditions of life *demand* innovation and creation from social agents. Interactions generate a pressure for change. But such demands are only able to have their effects upon conduct and habit because of the agent who is capable of meeting them. There is something more to agency than the concept of habit can fully capture; a creative and generative dynamic which makes and modifies habits. And we therefore need to locate our concept of the habitus within this broader conception of agency.

It is important to emphasise the role of action in this creative process and to distance my comments from naive forms of humanism or the philosophy of consciousness. I do not mean to imply mysterious creative urges and forces, less still to suggest that creative acts translate 'ready made' thoughts into practice. It is not my intention to decontextualise creative acts by suggesting that they are anything other than purposive and innovative 'replies' to unusual situations, which modify existing habits and remain firmly rooted in the logic of a situation. My point, rather, is that periodically actions and interactions give rise to new cultural forms and repertoires, often to the surprise of their 'creator', such that field and habitus 'move on'. This is both undeniable and important.

It is because Bourdieu ignores this generative role of agency, in my view, that he leaves himself vulnerable to the charge of determinism. Without a more elaborate conception of the agent whose actions generate habits, it is impossible for him to explain how habits are generated, modified or indeed fitted to the exigencies of material life circumstances. He is left appearing to suggest, for example, that conditions of material scarcity produce habits of this or that kind automatically, where a stronger focus upon generative agency would bridge the gap between habits and their material conditions of existence, allowing him to say that 'these habits' emerge in 'these conditions' as a result of the creative and adaptive work of 'this' particular set of agents. Much of this is implicit in his work, I believe, but it must be drawn out into the open and discussed if misunderstandings are to be avoided and a deeper exploration of the habitus is to be conducted.

There is a further aspect to this point, stemming from remarks Bourdieu has periodically made with respect to non-habitual actions. When discussing the critiques which emerge in times of social crisis, for example, he seemingly points to a non-habitual element of agency. This is alluded to in a very recent interview, in which he reflects upon the growing resistance to processes of globalisation:

> The habitus is a set of dispositions, reflexes and forms of behaviour people acquire through acting in society. It reflects the different positions people have in society, for example, whether they are brought up in a middle class environment or in a working class suburb.
>
> It is part of how society reproduces itself. But there is also change. Conflict is built into society. People can find that their expectations and ways of living are suddenly out of step with the new social position they find themselves in. This is what is happening in France today. Then the question of social agency and political intervention becomes very important. (Bourdieu 2000: 19)

We also find a more theoretical and studied version of the same claim at numerous points in his work:

> ... habitus is one principle of production of practices amongst others and although it is undoubtedly more frequently in play than any other – 'We are empirical', says Leibniz, 'in three-quarters of our actions' – one cannot rule out that it may be superseded in certain circumstances – certainly in situations of crisis which adjust the immediate adjustment of habitus to field – by other principles, such as rational and conscious computation. (Bourdieu 1990: 108)

I have two criticisms of this claim. Firstly, Bourdieu underestimates the extent to which 'rational and conscious calculation', indeed reflexivity, enter into everyday life as a matter of course. The metaphor of the 'feel for the game' which he uses to make sense of the vast amount of social action and uses as a shorthand definition of habitus is extremely powerful and seductive but it loses what is so suggestive about it when it is made to do too much work. Individuals have choices to make everyday of their lives, for example, about jobs, money and leisure activities. And this is all the more so in the present, given the new demand for 'flexibility' in economic and political life. We cannot therefore make choice an exception in the way he seems to want to do. Choices, albeit rooted in a feel for the game, routinely enter everyday life in interaction with more spontaneous tactical manoeuvres. Secondly, the notion that we are 'empirical in three-quarters of our actions' is an extremely unhelpful way of formulating the distinction intended here. If treated with the slightest seriousness it would lead us right back into the philosophical problems that the notion of habitus is supposed to resolve. If we are empirical in three-quarters of our actions then what are we in the remaining quarter? Transcendental?

In making this claim Bourdieu appears to lead us back into some of the most problematic territory of the philosophical tradition. Furthermore, posing the issue of choice the way he does seemingly suggests that reflective choice and reflexive analysis are somehow radically divorced from the realm of habit when they are not. They too are habitually rooted, as I argue later.

This reference to non-habitual aspects of agency begs the general question of agency ever more urgently and raises, in a slightly different way, the question of reflexivity raised by Kogler (see p. 113 above). Kogler was wrong to suppose that Bourdieu does not allow for reflexivity and self-criticism in his theory of agency. He does. Unfortunately the way in which he does it raises serious problems. We therefore need to deepen our understanding of habitus by reference to a broader understanding of both embodied social agency and reflexivity.

My final point of criticism relates to Jenkins' concern with the subjective understanding of social agents. Bourdieu's use of the concept of the habitus to identify the role of perception, expectation, know-how and so on in agency and structure building is a very strong and important aspect of his work. It is also evident, in his work as a whole, that he is concerned to bring an analysis of these subjective structures into his investigations. Notwithstanding this his work to date offers us relatively little in the way of an analytic toolbox for opening up and exploring the subjective side of the social world. The concept of the habitus hints at the possibility for a hermeneutic dimension to social analysis but sadly does no more than hint.

Conclusion

Having identified these problems I want to turn now to their solution. It is my contention that Bourdieu's perspective can acquire the enrichment it needs from phenomenology. Though far from perfect as a sociological perspective, and open to criticisms of exactly the type Bourdieu levels against it, phenomenology, and particularly the phenomenological analysis of habit, can fill in some of the important gaps in his work. It is my intention, in the next chapter, to demonstrate this. It may be that in doing this I am doing nothing more than filling in blanks in the interpretation of Bourdieu. He has often complained that he is misunderstood by English speaking commentators, and Wacquant (1993) has echoed this point, putting particular emphasis upon the failure of anglophone critics to identify the phenomenological (amongst other) roots of his key concepts. Furthermore, a number of important commentaries on Bourdieu's work have identified its overlaps with phenomenology; particularly the work of Merleau-Ponty and Heidegger (for example, Wacquant in Bourdieu and Wacquant 1992, Dreyfus and Rabinow 1993, Dreyfus 1993). I agree with these interpretations. The influence of phenomenology upon Bourdieu is only too evident to anyone acquainted with this philosophical tradition. My analysis will not be exegetic, however. I am not claiming to interpret Bourdieu correctly or to offer a pure reading of his work. The problems I have identified with Bourdieu's work stand, in my view, whatever his influences. And the way to resolve those problems is to return to the phenomenological literature, where a broader and deeper understanding of habit is to be found. We need to bring the insights of phenomenology into the otherwise very powerful theory of practice that Bourdieu has developed.

7

HABIT, INCORPORATION AND
THE CORPOREAL SCHEMA

Having raised a number of doubts regarding Bourdieu's work in the last chapter I want to return, in this chapter, to the work of Merleau-Ponty. It is my contention that his conception of habit affords us the opportunity to deepen Bourdieu's account and, at the same time, address its main weaknesses. In addition, for the same reason, I will be introducing a number of ideas on habit from the work of Husserl and Schutz.

Merleau-Ponty's account of habit stems from his analysis of the 'corporeal schema' and it is necessary, therefore, that our exposition begins with this concept. Before doing so, however, it is important to situate Merleau-Ponty's account of habit more broadly. One of my key doubts about Bourdieu was that he tends to pre-empt the notion of agency with the concept of the habitus. I do not want to repeat that problem here, by seeming to discuss Merleau-Ponty's conception of habit in abstraction from his broader view of the embodied agent. I wish to stress therefore that what follows is an extension of the discussion of embodiment and agency opened up in Chapter 5. In many ways Merleau-Ponty's conception of the agent is more habit focused than Bourdieu's; at least he, in contrast to Bourdieu, does not make habit one of a number of principles which might root our actions, applicable to only three-quarters of our actions. All of our actions have a habitual aspect for Merleau-Ponty. On the other hand, he goes much further than Bourdieu in seeking to consider that and how habits take shape within the context of the on-going activities of embodied social agents, such that they are as much shaped by action as shaping it. Habit, Merleau-Ponty reminds us, is a residue or sediment of action and, as such, its relation to action is necessarily dialectical. If our present actions are shaped by habits it is only because our previous actions have given rise to those habits; and insofar as our present actions mutate into new patterns they can give rise to new habits which will shape our future actions. The improvised and innovative nature of action, in other words, is such that, on occasion, it gives rise to new and novel habits and dispositions, 'coherently deforming' (Merleau-Ponty 1962) or transforming the structure of a given domain of practice. I return to this dynamic later in the chapter. The point for now is merely to stress that my exposition of

Merleau-Ponty's account of habit should be read with the broader context of his theory of agency (see Chapter 5) in mind.

In addition I wish to emphasise, again with reference to Chapter 5, Merleau-Ponty's critique of the mechanistic conception of human action posited by the behaviourists. Like Descartes, but in contrast to the behaviourists, Merleau-Ponty was deeply concerned with the prospect that the deterministic and mechanistic worldview advocated within the physical sciences might (falsely) reduce all of human life within its schema. Unlike Descartes, who sought to escape this implication by separating mind (which is freed from the material realm of physical causation) from body (which is subject to the laws of nature), however, Merleau-Ponty sought to show that and how the structure of human behaviour, that is, the structure formed out of the interaction of a human organism with its environment, constitutes a higher level physical structure which requires a relatively unique framework of understanding. Determinism, in any strict sense, is only appropriate to lower level structures of the physical world, he argued. In place of cause and effect the most parsimonious way of accounting for action within human behavioural structures is by way of purpose and meaning (see Chapter 5). Later in this chapter I will suggest that this argument can be invoked to defend a habit or habitus based theory of agency against the charge of determinism, though I will also seek to establish that this position equally shuns the metaphysical notion of 'free will'. With this said we can turn to the corporeal schema.

The Corporeal Schema

One is one's body according to Merleau-Ponty (1962) and, contra Descartes, one does not relate to it as to an external object (see Chapter 2). If I wish to move my arm, for example, I do not have first to locate it or think about lifting it. I do not do something in order to move it, as when I move the book on my desk by first moving my hand towards it and grasping it. Only one thing occurs: my arm moves. The act, we might say, is intentional; but it is a single and unified whole: an intentional-action rather than an action added to or caused by an intention. And, as such, the intention need not be formulated either linguistically or reflectively. I need not think about my action:

> When I motion my friend to come nearer, my intention is not a thought prepared within me and I do not perceive the signal in my body. I beckon across the world ... (Merleau-Ponty 1962: 111)

Knowledge is clearly involved here but it is not the reflective knowledge of which the intellectualist speaks. I know where my hand is and it is mobilised with all the necessary postural adjustment required to execute my action whilst maintaining my balance. Indeed, many acts involve a whole complex of knowledge. To comb my hair, for example, I must know where my hand is, where my head is, how far and at what angle I must reach to grasp the comb and so on/But this is not conscious or reflective knowledge. My act is (usually) perfectly 'fitted' to the exigencies of my circumstances but I have not had to think about how to make it so or to reflectively articulate the principles upon which my action is based.

What Merleau-Ponty refers to here is the scientifically well documented phenomenon of proprioception; a phenomenon which he explores in part through a consideration of the strange and sometimes drastic consequences of a failure of this particular mode of knowledge. That we ordinarily 'know without knowing' where our various body parts are relative to both the whole and to the wider environment is nowhere more dramatically illustrated than in those rare instances where an individual does not know these things (see also Sacks 1984, 1985). Such observations are established facts and Merleau-Ponty is in no way unique in referring to them. Where he is highly innovative, however, is in the implications he draws from this. This embodied form of 'knowing without knowing' challenges the Cartesian worldview, he observes, and not only because it reveals our relationship to our bodies to be other than that of a subject to an object. It is a form of knowing which transcends the subject/object duality; a form of unformulated and perhaps unformulable knowledge which consists only in the capacity to do and which, for that reason, is indissociably 'tangled' with that which it knows. On this point he rejoins Ryle's (1949) observations on know-how (see Chapter 4).

It is not only my own body that I 'know' in this way, Merleau-Ponty continues, I have a pre-reflective sense or grasp on my environment, relative to my body, as is evidenced by my capacity to move around in and utilise that space without first having to think how to do so. Our relation to technological objects, such as word processors, provides an interesting illustration of this. I can type and to that extent 'I know' where the various letters are on the keyboard. I do not have to find the letters one by one, as when I first bought the thing. My fingers just move in the direction of the correct keys. Indeed, when I am in full flow I seem actually to be thinking with my fingers in the respect that I do not know in advance of typing exactly what I will say. It is not just that I *do not need* to think about where the keys are, however. The break with reflective thought is more severe than this. *I could not give a reflective, discursive account of the keyboard layout.* I do not 'know' where the keys are in a reflective sense and to make any half-decent attempt at guessing I have to imagine that I am typing and watch where my fingers head for when I come to the appropriate letter. The type of knowledge I have of the keyboard is a practical, embodied knowledge, quite remote and distinct from discursive knowledge. It is also a functional and 'interested' form of knowledge; a form of knowledge of the space surrounding me which constitutes and subordinates that space in accordance with my practical interests, allowing me to do whatever I am doing. Whilst the keyboard has clearly been designed for typing, for example, there is equally a sense in which that chunk of plastic depends upon my 'knowledgeable hands' for it's practical meaning. My hands turn it into a space for typing, subordinating it to this human function (see also Sudnow 1993).

It is this fundamental co-ordination of the embodied agent with both self and world which lies at the root of Merleau-Ponty's (1962) conception of the corporeal schema. The corporeal schema is an incorporated bodily know-how and practical sense; a perspectival grasp upon the world from the 'point of view' of the body. Furthermore, it is a point of view which may be enlarged or diminished through the incorporation of alien elements. Car driving allows us to demonstrate this in a relatively mundane and uncomplicated way. When I drive I 'know without knowing' where the various controls of the car are and how and when to use them. I do not need to think about it and, as becomes apparent if I try to instruct a learner, I cannot really formulate this embodied knowledge in linguistic form. As far as I, *qua* 'driving instructor', am concerned, 'you just do it!' My experience of driving involves more than a practical mastery over and functional subordination of the internal space of the car, however. Not only do I incorporate the internal space of the car, such that pushing the breaks becomes as 'natural' a way of stopping to me as halting in my stride, but I incorporate the external space of the car; its power, velocity and acceleration. When I park, overtake or pull onto a roundabout, for example, I 'know without thinking' how big the car is and how fast it will accelerate. I feel its size and speed as surely as that of my own body, moving only into those spaces in which I will fit and have the time to reach. I do not think *about* the car. I think *as* the car, *from the point of view of the car*. This must necessarily be so because I could not concentrate on the road if I needed to think about the car. The car has been incorporated within my corporeal schema and thereby become an extension of my body, akin to the blind man's stick:

> The blind man's stick has ceased to be an object for him, and is no longer perceived for itself; its point has become an area of sensitivity, extending the scope and active radius of touch, and providing a parallel to sight. In the exploration of things, the length of the stick does not enter expressly as a middle term: the blind man is rather aware of it through the position of objects than of the position of objects through it. (Merleau-Ponty 1962: 143)

None of this is revealed to me if everything runs smoothly. There is no reason that it should. But when things go wrong everything is revealed. My feel for the acceleration and size of the car is revealed when I inadvertently pull away from the lights in second gear, for example, and find myself nowhere near where I need to be to avoid collision. Similarly, my feel for the computer is revealed every time my software is updated and I find myself once again dazed and disorientated before an incomprehensible plastic box. The fit between my embodied know-how and milieu has broken down and I am stuck.

The situation revealed by these technical examples is no different when it is other agents we are interacting with. Social interactions are more complex, in the respect that each party 'reads' and communicates with the others, such that they are genuinely inter-active. Moreover, matters of social structure and, for example, decorum and power enter in such circumstances. Nevertheless, the corporeal schema is still very much the active ingredient of agency in such situations, situating agents perceptually, linguistically and through motor activity. Agents are knowledgeable of their situation and their knowledge is integral to the successful accomplishment or 'doing' of that situation, but it is an embodied know-how that we are referring to here whose operation might be unnoticed by even the agent herself and whose 'principles', like the position of the letters on the keyboard, need not be known to reflective-discursive consciousness. Agents 'know-how' to read the signs, broadly conceived, in their contexts of interaction. And their responses, however 'perfect', are often generated as if by instinct. Furthermore, just as we can incorporate the dimensions of a car within our corporeal schema, we can incorporate a social group. The notion of an *esprit de corps* illustrates this. Blumer (1969) uses this notion to capture the sense of solidarity that develops in social movements and Bourdieu (1996) uses it to describe the solidarity between pupils and ex-pupils of elite schools. What is evident in both cases is the manner in which the dimensions and *raison d'être* of the group are incorporated into the corporeal schema of the individual agent. The agent thinks, in these cases, *from the point of view of the group*. The group bestows a collective power upon its members and each member feels and wields this power, perhaps unknowingly, in their individual actions. As when driving their cars they assume the 'vital statistics' of the group – its reputation, size and force – as their own, even in the most spontaneous of their actions. Moreover, attacks upon the group are experienced as personal attacks and the needs or demands of the group exert a magical power of mobilisation upon its members.

As with the computer example cited above, anomic situations function to reveal the importance of this embodied social 'feel'. One is at no time more aware of know-how and the ease bred of competence than in those situations where they are missing. Games provide another important source of examples. Our experience of learning and playing games clearly illustrates the way in which we can incorporate arbitrary social structures in the form of perceptual, linguistic and motor schemas, absorbing the imperatives and goals of the game as deep rooted motivations of our own actions: for example, we desire to score a goal or 'roll a six' as if our life depends upon it. It illustrates how spontaneous actions can simultaneously combine ruthless tactics or strategy with rigid adherence to highly specific and arbitrary norms, values and 'forms of life'. Finally, fast moving games demonstrate how all of this is a matter of pre-reflective and embodied know-how, acquired by way of playing the game, rather than reflective or intellectual mastery. A good footballer, boxer or hockey player has no time to think before acting. They must 'feel' the game in their bones. Games are, of course, different to 'real life', not least because we recognise that they are only games. However, as we saw in Chapter 6, with

Bourdieu's notion of 'fields', social spaces are akin to games. They manifest the same culturally arbitrary 'shape' (see also Huizinga 1950, Winch 1958, Garfinkel 1967, Elias 1978, Mead 1967, Bourdieu and Wacquant 1992). This, I believe, is what Merleau-Ponty is suggesting too when, as I discussed in Chapter 5, he identifies the 'symbolic' nature of human existence. The arbitrariness which he identifies with the symbolic is the arbitrariness of a game. And his notion of the corporeal schema allows us to see how, as agents, we are fitted to and for those games as players. We are players who feel the game and we do so because we have incorporated the structures of the game within our corporeal schema.

Habit and Corporeal Schema

This account of the corporeal schema already includes much of what Merleau-Ponty means by habit. Habit involves a modification and enlargement of the corporeal schema, an incorporation of new 'principles' of action and know-how which permit new ways of acting and understanding. It is a sediment of past activity which remains alive in the present in the form of the structures of the corporeal schema; shaping perception, conception, deliberation, emotion and action.

This notion of habit is central for Merleau-Ponty because of the path it allows him to forge between the equally untenable views of action posited by the 'intellectualists' and 'behaviourists' respectively. The behaviourists have a concept of 'habit', of course. For them it denotes a conditioned reflex; a mechanical tendency to respond to fixed stimuli in a fixed way. Even complex behaviour patterns are composed of a mechanically linked chain of simple and atomised reflex mechanisms and as such, all habits are localised; organisms respond to identical stimuli in an identical way, with the same movement and same 'body part'. Merleau-Ponty has many criticisms of this approach, some of which are covered by my discussion of his critique of behaviourism in Chapter 5. For present purposes it will suffice to draw out three additional points. Firstly, he is critical of the behaviourist account of learning. They conceptualise learning as a process whereby accidental responses to situations lead in some instances to 'rewards' which 'reinforce' them, and do so on a sufficient number of circumstances that they become habituated. There are a number of problems with the internal cogency of this account. In particular it seems to presuppose a purposiveness and future orientation (that is, acting for an anticipated reward) that is incommensurable with the atomistic and mechanistic assumptions of the behaviourist account, and a power of co-ordination, required to mobilise rewarded actions, which is at best unexplained. To make their account work the behaviourists would need a model of the organism more akin to Merleau-Ponty's. More centrally, however, this account of learning simply does not 'fit the facts'. It cannot account, for example, for the process of 'refinement' which often accompanies learning. If a human or other animal does accidentally stumble

upon a means of bringing about a particular end, this means is often
clumsy and inefficient, as the notion of an accident suggests; but they do
not stick to this clumsy *modus operandi* as behaviourism must logically
predict. Their very next action, following the 'accident', will often improve
upon its *modus operandi*, perhaps modifying it considerably. And successive actions will continue to refine the skill. Having clumsily knocked a
lever with one's elbow, for example, one may subsequently push it with
one's hands and even flick it with one's fingers. Indeed, the lessons
learned from an experience may be further removed still. A child who
withdraws their hand from a hot object and thus relieves the pain caused
by the heat does not thereby learn to retract their hand from hot objects;
they learn not to touch such objects in the first place. Everything happens
in the process of habit acquisition, Merleau-Ponty writes, as if it were a
principle that had been acquired. Certainly it is not a mechanical reaction
as the behaviourists suggest.

Secondly, failure to achieve an end is often insufficient, in the first
instance, to prevent an agent from repeating the action successively, thus
suggesting that initial actions are not always accidental in the manner
behaviourism suggests. Studies reveal that animals will try out the same
solution to a problem many times before giving up, suggesting that they
'expect' it to succeed:

> Everything happens as if the animal adopted a 'hypothesis' which 'is not
> explained by the success since it is manifested and persists before the success
> can confirm it'. (Merleau-Ponty 1965: 100)

The animal 'tries out' a possible 'solution' to its situation based upon the
habits already incorporated in its corporeal schema. It puzzles over new
and difficult situations, mobilising previously acquired and habituated
solutions in an effort to resolve them, and sometimes 'breaking through'
to a new solution in the process. This may entail a degree of luck but it is
far cry from the random contingencies envisaged by the behaviourist.

Thirdly, Merleau-Ponty objects to the behaviourist argument that structures of behaviour are decomposable into the sum of the individual
behaviours which they entail. Not only is such a view philosophically
untenable, he argues, but it is falsified by studies which show that agents
who learn parts of a routine independently are not competent, on the
basis of this, to perform the whole. They do not grasp the whole.
Habituated 'structures' of behaviour are greater than the sum of their
parts. This relates to the final major problem with the behaviourist conception of habit, which is that what is acquired in the process of habituation is never a mechanical response to a fixed stimulus but rather a general
and flexible power of responding to situations of a general sort:

> Any mechanistic theory runs up against the fact that the learning process is
> systematic; the subject does not weld together individual movements and
> individual stimuli but acquires the general power to respond with a certain type
> of solution to situations of a certain general form. (Merleau-Ponty 1962: 142)

This point rejoins the critique of behaviourism outlined in Chapter 5. To acquire a habit is to acquire a purposive orientation towards situations with a specific meaning; to develop a new form of understanding, in Ryle's sense (see Chapter 4), grasping in a pre-reflective way the principles of a particular situation or way of acting; and to develop the various forms of know-how and skill to 'play the game' competently in those situations. Habits admit of a great deal of improvisation as the example of the skilled game player illustrates. Moreover, they are 'transferable' in at least two respects. Firstly, we can transfer skills acquired in one 'region' of the body to another, as when we write in the sand with our feet, turn on a light switch with our forehead or untie a knot with our teeth. They are not, in other words, localised in specific body parts, as behaviourism suggests that they are. The acquired principle can be realised in a multitude of ways through a number of different bodily parts and systems. Secondly, we can, by way of a practical analogy, treat unfamiliar situations as if they were of a familiar type and apply our usual solutions to the problems they pose. Again this falsifies the mechanistic and localised view of habit which the behaviourist advances.

These various reflections lead Merleau-Ponty to adopt a radically different conception of habit to the behaviourists. Habit is not a mechanical response, he argues, but rather a form of embodied and practical understanding or know-how which manifests in and as competent and purposive action, and which 'attaches' to the world by way of the meaning it discerns therein. To acquire a habit is to grasp and incorporate, within one's bodily schema, a tacit and practical 'principle':

> We say that the body has understood and habit has been cultivated when it has absorbed a new meaning and assimilated a fresh core of significance. (Merleau-Ponty 1962: 146)

He is equally clear, however, that he does not intend these notions to be understood in an 'intellectualist' fashion, where they would be associated with the supposedly self-transparent activities of a reflexive, epistemological subject. Knowledge and understanding, as Merleau-Ponty understands them here, are capacities for acting; know-how belonging to an agent whose primary relation to their environment, as we discussed in Chapter 5, is that of active, pre-reflective and practical involvement. The principles and meanings to which he refers are 'incarnate', 'motor' principles and meanings, whose full sense is only ever expressed in the actions to which they belong:

> If habit is neither a form knowledge nor an involuntary action what then is it? It is knowledge in the hands, which is forthcoming only when bodily effort is made, and cannot be formulated in detachment from that effort. The subject knows where the letters are on the typewriter as we know where one of our limbs is, through knowledge bred of familiarity which does not give us a position in objective space. (Merleau-Ponty 1962: 144)

> We said earlier that it is the body which understands in the acquisition of habit. This way of putting it will appear absurd, if understanding is subsuming a

sense datum under an idea, and if the body if as an object. But the phenomenon of habit is just what prompts us to revise our notion of 'understand' and our notion of the body. To understand is to experience the harmony between what we aim at and what is given, between the intention and the performance – and the body is our anchorage in a world. (ibid.)

This anti-intellectualist point is reinforced by a consideration of the nature of learning. We learn, Merleau-Ponty argues, not by thinking about things but by doing them. Learning is, as we said above, incorporation, an absorption of new competencies and understandings into the corporeal schema which, in turn, transform one's way of perceiving and acting in the world. This is obvious in the case of certain sorts of activities; one does not learn how to dance or play the guitar by reading, but rather by dancing and playing. Even if a reading element is present in such learning activities it must be translated into practice to become significant. Much the same is true of even the most 'intellectual' activities such as science and philosophy, however, as many philosophers of science now suggest (Kuhn 1970, Polanyi 1966). Intellectual activity is still 'activity' and always presupposes a competence in particular ways of reading, reasoning and responding; a competence at specific language games which is acquired by playing those games and incorporating their principles, as habits, within one's corporeal schema.

These points rejoin Merleau-Ponty's aforementioned critique of intellectualism (see Chapter 5) and his attempt to reveal and explore the nature of pre-reflective embodied agency as a 'third term' between object and subject. Habit is not a mechanical response and is not acquired in a mechanical fashion, but neither is it a reflective or intellectual phenomenon. It is a phenomenon which forces us to abandon each of these false alternatives in favour of a more existential focus upon our simultaneously meaningful and embodied manner of being-in-the-world.

The Nature of Nurture

A further false dualism, also challenged by this conception, is that between nature and culture. In emphasising habit and giving it a prominent role within his theory of agency Merleau-Ponty agrees with those sociologists who have stressed the plasticity of the human organism and argued for the primacy of nurture over nature (for example, Parsons 1966). Notwithstanding this, having stressed the importance of plasticity and habituation, Merleau-Ponty notes that these features of human life are our natural endowment and disposition. It is our nature to be cultural beings:

> Although our body does not impose definite instincts upon us, as it does other animals, it does at least give to our life the form of generality, and develops our personal acts into stable dispositional tendencies. In this sense our nature is not long-established custom, since custom presupposes the form of passivity derived from nature. (Merleau-Ponty 1962: 146)

We could advance upon this claim by speculating that this natural mechanism of habituation is our specific evolutionary mode of adaptation. In contrast to the fixed instincts which appear well suited to fitting other animals to their environments, our adaptive advantage is our capacity for habituation. This equally entails they we do not simply adapt to our environments but adapt them through the construction of material culture:

> ... behaviour patterns settle into that nature, being deposited in the form of a cultural world. Not only have I a physical world, not only do I live in the midst of earth, air and water, I have around me roads, plantations, villages, streets, churches, implements, a bell, a spoon, a pipe. (Merleau-Ponty 1962: 346)

Such physical transformations of nature only function as culture to the extent that they are used by agents in a way which accords with their 'meaning' and this, in turn, presupposes that their meaning has been incorporated within the corporeal schema of the agent. Pipes are only pipes and churches only churches so long as agents are disposed to smoke them and prey in them respectively. Nevertheless, as Burkitt (1999) has argued, our interaction with and incorporation of artefacts effects a further and crucial transformation of our ways of being in and experiencing the world. As with the above-mentioned blind man's stick, they become extensions of our bodies.

This capacity for habituation is twinned with the capacity, hinted at in the above critique of behaviourism, for innovative and creative praxes which give rise to modes of acting worthy of conserving through habit. Many of our habits are acquired from the collective pool in our society, which we see being performed around us and are able to copy, Merleau-Ponty notes. Indeed, one mode of the intelligence of the human organism is its tendency to replicate solutions to action problems which it perceives others performing. But aside from this, or running parallel to it, there is a dual tendency in human behaviour: towards innovation and creation on the one hand, and towards habituation on the other. These two tendencies work together, since habit allows innovation to be conserved and built upon, whilst innovation, or at least action, provides the raw materials for habituation. Innovation gives the agent something to turn into a habit. Furthermore, innovation and creativity in praxis generally entail a modification or transformation of existing habits, or at least a process of building upon them. This is particularly evident in relation to linguistic behaviour. Agents incorporate language as infants and, for the most part, reproduce it by way of their speech; transmitting it to future generations in the same way as they inherited it from past generations, and mutually reinforcing its form and structure in their every interaction with others. However, languages change. Some linguistic uses are innovative and creative. They 'coherently deform' the language, changing aspects of it and giving rise to new (collective) habits and schemas. Thus, as noted in Chapter 5, language is a moving equilibrium.

The extent of these innovations and creations, especially on an individual level, is likely to be very small. And this mode of change is gradual. Nevertheless, it is sufficient to persuade us to view the habitus itself as a 'moving equilibrium'. Old habits, as the saying has it, die hard. And agents will take many habits, acquired in infancy, to their grave. But the habitus of both the individual and the group is in a process of constant, if slow and gradual, change. And the proximate source of that change is the innovative praxis of the agent.

Merleau-Ponty's discussion of habit formation tends to focus upon the pre-reflective level. Other phenomenologists, most notably Husserl, have extended the point into the predicative realm to cover such matters as choice, judgement and reflective attitudes. Our more important choices and judgements sediment within our habitus, Husserl argues, steering all subsequent decisions and actions. A decision, by way of the process of habituation, can become a conviction or commitment:

> If, in an act of judgement, I decide for the first time in favour of a being and a being-thus, the fleeting act passes; but from now on *I am abidingly the Ego who is thus and so decided*, 'I am of this conviction.' That, however, does not signify merely that I remember the act or can remember it later. This I can do, even if meanwhile I have 'given up' my conviction. (Husserl 1991: 67, original emphasis)

By virtue of habitus, he continues, the act of judgement has altered his manner of being. He is now a different agent to that which he was:

> As long as it is accepted by me, I can 'return' to it repeatedly, and repeatedly find it as mine, habitually my own opinion or, correlatively, find myself as the Ego who *is* convinced, who, as the persisting ego, is determined by this abiding *habitus* or state. (Husserl 1991: 67, original emphasis)

Not all judgements and decisions have such consequences, of course. Husserl makes a distinction between fleeting judgements or opinions and those which sediment within our being, forming our habitus. Even fleeting opinions have a relative durability, for Husserl, as is evidenced by our capacity to 'pick up' tasks and conversations 'where we left off', even when a considerable passage of time has elapsed. The mechanism of habituation is the very basis of the temporal continuity of our lives and thus of our history. Today follows yesterday and prepares for tomorrow because the past is always carried into the present by the body in the form of habitus.

Habit and Expectation

Habits do not merely regulate the way we act. They shape the ways in which we make sense of our environment too, manifesting as expectations and interpretative methods. We saw this in Chapter 5 when we discussed Merleau-Ponty's reflections upon the habitual root of perceptual and linguistic activity. We can push this analysis further now, however, by reference to Husserl's (1970, 1991) discussion of 'apperception' and 'typification'.

The best way into this issue is by reference to the sense of shock we sometimes experience when our perceptual expectations are confounded. Suppose, for example, that we try to lift what looks like a heavy object, perhaps a dumbell, only to find that it is actually made of polystyrene and very light. In such a case we may tumble backwards on account of the excess force and inappropriate lifting technique we have applied to such a light object and we would almost certainly experience a sense of shock that something so 'heavy looking' was actually so light. Similarly we might experience a sense of shock if we reached for a book from a friend's shelf only to find that it was entirely ornamental; a spine of a classic book glued to a wooden block and placed on a shelf to lend our friend's room a scholarly appearance. A great deal of comedy, not to mention detective stories, are based precisely on this sense of things turning out to be not quite what they seem. We assume certain facts of the matter on the basis of what we see and hear, 'filling in gaps'. But we do this largely without knowing it such that we actually mistake our embellished perceptual experience for a raw percept. This allows us to be fooled, as is subsequently revealed when we discover that we filled in the gaps in a way which might be expected but which, in this case, was actually wrong. What this reveals, for Husserl, is a process, operative in all perception, whereby we bring habituated expectations to bear in such a way that our perception is altered or affected. All perception is perspectival and partial, he observes. We only ever perceive certain qualities of a percept and from certain angles. And yet, by force of habit and familiarity, we tacitly or unconsciously impute other 'hidden' qualities and dimensions such that our conscious perception is seemingly a perception of the 'whole' object, in all of its richness. In cases where such habitual expectations are born out this is very useful, of course, and it passes largely unnoticed. But it is a defeasible process and one which makes us vulnerable to deception and shock. I am fooled by my friend's ornamental book spine, for example, because I do not see a book spine, as such. Rather, my habitual familiarity with books and the habitus formed on this basis leads me to perceive a whole book, albeit from the point of view of the spine. When it turns out not to be a book the work of the habitus becomes apparent to me, but only then. Similarly with the dumbell. It 'looks' heavy to me and under normal circumstances that is a good thing because it ensures that I approach it, to lift it, in a way which will be appropriate and safe. But of course the kinaesthetic quality of heaviness is not really seen by me precisely because it is a kinaesthetic and not a visual quality. It is rather imputed on the basis that objects looking like that have, in the past, turned out to be heavy. Not that I think to myself 'that is heavy', of course. By force of habit I just perceive the object as heavy.

Any number or type of qualities and dimensions may be apperceived in this way, including important social dimensions. We often apperceive an agent's role on the basis of their appearance and context, for example, such that a man standing outside a night club wearing a dinner jacket and bow tie would be perceived as a bouncer. Similarly, we may perceive an agent's station in life or social standing from the way they look. And much of the less conscious aspects of various forms of prejudice and discrimination work in exactly this way. We apperceive individuals as representatives of an abstract group, on the basis of markers we associate with that group, and we attribute the supposed properties of the group to them. As in the physical examples this process of habituation is as essential as it can be dangerous. We simply couldn't function without these inductive habits and yet they can be wrong and can generate harmful consequences either for ourselves or for others.

Apperception draws upon processes which Husserl (1991) refers to as 'typification' and 'pairing'. Typification entails the formation of habitual perceptual schemas which simplify complex perceptual input. In effect the uniqueness and particularity of each new moment of our experience is simplified by being subsumed into a general category or 'type'. Thus, even when we approach objects which, strictly speaking, we have never encountered before, we will see them in terms of the broader type to which they belong. Moreover, newly typed objects are 'paired' with objects of the same type which we have experienced in the past, and properties and qualities attributed to them accordingly. When I get in your car, for example, I will not think to ask if it has a gear stick and clutch or even look for them. I will just reach for them because I will assume them to be there. In this sense my typification overlaps, as is most usually the case, with my practical know-how and competence of car driving.

Perceptual experience, in this respect, is structured by biography and, more specifically, biographically acquired habit. What I have experienced in the past shapes my current experience. And, by the same token, what I experience now sediments in the form of habitus which will shape my future experiences if so called upon:

> This lived experience itself, and the objective moment constituted in it, may become 'forgotten'; but for all this it in no way disappears without a trace; it has merely become latent. With regard to what has become constituted in it, it is a *possession in the form of a habitus*, ready at any time to be awakened anew by an active association. (Husserl 1973: 122, original emphasis)

Each experience sediments into a form of habitual and practical knowledge, a form of know-how which entails both ways of seeing and responding to what is a seen; and which therefore disposes the agent to respond in 'typical' ways to 'typical' situations:

> The object has incorporated into itself the forms of sense originally constituted in the acts of explication by virtue of a *knowledge in the form of a habitus*. Thus all contemplation which enters into an object has *a lasting result* with regard to the object. The subjective activity which has been realised remains attached to the object *qua* intentional by virtue of a *habitus*. (Husserl 1973: 122, original emphasis)

Some typifications and pairings may have an individual element to them. As no two people's experience is identical, no two agents' habitus will be exactly the same. Notwithstanding this, typifications and pairing, as well as know-how and agentic dispositions more generally, usually arise out of social interactions within collectivities and, as such, tend to be shared.

Most aspects of our individual habitus', as Bourdieu has done most to show, are rooted in the shared habitus of the groups to which we belong.

Language is central here. It is necessary if ideas are to be communicated and taught. More centrally, however, languages are concrete embodiments of our schemas of typifications (Husserl 1970, Mead 1967, Schutz 1970). Languages and language games, as philosophers from Marx, through Mead, the phenomenologists and Wittgenstein have all argued, are the embodiment of the shared practical sense of a society or social group. They give durable form to habits of perception, conception and reflection which have formed within the group. When a child acquires language it acquires not only a new use of its body, but a use which enjoins it to the collective life of its society by affording it the opportunity to 'think' according to the shared schemas and prejudices of the group.

Within sociology it is Schutz (1970, 1972) and the ethnomethodologists (Garfinkel 1967) who have done most to explore these sense making habits and their significance. Schutz's explicitly appropriates Husserl's notion of typifications, for example, as a way of deepening the (Weberian) theory of action. And he develops a range of concepts which manifest this same concern with habitual forms of knowing and understanding: for example, 'recipe knowledge', 'thinking as usual' and (again from Husserl) the 'natural attitude'. Similarly with ethnomethodology though the ethnomethodologists have sought to develop these ideas empirically. They have sought to reveal, in practice, the sense-making methods and assumptions which social agents routinely and habitual deploy in order to render their situations manageable and accountable.

Freedom and Habit

It is important, at this point, for us to locate the concept of habit in terms of yet one further dualism which haunts the sociological world: freedom and determinism. We saw in Chapter 5 how Merleau-Ponty challenges the mechanistic determinism of the behaviourist. Naive attempts to explain human behaviour in terms of physical causes and effects, he argued, simply fail at the empirical level. The concepts of purpose and meaning prove to be a far more parsimonious framework for making sense of human behaviour, whether in a laboratory or anywhere else. We are now in a position to see that and how the purposes which manifest in human behaviour and the process of seeking out meaning in the environment achieve stability by way of the process of habituation. Many of the purposes which animate our behaviour are rooted in habit, as are the interpretive schemas we bring to bear in pursuing those purposes. Arguing this line makes no concession to determinism, however. Action could only be determined, if it were determined, by events or factors external to it and this does not apply to habits. Habits are part of our structure *qua* agents; part of what we are. This is not to deny that we are shaped by our external circumstances, of course. Quite to the contrary. As situated agents we are forced to 'reply' to events, as we perceive them, within our experiential field, and some of these replies will sediment in the form of habits, such that these events indirectly shape who we are. Similarly, through our interactions with others, and particularly the imitation of others, we 'pick up' the habits which prevail within our immediate environment. We will inherit the language of our particular society, for example, and the accent of our geo-social group. Nevertheless, to make sense of these processes we must necessarily make reference to the activity of the embodied agent who is influenced in this way. Agents reply to situations and emulate others; that is, they act and do so purposively and meaningfully. There is no space here for determinism.

However, this conception of agency is not based upon a metaphysical notion of 'free will', or absolute freedom either. Indeed, in a number of his works Merleau-Ponty launches a staunch attack upon the notion of absolute freedom advocated by his friend and colleague, Sartre (1969). Any meaningful conception of freedom necessitates a notion of choice, Merleau-Ponty argues. Freedom without choice would amount to random indeterminacy. But choice presupposes a prior engagement with and belongingness to the world which cannot, if infinite regression is to be avoided, be chosen itself: it presupposes a meaningful view of and grasp upon the world, a set of preferences and a means of deliberation. Without these components in place we could not meaningfully be said to choose, but for that very reason they cannot themselves be chosen, at least not in the final instance. Choice cannot, therefore, be absolute and neither can freedom. Furthermore, our choices must not simply be rooted in the world; they must take root in the world if we are to speak meaningfully of freedom. An individual who approaches each day or each hour anew has no freedom as none of their projects would ever come to fruition. True freedom entails that by acting we commit ourselves, transforming both ourselves and our circumstances in relatively durable ways which cannot be simply erased or undone.

As might be expected, habit plays a crucial a role in this critique. Habits root us in the world, providing the necessary background of meaning and preference which makes choice possible. Furthermore, it is our tendency towards habituation which makes those choices meaningful by affording them durability.

None of this seeks to challenge the notion that human beings are, in a sense, free. But it suggests a 'situated' rather than an absolute freedom. Human beings transcend the given by way of their projects, for Merleau-Ponty. They are capable of both creative action and choice. But they are always situated within the world, anchored by their habits, and are never 'suspended in nothingness'. This renders their actions predictable and more or less probable:

> Generality and probability are not fictions, but phenomena; we must therefore find a phenomenological basis for statistical thought. It belongs necessarily to a being which is fixed, situated and surrounded by things in the world. ... this

past, though not a fate, has at least a specific weight and is not a set of events over there, at a distance from me, but the atmosphere of my present. (Merleau-Ponty 1962: 442)

This is far truer to our sense of history than Sartre's (1969) model. *Being and Nothingness* points to an absurd situation, in Merleau-Ponty's view, in which any event is equally likely at any time and we have no reason to suppose that states of affairs might not be transformed into their opposite at any moment. Dictators might become democrats and stable social orders might explode in revolutionary fervour at any moment. Merleau-Ponty's habit focused concept of agency permits a more sociological view. It allows us to consider how patterns of behaviour become stabilised both individually and in the form of institutions. This is not deny the possibility of radical change. Merleau-Ponty offers this reflection in the midst of a discussion on the possibility of revolutionary transformation – a prospect which, in the 1940s, he still deemed possible in the capitalist west. The point, rather, is that such transformations, as any number of sociological studies suggest, do not happen 'spontaneously'. They must be prepared within the social formation over time, events building upon events and opening up spaces of opportunity. This is only possible, however, if the events of the present do not pass away into nothing but rather cumulate and sediment; if the actions of today have a durable impact upon the actions of tomorrow. And this, in turn, is only possible if we are creatures of habit. Habit is as essential to the movement of history as innovation and creation, since history, even a history of rapid change, presupposes the sedimentation of actions which allows them to build upon one another. History is not the succession of discrete events, past and present, but their cumulative penetration in an unfolding process, and it is habit, as the sedimented effect of the past within the present, that allows this penetration and unfolding to occur.

The concept of situated freedom that Merleau-Ponty outlines is, in my view, a fundamentally pragmatic conception. Like Ryle (see Chapter 4), he recognises the senselessness of debates on human freedom which take a general or abstract turn. Questions of freedom become meaningful for him only in the context of specific issues; when, for example, we are inquiring into the responsibility of a particular agent for a particular event, and wish to know if they could or should have acted differently – a question which is ultimately about their circumstances, knowledge and competence; or perhaps when we are enquiring into the opportunity which a specific group has to realise their potential and take control over their own lives.

Conclusion: Phenomenological Habits and the Theory of Practice

The purpose of this chapter has been twofold. Firstly, to build upon the exposition of Merleau-Ponty's theory of agency, outlined in Chapter 5, so as to complete our outline of an embodied, post-Cartesian and non-dualistic theory of social agency. Secondly, to consider how his conception of habit and agency allows us to overcome some of the shortcomings of Bourdieu's approach, as outlined in Chapter 6. In this concluding section I will reflect briefly upon this second aim.

In my critique of Bourdieu I outlined four weaknesses of his approach. Firstly, though I suggested that his work was not deterministic, I argued that he had never spelled out his opposition to determinism in any detail nor elaborated upon the manner in which his theory of habitus allowed us to avoid determinism without slipping into the absolute voluntarism of the early Sartre (1969). This is exacerbated, I argued, by the second problem of his approach, which is that he tends to portray the relationship of habit to action in a very one-directional manner; habits, though constructed through practice, are deemed generative of practice and there is little recognition of the potential for creative actions or praxes which modify both habitus and practice. Thirdly, I observed that Bourdieu has done little, despite his assertions, to consider the ways in which the habitus shapes our subjective worlds and interpretative practices. Finally, I argued that Bourdieu renders his notion of habitus problematic by posing it as one structure of action, to be set against more reflective and reflexive possibilities.

In response to the first two problems I suggest that Merleau-Ponty's work could clearly be helpful. As I have said, he offers a clear and strong critique of mechanistic determinism, arguing that human behaviour is not caused by events external to it but rather responds purposively to those events, in accordance with the meanings they have for it. These meanings and purposes are, in turn, rooted in habits, as we have seen in this chapter, but we still avoid determinism because our habits are simply part of our constitution. They are integral to what we are and thus cannot count as an external cause acting upon us. We have also seen in this chapter, however, that Merleau-Ponty refuses the absolute voluntarism of Sartre. Absolute notions of freedom are incoherent, he shows. Habit is invoked again in this account since Merleau-Ponty argues that any meaningful conception of human choice must presuppose the habitual schemas which function to make our world meaningful us and afford a grasp upon it (giving us a situation in which to choose), as well the acquisition of stable preferences and means of deliberation. Moreover, he argues that choice is only meaningful if it sticks, and that again involves habit. In this respect his position overlaps with that of Husserl, who, as I indicated, is concerned with the way in which decisions and judgements acquire the status of convictions and commitments by way of the process of habituation. In effect then, Merleau-Ponty forces us to abandon the terms of the freedom/determinism debate. Neither option fits the realities of human agency. In their place we need to learn to think of agency in terms of purposive and meaningful conduct, shaped by habit. Here he rejoins Bourdieu, providing him with the philosophical support which needs to sustain his claim that the concept of the habitus dissolves the freedom/determinism debate.

A further advantage of Merleau-Ponty's conception of habit, however, is that he situates it within a broader conception of agency. Habits arise, for Merleau-Ponty, out of the interaction between the organism or agent and the world. Some are the result of imitation but some are the result of innovative and creative praxes, and many are the result of a combination of the two. In this respect the agent is not wholly pre-empted by the notion of the habitus and the habitus is conceived as a 'moving equilibrium', subject, by virtue of action, to 'coherent deformations' which alter its structure. Furthermore, with his notion of the potential creativity of praxis, Merleau-Ponty is able to account for the way in which habits and practices are fitted to whatever material circumstances the agent occupies. The mystery of how habitus are shaped by circumstances, which we find in Bourdieu and which allows his critics to level the charge of determinism at him, is resolved in Merleau-Ponty by way of a consideration of the adaptive responses which the agent makes to her circumstances.

Merleau-Ponty's discussion of the habits of perception and linguistic articulation also go some way to allowing to see how the subjective life of the agent is shaped by habit. In this chapter, however, we have also considered the work of Husserl. Husserl's reflections on typification and apperception afford us a strong grasp upon the way in which habit enters into our subjective life. And both his work, and that of Schutz and the enthnomethodologists, offer us a range of tools by which we might open up and further explore this domain, adding a more substantive subjective dimension to our research. They look more deeply 'inside' the habitus, at its role in the construction of experience and interpretation.

This leaves one issue remaining: Bourdieu's treatment of reflection and reflexivity. Bourdieu is wrong to posit reflection and choice as different modalities of action to those rooted in habit. Against this we must insist rather upon the habitual root of reflexive and reflective forms of behaviour; that is, upon reflective, reflexive and both habit busting and habit forming habits. I will deal with this issue more extensively in the next chapter, where I consider reflexive habits, self-hood and processes of self-formation. Using the work of Mead (1967) I will discuss the manner in which reflexive possibilities are incorporated within the habitus. For the moment, however, I will briefly identify three arguments, already outlined in this book, which point to the reflective and reflexive possibilities entailed in the concept of the habitus.

Firstly, the incorporation of linguistic schemas within the habitus gives rise to reflective possibilities. As I noted in Chapter 5, the acquisition of language entails that the agent learns to substitute certain of their immediate responses to situations with linguistic formulations. They acquire the habit of inhibiting immediate responses. The use of language brings the agent into a different relationship with their self. Not only does language make their possibilities for action and 'intentions' perceptible to them but, having incorporated as habitus the process of dialogue, they can actually enter into a process of dialogue with their self. This is precisely what reflection and reflective decision making are; dialogues with oneself.

We can also add to this that whatever choices are made in this reflective mode are necessarily shaped by habit. Habits enter into choice, as we have seen, by way of our ways of making sense of our situations of choice, the technique of deliberation we use and the preferences we have. Choices are forms of social practice which arise out of practical contexts of action and, as such, they are structured by way of habits on all fronts.

The same is true of more radically reflexive projects. We could cite Bourdieu himself on this point. It is evident, for example, that he does not view the reflexivity achieved by way of sociology as a mysterious act of a transcendental subject. To the contrary, he views sociology as a craft and argues for the superiority of its views of the social world on the basis of the specific methodological practices it adopts (see Chapter 6). Sociological reflexivity is something that we achieve, for Bourdieu, by way of specific (sociological and scientific) forms of practice, and like any forms of practice these are rooted in habits. We learn how to conduct surveys, use statistics, deconstruct texts and so on. We find a similar argument to this in Husserl's phenomenology. Phenomenology is a reflexive form of philosophy *par excellence*. It entails an inspection of the various habits by which the sense of the world is constituted for us, making explicit all that is ordinarily habitually taken for granted in our 'natural attitude'. In this respect phenomenology frees us from our habits by making us aware of them as habits. We take a step back from our habitual ways of being. And yet, as Husserl (1970) emphasises, phenomenology is a technique which individuals must acquire as a habit if they are to engage in it successfully. Moreover, it is a technique which emerges out of the history of philosophy, building upon the habitual acquisitions of that history in much the same way that an agent builds upon the habitual acquisitions of their own individual history. In other words, however much phenomenology may free us from our habits, or some of them, it is nevertheless itself a habit. It is a reflexive habit; a disposition towards reflexivity. Nothing would be altered if phenomenology entailed a technique for altering habits, as indeed it does in its psychotherapeutic application. It might then be a 'habit-busting habit', but that is still a habit or technique, albeit perhaps a 'second order' habit. To suggest otherwise would be to suggest that we can disconnect from our embodied manner of being and thus to fall back into the Cartesian trap of assuming that we are something other than that embodied manner of being.

It would be a mistake to believe that such forms of radical reflection and reflexivity are a routine or mundane feature of everyday life. Bourdieu is right to suggest that they tend to occur either in the context of academic life or at periods of crisis, when much that is taken for granted is raised to the level of discourse. However, the point still stands that even these more radical forms of reflexivity belong, in the final instance, to the habitus.

The arguments I have put forward in this chapter and the issues and perspectives I have discussed are not intended, in any way, to displace the work of Bourdieu. To the contrary, I believe that his is the most promising approach to sociology we have. My intention has simply been to consider ways in which we might deepen and strengthen his position. I believe that this rather limited aim has been achieved, though, of course, there doubtless remains much to be done to extend and deepen the theory of practice.

8

REFLEXIVE EMBODIMENT: BEING, HAVING AND DIFFERENCE

The central theme and argument of this book hitherto has been that we are our bodies and that everything we are and do assumes an embodied form. This is an important argument and I do not wish to detract from it in anything that I will go on to argue in this final chapter. It would be inadequate to state simply that we are our bodies, however, if that involves ignoring the significant ways in which we might be said to 'have' bodies too. Descartes points us to this aspect of embodiment. He was wrong to differentiate himself, *qua* mind, from his body; but the fact that he was able to make a case for dualism and that many people agreed with him points to a phenomenologically real dimension of our being. The human body does not simply exist 'in itself'. It exists 'for itself' too; as a focus of its own projects, concerns and contemplation. We inspect ourselves before the mirror, worry about ourselves; about our health and well being, appearance and demeanour. And we work upon ourselves to effect change. We build up our bodies through exercise, for example, and slim them down through diet. We adorn them with clothing and jewels. Some even go so far as to have them surgically altered. The mistake of the dualist is to be misled by this state of affairs into believing that their 'real self' must therefore be elsewhere, transcending this observable empirical manifestation, when in fact the trick is achieved by a reflex process in which we, as embodied beings, turn back upon ourselves to inspect ourselves:

> … I am not in front of my body, I am in it, or rather I am it. … If we can still speak of interpretation in relation in relation to the perception of one's own body, we shall have to say that it interprets itself. (Merleau-Ponty 1962: 150)

This duality of being and having applies to habit too. I am my habits in the sense that everything I perceive, think, feel or otherwise do emerges out of behaviours which follow a habituated pattern. Yet, as an individual, a citizen and a sociologist, I am in the habit of reflecting upon and attempting to change certain of my habits. Amongst the habitual schemas that make me what I am are reflexive and 'habit-busting' habits; habits which both equip and incline me to question and change the way in which I live my life. Thus I may decide to make myself more assertive or perhaps to adopt a healthier lifestyle. I may elect to be more reflective about my life, or perhaps less reflective. My habits, in this sense, strike me as something that 'I have', like my body, and something that I can work upon and change.

It is not just we who have our bodies and habits, however. As embodied beings we are perceptible to others. We fall within their perceptual field and, in this sense, they 'have' us too. Our embodiment is thus necessarily alienated. We are never in complete possession of ourselves. More to the point, our perceptible being is captured in schemas of collective representation. From the moment of birth, and even before, our anatomical state and embodied visibility are made to signify social meanings and we, accordingly, are positioned in social space. Indeed, we only come to have ourselves by first enjoining this intersubjective order and learning to see ourselves from the outside, as 'other'.

In this final chapter I explore these issues. The first half of the chapter focuses upon the question of self-consciousness, reflexivity and the various ways in which we come to 'have' a sense of our self, body and habits. This part of the chapter continues the arguments about reflexivity raised at the end of the previous chapter, and seeks to further advance the model of agency that has been developed in the book. In particular I seek to show that and how our reflexive capacities are rooted in our corporeal schema in the form of habit, and I use the work of Mead (1967) to establish this point. The second part of the chapter then focuses upon what is perhaps the more negative aspect of my argument. It examines the way in which human bodies are codified and classified in societies and the effects which this has upon both agency and the determination of life chances. Moreover, I suggest that bodily differences, codified in this way, can be understood as embodied forms of symbolic capital. I begin the chapter with a brief reflection on self-consciousness and a recap of the arguments we have already considered with respect to it.

The Problem of Self-Consciousness

For Descartes there is no problem of self-consciousness. As we saw in Chapter 2, he believes that he enjoys a special form of access to the contents of his own mind and that nothing could be more certain than this immediate knowledge. Unlike his external perceptions, which are prone to error, he cannot be mistaken in his peek inwards as he has no need to rely upon his unreliable senses. That this theory precludes the possibility of both self-deception and degrees of personal insight, not to mention moments of personal revelation, should be sufficient to warn us against it. As we saw in Chapter 4, however, there are further, strong reasons to challenge it. Our psychological life is not an internal theatre production which we are free to observe. Rather, it consists in our behaviour, dispositions and externally focused or 'intentional' sensations, perceptions and imaginings. Furthermore, none of these aspects of our psychological life come with a label readily attached and all derive their meaning from their relationship to contexts and circumstances. There is no determinate sensation or behaviour which merits the label 'jealousy', for example. Many types of sensation or behaviour might signal jealousy, depending upon context, but none will necessarily do so. Insofar as we achieve a sense and knowledge of self, therefore, we must monitor our own conduct and sensations in relation to the contexts in which they unfold. And there is no guarantee that our assessment will be correct, not least since the language games of psychological assessment, whether focused upon self and other, are generally moral in nature. To describe a response as 'jealous', for example, is less a matter of description and more a matter of reprimand. And many of us are disinclined from being too harsh upon ourselves.

To this anti-Cartesian argument we can add another; namely, that the possibility of self-reflection is derived and secondary. Consciousness is not, in the first instance, self-consciousness. Merleau-Ponty expresses this point in the following way:

> For myself I am neither 'inquisitive', nor 'jealous', nor 'hunchbacked', nor a 'civil servant'. It is often a matter of surprise that the cripple or invalid can put up with himself. The reason is that such persons are not for themselves deformed or at death's door. Until the final coma, the dying man is inhabited by a consciousness, *he is all that he sees*, and enjoys this much an outlet. (Merleau-Ponty 1962: 434, my emphasis)

What Merleau-Ponty is arguing here is that whatever attributions we might make about ourselves, whether about our basic physical state ('hunchbacked'), our psychological state ('jealous') or our social role ('civil servant'), always presuppose an outside view; an objectification of one's self which is not basic to our experience. As embodied beings we look out upon the world in which we are situated but, as such, we are always our own blind spot. The eye does not see itself and as perception and motility are the basis of human subjectivity neither therefore does the I. Eye and I are turned outwards towards the world and their experience is an experience of this world. Furthermore, my experience of the world is the only experience I have, such that any deficiencies, peculiarities or 'distinguishing features' it might manifest could not be apparent to me 'from within'. I can only get a handle on my experience by standing back from it and comparing it with other possible experiences; that is, by objectifying it.

This is not to deny that we have a tacit sense of self within our corporeal schema. I only duck to avoid low doorways and stray cricket balls because my perception of them entails, within it, a sense both of myself and of the likelihood that they will collide with me. Similarly my perception of objects as 'far away' or 'to the left' entail a tacit reference back to myself as the observer of them. They are far away from or to the left of 'me'. My sense of 'me' is not thematic in these experiences, however. And it only becomes so, for Merleau-Ponty, by way of my involvement in an intersubjective world, with others:

Consciousness can never objectify itself into invalid consciousness or cripple consciousness, and even if the old man complains of his age or the cripple of his deformity, they can do so only by comparing themselves with others, or seeing themselves through the eyes of others, that is, by taking a statistical and objective view of themselves, so that such complaints are never absolutely genuine ... (ibid.)

There are two aspects to this claim. Firstly, the characteristics of the embodied agent are relational and comparative. This point concerns our subjective sense of ourselves, in the respect that we can only experience aspects of our bodily being as deficient insofar as we can compare them with preferable states which we perceive in others. I can only 'feel' short, for example, if others around me are taller than me. Secondly, it addresses the broader issue of objective bodily states. 'Deficiencies' can only strike us as such, even in objective analyses, relative to norms which are, in turn, derived from average states of the collective to which the 'deficient' body belongs. Indeed, whatever attributions we may make depend for their positive content upon a contrast with something other. If everything in the world were red then the word 'red', no less than 'colour', would be redundant as it would cease to distinguish anything. In addition to this, however, Merleau-Ponty takes the further step of indicating that we can only feel or otherwise experience ourselves in terms of these categories insofar as we come to see ourselves *'through the eyes of others'*. That is, we must step out of the particularity which is the primary state of our conscious being-in-the-world and turn back upon ourselves to experience ourselves as other.

At one level this entails, as Cooley (1902) famously argues, that we derive our sense of self from the image of our self that others reflect back to us in interaction. I may be my own blind spot but others have a direct experience of me. They are direct witnesses to my various moods and pre-occupations. I am an object in their perceptual field; an object which they must and will typify and classify along with all other objects of their experience. And they will communicate their experience of me, their judgements and types, back to me in the course of our interactions. This may be direct, as, for example, when they explicitly label me. But it could be indirect. The view they have of me is embodied in the way they act towards me and that view is thereby conveyed to me. This is not to say that the agent must accept each and every label that is thrown at them. They may resist labels and/or attempt to negotiate the specific labels that are applied to them. Moreover, as Goffman's (1959) work illustrates, agents may go to great lengths to create particular impressions of self and to manage the flow of information about their self that circulates in any social situation. Notwithstanding this, the only court of appeal regarding 'self' that is available to agents, even if they only wish to convince or persuade themselves, is the realm of (potentially) publicly available action. To repeat, there is no 'inner sanctum' of self for them to consult and their conception of self is therefore dependent upon the same types of evidence as others might use with respect to them. Furthermore, given this, it is always possible that others may have spotted things about them that they have not noticed for their self.

In the modern context the existence of mirrors and other reflecting surfaces adds to this basic 'mirroring' from others and potentially intensifies the relationship which an agent may enjoy to their self *qua* embodied being. As Romanyshyn (1982) has noted, the mirror is a crucial mechanism for 'self work' in the modern context. We use the mirror to style the self we want to be; to create the image which will make others see us as we want to be seen, thus allowing us to be that self for ourselves. There is more to the notion of self than this, however. These accounts of 'mirroring' and *a fortiori* the notions of self-presentation and resistance to labels presuppose a basic sense that we have of ourselves, to which we relate this incoming information. Moreover, it presupposes that we experience others as experiencing beings; that is, that we experience them as experiencing us. To consider how this is possible we must turn to the work of George Herbert Mead (1967, see also Crossley 1996a, 2000b).

Embodiment, Imagination and Play

Mead's account of the emergence of the self is very much a continuation of the 'looking glass' conception advocated by Cooley (1902). It pushes Cooley's basic idea much further, however. Even our basic capacity for reflecting upon ourselves derives from interaction, Mead argues; and from an incorporation during childhood of what he variously calls the 'attitude' or 'role' of others. Mead theorises this, in the first instance, in terms of play. Children, he observes, routinely play at being other people. Both when alone and with other children they imitate others, acting out the roles of those others. Moreover, when doing so they very often take on many roles at once, alternating between them and juggling them in what, from the outside, appears like an immensely complex debate. Multiple voices are brought into dialogue as the child switches between roles. Such play is crucial for Mead. It allows the child to develop a sense and mastery of the intersubjective texture of the social world, affording it a sense of different social roles, of otherness and, almost by default therefore, of itself. The child learns to see the world as being composed of different points of view by literally acting out the roles or 'characters' of others and discovering 'within' the role the particular view of the world that goes with it. Like a method actor, but without the reflective intention, the child gets inside others by 'being' them; that is, by putting itself in their shoes, copying what they do and thereby learning to occupy and perceive the world as they do. This gives the child a sense of its own particularity by default; grasping the place of others establishes a place and a sense of self. But this is further enhanced when the child is able to bring its own role into dialogue with those of the others it plays at, such that it looks at itself from the point of view of the other. It might play at being mother or father to itself, for example, and thereby look at and objectify itself from their point of view. Furthermore, through frequent repetition of such play these simulated others and their perspectives sediment within the corporeal schema of the agent in the form of habit. The agent acquires a durable capacity for talking to and reflecting upon their self, and indeed for viewing problems and situations from different points of view. Their habitus is modified and acquires an intersubjective dimension.

It is important to emphasise the habitual root here. Mead is often read as a theorist who puts great emphasis upon the human capacity for choice and reflection and this is correct. But for Mead this capacity and tendency towards reflection is acquired through experience in the form of habit:

> Our past stays with us in terms of those changes which have resulted from our experience and which are in some sense registered there. The peculiar intelligence of the human form lies in this elaborate control gained through the past. The human animal's past is constantly present in the facility with which he acts ... (Mead 1967: 116)

We have reflective and reflexive habits.

What Mead suggests regarding the incorporation of others within the habitus overlaps with what many psychoanalysts have argued regarding identification and the introjection. Furthermore, he insists that authority figures or those who have the most direct impact upon the child are most likely to be incorporated in this way, thereby confirming the psychoanalytic emphasis upon the role of the 'father figure'. There are traces of Husserl (1991) and his 'empathic intentionality' in here too, as the child is learning to put itself into the shoes of the other (see also Crossley 1996a, 2000b). What is particularly impressive about Mead's version of this familiar theme, however, is the manner in which he embodies these 'mental' processes and thereby demystifies them by revealing their mechanism and medium. The child does not 'introject' the father, as such, nor does it engage in any complex process of analogical or empathic reasoning. It plays. It mimics what it sees and derives great pleasure from doing so. But this has the unintended consequence that the role of the father or whoever is being played at is habituated within its corporeal schema. The psychological leap from father to child is bridged by the bodily activity of play and mimicry. Play is the embodied vehicle of the imaginative process that links the child to others and to the world. It is important to emphasise that this 'conception' of the perspective of the other which the child achieves is a lived and embodied sense which takes root within the habitus or corporeal schema. The child does not think about the perspective of the other but rather, having played the role of the other, it incorporates that perspective, achieving a felt sense of the world as intersubjective and multi-perspectival. This has the effect of distancing the child from its own position, thereby allowing it both to form a perspective, or perhaps multiple perspectives, upon itself. By taking the role of the other the child can become other to itself and achieve the outside perspective on itself that is required for it to relate to itself in categorical or objective terms: as 'jealous', 'hunchbacked' or a 'civil servant', for example.

Games, Norms and Laws

What is achieved by way of play is further extended, according to Mead, by way of games. In play the child learns to see itself from the point of view of specific other people or roles. This is important as it allows the child to develop a pre-reflective corporeal 'map' of the positions of the social world and its 'place' in it. It develops a 'feel' for the different types of person it will encounter in the social world and of their various relationships to both itself and each other. The structure of the social world is incorporated within its habitus. Moreover, it incorporates the sentiments and identity of the social group to which it belongs; that is, the *esprit de corps* referred to in Chapter 7. This sense of the social world is, in some respects, still quite particular. With games, however, particularly team games which involve both rule structures and multiple team positions, the child learns to see itself from the point of view of the 'generalised other'; that is, from the point of view of the team as a whole and from the point of view of the game and its rules. It learns to apply the rules and the general aspirations of the group to itself; to take up a place in the team and to experience itself as so positioned. This is important, for Mead, because it prefigures the relationship which the child must develop to its community and the law of that community. Indeed games, for him, provide for the passage of the child to the rule of law. In learning to play games and incorporating the structure of the game into its habitus, such that it can both play unreflectively within the parameters of the game and also reflect upon itself from the point of view of the game and its community of players, it prepares for the incorporation that will be demanded of it within the wider society it is destined to join.

This reference to games and their role in the construction of self resonates strongly with the game metaphor that I have used at numerous points already in this book. If the different fields that comprise the social world are akin to games then playing games is, of course, the ideal way of fitting a child for participation in the social world. Furthermore, as play and games are both modalities of learning for Mead, we can equally see how, from his point of view, one's stock of habits might be modified and certainly added to through the course of everyday participation in the games that comprise the social world; that is, through participation in different social fields.

The Embodied I and Me

By assuming the roles of others and interacting with them in structured game situations, combined with its acquisition and learning of a language, which includes both its own name and personal pronouns, the child learns to take a perspective upon and forms an image of itself which

Mead calls its 'me'. This me or rather the process of inspecting it is, in effect, the basis for self-identity; it is our self as we learn to know and experience our self. Self-hood is a process, for Mead, in which 'I' adopt the role of the other as a means of turning back upon myself, to reflect upon myself as 'me'. I develop a concept of myself (me) by acting (*qua* I) out the role of the generalised other.

Giddens (1991) has suggested that Mead's I and me are the unsocialised and socialised aspects of the self, respectively, and that they correspond with the Freudian distinction between id and ego/super ego. This reading captures one important aspect of the distinction which Mead is attempting to draw; namely, that agents can become torn between their own private utilitarian interests and the demands and expectations of their group, which they have incorporated within their habitus as a sense of duty. In reflecting upon themselves (*qua* me) they apply the rules of the group to their own proposed actions. Like Durkheim (1915), Mead (1967) conceives of agency in terms of this tension between the individual and the group, the particular and the universal. His way of formulating it is quite distinct and wholly more preferable to the Freudian model imputed to him by Giddens, however. There is no unsocialised aspect of the self, for Mead, though that does not mean that our behaviours are simply reducible to learned roles.[1] The split between I and me is between a sensuous and socialised bodily agent and the image which that agent is able to form of itself. The I is not a 'part' of the self; it is everything that I am. And the me is not a part of the self but rather the representation of myself which I (*qua* I) form of myself: my mirror image. The relationship between the two, it follows, is not a spatial relationship between two parts of self which are competing for predominance, but rather a temporal and reflexive self-relationship of an agent who chases her own shadow. Moreover, it is a relationship defined by a 'lag' because, as I have noted on numerous occasions in this book, the agent who chases her own self-image will never quite catch up with herself. At the very least, as our discussion of Ryle (1949) in Chapter 4 revealed, the act of self-reflection must necessarily fail to thematise or reflect upon itself, such that it is always one step behind. The I enters into its own stream of experience as 'me'

> ... but it is a 'me' which was the 'I' at an earlier time. If you ask then, where directly in your own experience the 'I' comes in, the answer is that it comes in as a historical figure. It is what you were a second ago that is the 'I' of the 'me'. [the 'I'] is not directly given in experience. (Mead 1967: 174–5)

The distinction that Mead makes here sounds like the Kantian or Husserlian distinction between the empirical and transcendental egos and it is similar in certain respects. Mead's elusive 'I' is thoroughly empirical, however, and like Ryle's elusive I, discussed in Chapter 4, not remotely mysterious. It is only elusive because it consists in what we do and experience in the immediate present and because self-reflection is a process of retrospection which necessarily precludes the immediate present. Self-reflection focuses upon the historical image of ourselves which Mead refers to as the 'me', or rather, it builds up such a sense and image.

However, it could be this experience of elusion and tension which gives rise to the sense that we have of a transcendental ego or indeed an immaterial mind. Indeed, this is precisely what Durkheim (1915) argues with respect to the soul in the *Elementary Form of Religious Life*. There is no soul distinct from the body, for Durkheim (1974). Though his thoughts on the matter are few and far between he seemingly posits an argument very similar to that argued in this book; namely, that our psychological life is a whole greater than the sum of its physical parts, just as society is a whole greater than the sum of its psychological parts (ibid.). Having said this, however, in his attempt to explain the emergence of the idea and the sense that we have of the soul he suggests that it stems directly from the feeling that we have of 'alien' elements within us; elements generated by the incorporation of 'collective representations' or, to put it in Mead's terms, the 'generalised other'.

Reflexivity

The I and the me manifest two distinct forms of temporality: the I embodies and repeats its history in the form of the habits; the me, by contrast, is constructed in the web of narrative discourse and imaginative re-presentation which the I spins in its various reflexive activities and projects. And the two will by no means necessarily map neatly on to one another. Despite the considerable differences between Mead's perspective and that of Freud, this opens up the possibility of what we might refer to as an unconscious; that is, of historically derived schemas and interests which elude the conscious awareness of the agent whom they form. One is reminded of one of the definitions of the unconscious posited in the work of Lacan:

> The unconscious is that chapter of my history that is marked by a blank or occupied by a falsehood: it is the censored chapter. But the truth can be rediscovered; usually it has been written down elsewhere [such as the body]. (Lacan 1989: 50)

Mead's perspective is very different from Lacan's in many respects. But this quotation captures well a possibility which Mead's differentiation of I and me, and his conception of me as narrative history, opens up. The history of the agent is written on two registers; on the body in the form of the habitus and in language through self-narratives. And insofar as these two registers differ, the history of the agent may remain active in their present in ways which they are unaware of; ways which are unthematised in the narratives of the me which form the basis of their self-consciousness.

Notwithstanding this possibility of an unconscious, Mead's main emphasis is upon reflexivity and the way in which the self (*qua* I) becomes conscious of itself (*qua* me). By assuming the role of the other in relation to themselves social agents effectively objectify themselves and, to a certain degree at least, thereby liberate themselves from the worst excesses of their particularity and self-blindness. They come to see their own perspective upon the world as just one amongst others. Moreover, they can begin to reflect upon their self; upon their past, their future and their habits. Indeed, they may act upon their self so as to change their self. They can, as Husserl argues, harbour and use the 'laws' of their own psychological life to achieve new ends for their self:

> [The] transformation of the results of an originally intuitive apprehension into a *habitus* takes place according to a general law of conscious life, without our participation, so to speak, and it therefore takes place even where the interest in the explicated object is unique and transient [...] But it can also be that one strives to establish this *habitus* voluntarily. [...] Such an interest will give occasion to a *repeated running through* of the explicative synthesis ... (Husserl 1973: 123, his *italics*)

This will not necessarily be easy, of course. Old habits die hard, as the saying goes, and the struggle to establish new one's is often precisely that: a struggle. Nevertheless it is important to recognise this possibility, and the more general possibility of reflective and reflexive habits, if we are to fully realise the potential of a conception of agency rooted in habit and a reflexive sociology which claims to study these habits. In Chapter 6 I noted a critique of Bourdieu, by Kogler (1997), which suggested that he effectively assumes an epistemological privilege for sociology which threatens to undermine his whole schema. To put it crudely, Kogler suggests that Bourdieu's social agents, unbeknown to themselves, are victims of their habitus, whilst sociologists, by contrast, are the epistemological subjects who know this. I noted at the time that this criticism hardly does justice to Bourdieu. However, there is a problem, as I argued, concerning reflexivity and its relationship to the habitus in Bourdieu's work. Mead, I suggest, offers us a way out of this problem. The concept of habit does not preclude reflection or reflexivity in Mead's account. Indeed, we acquire the habit of self-objectification and reflection by way of our involvement in the social world. The project of a reflexive sociology, from this point of view, is simply an extension of that basic reflexivity, albeit one armed with more powerful techniques of analysis. Sociological objectification extends that form of self-objectification which gives us a sense of me, the objectification rooted in our incorporation of the role of the other, and it further extends the possibility of self-knowledge and mastery attainable by that route. Finally, it is because of our reflexivity, and because we can act upon ourselves so as to change ourselves, that the project of a reflexive sociology is a worthwhile endeavour. The critique offered by sociology can precisely feed back into the already existing reflexive projects of social agents, offering them insights (for example, the results of systematic studies) which are not apparent to reflective consciousness.

I do not mean to sound too idealistic here. The demands of everyday life are such that penetrating reflexions are often not on the agenda. Sociology is by no means always welcome or, indeed, helpful. The point of my argument has simply been to point to possibilities and potential.

There is another implication to Mead's work which complicates this issue of reflexivity further. If we acquire our own reflexivity by way of an appropriation of the view of the generalised other, then the limits of our own reflexivity are, in effect, the limits of the collective representations of our society. More to the point, our projects and self understanding are necessarily shaped by these representations and the way in which they classify and differentiate us. Indeed, even our bodies are shaped by these collective representations. In what remains of this chapter I want to explore this latter notion, considering how bodies are made meaningful in terms of social representations and then acted upon, largely from without, in ways which shape both their activity and ultimately their destiny. All societies, I will argue, involve basic systems of classification which are focused upon the body or particular 'markers' thereon. And these systems of classification both construct and enforce a particular definition of the me, creating significant forms of structural (vertical) differentiation. Bodies are classified according to gender, race, age and health status, for example. And with each of these categories comes a socially recognised meaning and a degree (or in some cases perhaps 'lack') of symbolic capital which affects life chances.

The Embodiment of Difference

Earlier in this chapter I cited a quotation in which Merleau-Ponty refers to the 'crippled body'. One never experiences one's body as crippled, at least in the first instance, this passage suggested, because one's body is one's 'point of view' on the world. It opens out upon the world but is, because of this, its own blind spot. One's body is, in a sense, all that one knows of bodily life and it can only seem deficient, if it does, by comparison. Indeed it will only seem deficient or different if one assumes the view of the other. This argument applies to all forms of bodily difference. One does not feel one's body intrinsically to be 'male' or 'female', for example, since each term only has meaning relative to the other. One could not know that one's body felt male unless one had a sense of what it is like for a body to feel something other than male and, as a male, one simply cannot have any such feeling, so any feelings of maleness one may have must come from within a comparative structure. Indeed, the very notion of male itself only makes sense in relation to female, such that the one can only exist relative to the other and such that one can only know that one belongs to one or the other side if one knows of the existence of both. The same applies to race, to disability and any other 'difference' one can imagine – precisely because these are *differences*.

Notwithstanding this, as embodied beings we are 'reversible'. We not only perceive but are perceived; we can be seen, touched, heard, smelled and tasted. And, as a consequence, we can be classified according to our perceptible qualities, or at least according to those perceptible qualities deemed salient within the forms of classification that have been constructed historically within our societies. Bodies are classified from birth and often before. Furthermore, this process of categorisation, irrespective of whatever biological differences it may map onto, effects a 'social magic'. Beginning with the very name an infant is given at birth, categories shape the way in which others act towards the child, their expectations and demands, and thus the opportunities, constraints and possibilities the infant will face throughout its life. Indeed, they shape the habits which the agent will acquire and, in this respect, affect the very core of the agent.

There are a number of points here which need to be drawn out. The first concerns categorisation. Anatomical and other visible differences are meaningful in human societies. Categorical schemas, sometimes complex but other times relatively straightforward and crude, are constructed around them such that they become signs in a signifying system or 'lexicon' (Barthes 1973). And what they signify is one's belonging to some social category or other. For the most part the outward appearance of one's genitals will be sufficient for one to be categorised male or female, for example. One acquires, on the basis of an anatomical difference, a social identity. And this will, in turn, have any of a number of effects upon one's life chances. In certain groups where females are particularly disvalued, for example, a female foetus may be aborted before birth. And the same thing may happen with respect to 'impaired' foetuses within our own culture. Indeed, with the prospect of antenatal gene therapy within Western societies abortion may become only one of any of a number of physical interventions that foetuses are subject to on account of the symbolic meaning attached to their anatomy, or rather to physical genetic markers on their DNA, by social systems of classification. Even setting aside these physical interventions, however, the social identities ascribed to individuals on the basis of their basic anatomical constitution (and differences) will have a multitude of social effects, ranging from the cosmetic to quite profound differences in life chances. Anatomical differences are made to make a social difference such that anatomy, to misquote Freud, is made destiny.

This is one very straightforward way in which the body, or rather specific bodily attributes, can function as 'symbolic capital'. And it is one very clear way in which certain key forms of structural inequality in modern societies, particularly gender and racial inequality, are best conceived of as an embodied form of symbolic capital. Bodily differences acquire a specific 'value' within any given social formation or social field, which may then be 'spent' or used in particular social fields. The boxing example which I discussed briefly at the end of Chapter 6 provides an interesting illustration of this. I noted, for example, that it is only very recently that women have been granted admission to this field, particularly as contenders. Their 'symbolic capital', as defined according to specified anatomical markers has, until now, been deemed insufficient or inappropriate for full consideration. Black men, by contrast, who have experienced comparable exclusion in relation to a whole range of different social fields, have found that their symbolic capital is more effective in granting them access to the boxing (and more generally the sports) field. In this case capital functions on a very simple inclusion/exclusion basis. It might equally function in more subtle and indirect ways, however. If colour and sex really do function as signifiers within our culture, as I have said, and what they signify is a specific symbolic value, then they inevitably enter into each and every interaction situation in which we engage, framing the ways in which we are seen, heard, judged and acted towards.

It might be objected against this that the bodily signs I am referring to are, in fact, real biological differences. I have argued that differences and deficiencies are not intrinsic properties of bodies but rather are arrived at by way of comparison, such that they are inevitably social constructions, but does this way of thinking not seek to shirk from the obvious truth that bodies are indeed different? That women are biologically equipped for childbirth and men are not? That the blind cannot see? I do not seek to deny such obvious truths. My point, rather, is that such states do not come with a meaning or significance already attached to them, and that the meaning or significance they acquire is one derived from the social world, in accordance with a wide range of interests, conflicts and concerns within that world. There is a degree of 'objectivity', for example, to skin colour. The human eye and perceptual system undoubtedly play an active role in discriminating between black and white but they can only do so because of real differences or resistances that they 'hook on' to; that is, because of differences in skin pigment. What it means to be black or white, however, the value attached to each state and the consequences likely to stem from them, is quite different in different societies. Being black in contemporary Britain has a different meaning to that which would have held true in the British colonies of the past, for example, or in the deep south of the USA prior to the civil rights movements; and one assumes that the meaning would be different again in a society which is predominantly black, whose elite groups are predominantly black and so on.

This point relates back to two important points, taken from Merleau-Ponty, which I discussed earlier in the book. Firstly, it relates to the notion that the nature of human existence is 'symbolic'; that is, that human beings respond to their environment in terms of the meanings they discern therein and that these meanings are, for the most part, conventional, such that human reality is a 'virtual' reality. This applies as much to the way in which human beings respond to one another as to other aspects of their environment. Aspects of the body become signs within the symbolic domain of culture and thereby have consequences in the organisation of conduct. Secondly, it reveals the reversibility of the flesh. Human beings categorise and respond to meaning but in the interworld of history this entails that they are categorised too, and that their very existence embodies social meanings which are beyond their control. One's basic anatomical constitution signifies and, as such, shapes the way in which one is acted towards and interpreted. This is not a matter of individuals but of societies and their collective representations. Merleau-Ponty's (1965) symbolic domain is a shared cultural domain. But it would be a mistake to fail to see that the distinctions and meanings operative in this domain exist only insofar as they are embodied, as incorporated habitual schemas of perception and discourse, in the corporeal schemas of the agents who comprise that domain at any point in time.

From Categorisation to Hexis

Much contemporary work on the categorisation of bodily differences and/or their devaluation and rejection is associated with post-structuralist and post-modern philosophies. There is little need for them to be couched in this way, however, as the post-structuralists are, in this as in many other respects, reinventing a much older and more general sociological wheel. As early as 1951, for example, Lemert wrote of the social meaning which becomes attached to bodily differences, and the consequences which follow from this. On disability, for example, he writes:

> There is nothing intrinsic in a disfiguring scar or in extreme hairiness on the body of a woman which interferes in any way with physiological activity or with the potential fulfillment of social roles. Nevertheless a culture may *impute* a set of mythical physiological limits to such differentiae and thus cause them to become criteria for social exclusion and penalty.
>
> It is likewise true that those biological differentiae which have a demonstrable handicapping upon behaviour are overlaid with culturally conceived ideas as to how far the handicaps go. In fact, it is these cultural stereotypes which give the larger part of the social meaning to physical handicaps. (Lemert 1951: 29)

Lemert's discussion of this issue adds a very important point. The way in which an agent is classified not only affects the way in which others act towards them and thus their 'external' life chances. These interactions, in turn, shape both the habitus and self-identity of the agent such that they come to embody their difference in a secondary way too. They are effectively forced to 'act out' the meaning assigned to their anatomical signs and thereby to incorporate such differences within their corporeal schema. Having been defined as female on the basis of visible anatomical markers, for example, a girl is expected to act like a girl; that is, to identify with femininity as a self-identity and to incorporate typically female dispositions. Her 'natural' signifiers of gender are amplified by secondary, acquired markers (Oakley 1972, Sharpe 1976, Hughes and Witz 1997, Witz 2000).

In Lemert's work, which focuses primarily upon the labelling of 'deviance', such imposition is generally to the perceived detriment of the labelled individual. Labels are negative and the dispositions cultivated on their basis are disadvantageous, not least because they ensure that the agent remains fixed within the negative category. Bourdieu (1996) has described a very similar process with respect to elite schools, illustrating how the embodiment of difference may work to an agent's advantage. The difference between individuals accepted for these schools and those not may be very small in terms of marks on an entrance examination, he notes, but they acquire a great symbolic value. A difference of two per cent on an exam may determine whether an agent passes and enters the school or fails, and thus whether they acquire the status of the consecrated or not. Furthermore, the school will make big differences out of these little differences. It will work upon the bodies and particularly the dispositions of its pupils, fully expecting them to do likewise to themselves. In this way it will carve out visible differences in the modes of bodily comportment of those pupils, their *hexis*, and, as with more natural bodily differences, a meaning will be attached to these differences too. In particular they will be valued and the schools will encourage their pupils to value and perpetuate them.

As this latter example illustrates, even social differences which have no obvious anatomical or physical marker, such as class differences, can become embodied in this way. Socially distinct groups mark out their differences through their 'body techniques' (Mauss 1979) or 'hexis' (Bourdieu 1992a). One need only think, for an illustration, of Liza in George Bernard Shaw's (1957) *Pygmalion*. She desires to be a lady and clearly has the right biological 'bits' to qualify. But she lacks the class background and must consequently incorporate lady-like ways, including a lady-like accent, into her habitus and bodily schema. She must learn to modulate her body in speech so as to talk like a lady:

> *Liza*:   [*almost in tears*] But I'm sayin' it. Ahyee, Buyee, Cu-yee –
> *Higgins*:   Stop. Say a cup of tea.
> *Liza*:   A capputu-ee.
> *Higgins*:   Put your tongue forward until it squeezes against the top of your lower teeth. Now say cup.
> *Liza*:   C-c-c – I can't. C-Cup.
> *Pickering*:   Good. Splendid Miss Doolittle.
> *Higgins*:   By Jupiter, she's done it at the first shot.
>
> (Shaw 1957: 50)

Hexis signifies value and position. It is, as Bourdieu puts it, 'political mythology realised, *em-bodied*' (Bourdieu 1992a: 69, his emphasis). And it naturalises inequality, or at least contributes to its naturalisation. Liza seems naturally to belong to a lower social order at the start of *Pygmalion* because she so obviously 'ain't a lady'. Her bodily movement, right down to the way in which she moves her tongue in speech, and perhaps especially there, fails to conform to the middle class norm and thus marks her out, for the middle class, as one who is not of them and is lower than them. It locates her amongst those believed to be 'ruffians', 'work shy good-for-nothings', the illiterate and uneducated. It is no surprise that she has no money given this, 'and no bad thing either!'

What we see again here, with this notion of hexis, is the manner in which bodily features, in this case behavioural and dispositional properties rather than anatomical differences, function within schemas of social classification – which are themselves embodied in the habitus of social agents of course – to produce specific forms of symbolic capital. The way an individual moves and speaks signifies their belongingness to specific status groups and thereby secures for them the power (or lack of it) which is attached to that group. As Liza Doolittle knows only too well, looking and sounding like a lady opens doors:

> The flower girl [Liza]: I want to be a lady in a flower shop stead of sellin' at the corner of Tottenham Court Road. But they won't take me unless I can talk more genteel. He said he could teach me. Well, here I am ready to pay him – not asking any favour – and he treats me zif I was dirt. (Shaw 1957: 23)

Walking Like a Man

Bourdieu's (1992a) discussion of gender and *hexis* amongst the Kabyle provides a useful example with which to explore this notion further. The opposition between male and female, he argues, is literally embodied in forms of posture and comportment, and perhaps even more so in the habitual, embodied schemas which form the basis for the perception and evaluation of posture and comportment. In particular the masculine is associated with the firm, the upright, the straight and the direct. And this is reflected in the way in which Kabyle men (and perhaps French and British men too) are expected to comport themselves:

> The manly man, who goes straight to his target, without detours, is also a man who refuses twisted and devious looks, words, gestures and blows. He stands up straight and looks straight into the face of the person he approaches or wishes to welcome. (Bourdieu 1992a: 70)

Here Bourdieu picks up Mauss's (1979) observation on the gendered and symbolically meaningful nature of styles of walking and elaborates it in a fascinating way. Habitual ways of walking, he shows, emerge out of gendered and sexualised symbolic economies, wherein they emit an ideological meaning. The way one walks communicates something about one. The manly man walks straight and in doing so he conveys his honesty. This is possible because straightness of posture can function as a signifier, akin to the word 'straight', thereby acquiring a positive ideological accent or connotation for itself, through a widely used linguistic play which links the moral and geometric senses of 'straightness'. In itself this is an intriguing idea which, in my view at least, resonates with many elements of British culture. Notions of standing 'chest out and shoulders back', of keeping one's 'chin up' and giving a 'firm handshake', for example, each make sense in these terms. There is much more to Bourdieu's analysis than this, however, since he equally indicates that this positive ideological accent is only available to the male because, at the same time that it signifies honesty, it equally signifies masculinity. The point, of course, is that masculinity is ideologically joined with the positive values of honesty and honour and that women are therefore placed in a double bind. Men, by being manly, are also rewarded by being deemed honest, but this road is not open to women. Indeed women might be punished by seeming to adopt a masculine posture and are thus condemned to signify dishonesty – which is also punished. Though Bourdieu does not explicitly discuss the matter, sexuality is also implicated here. In our own language homosexuality is often referred to, in a derogatory way, as 'bent', which also means criminal or dishonest. And gay men are referred to as, amongst other things, 'benders'. It is interesting, in this respect, that the caricature of the male homosexual also focuses very much upon posture: for example, the limp wrist and mincing walk.

It is important to put this into perspective. The social world is never quite so simple and its rigidities and boundaries are never quite so straightforward, not least because its members are often all too aware and critical of them. The once socially powerful comic genre 'grotesque realism', as described by Bakhtin (1984), for example, is clearly one manifestation of a social form which can challenge and subvert ideological connotations, such as those attached to straightness and uprightness. Grotesque realism, which originated as a folk tradition, functions by bringing the more excessive aspect of embodiment and the 'lower bodily stratum' into the official world which so often denies them, and playing havoc with the meaning systems of the official world by inverting them for the purposes of the generation of laughter. Whether or not it is possible to refer to such grotesque realism in the present it is evident that much contemporary comedy has been based around a subversion of masculine postural norms in the way that this suggests. Monty Python's famous 'lumberjack' sketch[2] is just one example; the humour of the sketch precisely resides in a process of 'degeneration' from a form of masculinity conveyed by a tough manual occupation, as well as comportment and posture, to effeminacy and transexualism. Indeed, a number of the most famous Monty Python sketches revolve around an 'unmasking' of masculine pretensions, often in the very context where the embodiment of those pretensions is central: for example, the military parade ground or wild and rugged countryside. In certain respects these sketches and the many others like them confirm Bourdieu's view. They are only funny because they trade upon and play with dominant forms of social categorisation which attach to and function through the body, thus presupposing both those forms and their dominance. They are funny because socially transgressive. On the other hand, they call for a more complex view of the nature of social classification and its political effects because they reveal the reflexive and critical purchase which social members sometimes have upon the categories that otherwise structure their lives.

Throwing Like a Girl

Bourdieu's account of hexis focuses very much upon the communicative function of such forms of comportment. It is important to note, however, that differences in bodily comportment are 'lived' too, with considerable consequences. This necessitates that we approach hexis from an existential-phenomenological, as well as a semiotic, manner. Iris Young's (1980) excellent paper, 'Throwing Like A Girl', is my main point of reference for this observation. Young develops Merleau-Ponty's account of embodied subjectivity through a phenomenological focus upon women's typical modes of bodily comportment and their differences from men. Amongst other things she suggests that women tend not to put their whole body into things, such that, for example, they might try to lift objects with their arms alone, where men would typically adopt a lifting technique which uses the power of the back and the legs. Similarly, she suggest that men, when engaging with objects, more typically move out towards those objects, whilst women, where possible, wait for the object to reach them:

> Men more often move outward towards a ball in flight and confront it with their own counter motion. Women tend to wait for and then *react* to its approach rather than going forward to meet it. We frequently respond to the motion of a ball coming outwards us as if it were coming *at* us, and our immediate bodily impulse is to flee, duck, or otherwise protect ourselves from its flight. (Young 1980: 143)

Young's analysis of these processes is complex and fascinating. I only have space to consider two central points, however, both of which have a bearing upon Bourdieu's analysis. In the first instance, Young reflects upon the consequences of 'throwing like a girl' for those who do so. She suggests, in brief, that this mode of bodily comportment is disempowering. Women do not maximise the physical power of their bodies, for example, and they greatly reduce their own capacity for achieving control over physical situations. This is important because it suggests that the inequalities manifested in different modes of hexis are more extensive than Bourdieu's investigation of their symbolism would suggest. Differences in comportment have direct consequences for one's agentic abilities. Secondly, in reflecting upon the reasons for these differences in posture she adds to a notion of decorum and socialisation, such as is suggested by Bourdieu's account, a notion of the sexual objectification of the female body and the self-consciousness this generates. The way a woman moves, she observes, reflects her need to protect herself in advance from male sexual interference, whether that be visual or involving touch and physical contact. Large or vigorous movements leave a woman exposed and vulnerable, at least visually, in a way that does not hold for men. Men are not publicly sexually objectified or ogled in the way women are.

This latter point draws off and develops the notion of 'the look' which Sartre (1969) develops in *Being and Nothingness*, and which Merleau-Ponty (1962, 1968a) picks up and develops at a number of points in his work. In essence this notion draws attention to the fact that our embodiment necessarily entails that we exist for others. We are perceptible to others; they can see, hear, touch and perhaps even smell and taste us. Moreover, it draws attention to the fact we can experience ourselves as being perceived or experienced by them. We might feel ourselves being looked at, for example, and feel the eyes of the other burn into our back. This is the primary form and indeed origin of self-consciousness for Sartre (1969), but it is equally alienating and effects a fundamental alteration in our structure. It forces us out of our pre-reflective ease, generating anxiety and making us acutely self-conscious. He illustrates this with reference to a character who, having been peaking through a key hole hears footsteps behind and realises that they, too, are being watched. As they are looking through the key hole, uninterrupted, Sartre suggests, the individual simply is the gaze. They simply are the doing of looking and have no self-consciousness. But the sound of the footsteps of the other changes all of this:

> Someone is looking at me! What does this mean? It means that I am suddenly affected in my being and that essential modifications appear in my structure ... I now exist as *myself* for my unreflective consciousness ... I see myself because somebody sees me ... (Sartre 1969: 260)

What Young adds to this notion is the observation that women, in particular, are positioned as objects of perception such they specifically become objects of unwanted attention. Moreover, this affects a woman's manner of being-in-the-world. Women cannot be comfortable 'in' their bodies in the same way as men are, she argues, and cannot enjoy the same degree of freedom of movement, because their bodies are objectified in a patriarchal culture and are experienced as such. Women are made to feel uncomfortable in their bodies, just as Sartre's peeping tom is, because they feel themselves captured and caught up in the gaze of the other.

Interestingly, a very similar point is raised in relation to black men by Fanon (1986) (who was also greatly influenced by Sartre and Merleau-Ponty):

> In the white world the man of colour encounters difficulties in the development of his bodily schema. Consciousness of the body is solely a negating activity. It is a third person consciousness. The body is surrounded by an atmosphere of certain uncertainty. I know that if I want to smoke I shall have to reach out my right arm and take the pack of cigarettes lying at the other end of the table. The matches, however, are in the draw on the left, and shall have to lean back slightly. (Fanon 1986: 111)

The action of the black man, at least prior to the emergence of black power and black consciousness raising was inhibited by the watchful gaze of the (white) other.

What I argued with respect to reflexivity and reflection in the first part of this chapter should suffice to indicate that there is nothing inevitable about these processes and that social agents need not necessarily be passive parties to them. Agents have the capacity to turn back upon their habits and practices, to reflect upon them and ultimately therefore to change them. Indeed, the fact that both Young and Fanon were able to formulate these critiques is evidence enough of this possibility.

Notwithstanding this, as both authors acknowledge, their critiques are aimed at extremely pervasive forms of power, forms which can come to invest even the most critically inclined of agents.

Conclusion

In the first part of this chapter, building upon my critical reflections regarding habit and the theory of practice (Chapters 6 and 7), I discussed the habitual and corporeal basis of reflective and reflexive thought. My aim was twofold. I wanted to counterbalance the emphasis upon the pre-reflective in the work of Bourdieu and Merleau-Ponty by flagging up the mundane and everyday forms of reflection and reflexivity woven into the social fabric, but I also wanted to establish, contrary to Bourdieu's claim that habit is only one modality of human action and that we are 'empirical' in only three quarters of our being, that reflexivity and reflection are themselves rooted in habit. This is not to deny that they free us, to a degree, from our habits and traditions, but it does challenge the notion that their source is anything other than habit and tradition. When human agents take up a reflective or reflexive posture they do not thereby cease to be creatures of habit.

The conception of reflection and reflexivity that I am using here is inter-subjective and is rooted in conceptions advocated by Mead (1967), Merleau-Ponty (1962) and ultimately Hegel (1979). I view reflection and reflexivity as achievements of a process tending from the individual or particular, towards the universal and social. To be reflective or reflexive is to transcend one's own particularity and we do this by assuming the role of others, particular, but more importantly, generalised others. The implication of this view is that progress can only be achieved through an openness to otherness and, thereby, further transcendence of particularity. However, this is an ideal rather than a concrete historical description. The desire for recognition which motivates us to participate in the social world simultaneously motivates multiple struggles for recognition, which in turn give rise to multiple forms of domination. There is no reason to follow Hegel in believing that these struggles and forms of domination will, of necessity, be dialectically resolved. The direction of history, such as there is one, is a contingent matter.

In the second part of this chapter I have attempted to reflect upon some of these various forms of domination and the ways in which they enter into the habits, reflexive and otherwise, which constitute us as social agents. I have argued that the limits of our reflexivity are the limits of our social world and that what we are and can be for ourselves is shaped by what we are for others, what we are in the schemas and collective representations of our society. Furthermore, I have attempted to map out the ways in which these representations are incorporated within our corporeal schemas in the form of habits.

The conclusions to this discussion need not be too pessimistic. Although the reality of forms of domination and their embodiment is only too apparent, so too is the resistance to those forms, in social movements, protests and 'identity politics'. There may be no final dialectical resolution awaiting us at the end of history but there is certainly always a dialogical interplay of claim and counter-claim, position and counter-position. The realm of social representations is not singular and forms of domination are seldom total or complete. Were there space this might lead us to consider the way in which resistance, and not just forms of domination, takes root in the body. As it is, that task must be deferred.

Notes

1. The I is 'socialised nature', which is to say nature transformed in various ways through participation in a social world: a natural appetite for nourishment, for example, which has been channelled into a desire for specific types of food, at specific times, eaten in specific ways.

2. Monty Python were a cult comedy team from the UK. The sketch referred to involves a lumberjack singing about his lifestyle and preferences. He begins in a typically 'masculine' way but this soon gives way to reveal his deeper feminine and transexual sides. Monty Python did a very similar sketch involving soldiers on a parade ground and, indeed, did 'grotesque' parodies of many of the more serious aspects of life including philosophy and sociology.

AFTERWORD: EMBODIED AGENCY AND THE THEORY OF PRACTICE

This book has focused upon two overlapping issues: mind–body dualism and the social theory of practice. The theme of dualism was dealt with, primarily, in Chapters 2 through 5. In these chapters I sought to explore the basis and nature of the dualist's argument; to challenge the claim that 'the brain' is the answer to the riddle of dualism; and to develop an alternative which focuses upon embodied agency. To achieve this alternative, I argued, we need both to exorcise the 'ghost' from the machine and also to challenge the portrayal of the body as a machine. I used the work of Gilbert Ryle, in particular, to challenge the ghost myth, and I identified Merleau-Ponty's work as the most effective challenge to the machine myth. Together these two writers allow us to conceive of the mental life of human beings in terms of an interaction of purposive behaviours, intelligent dispositions, meaningful configurations of sensation and the contexts of action and interaction in which these are embedded. Moreover, Merleau-Ponty in particular gives us a sense of the sensuous nature of human agency; that is, of our perceptions, desires and emotions.

Chapters 6, 7 and 8 focused most squarely upon Bourdieu's theory of practice and particularly his concept of the habitus. This theory of practice is, in my view, the most persuasive framework in contemporary sociology and it is not guilty of many of the problems which have been identified with it. There are problems with it, however, and my aim was both to outline those problems and to consider how they can be resolved in a manner which preserves the value of Bourdieu's approach. In particular, drawing upon the work of Merleau-Ponty, Husserl and Mead, I introduced: a notion of creative or generative praxis to explain how habits are formed, modified and transformed; a notion of reflective and reflexive habits which allows us to avoid positioning habit, problematically, relative to other non-habitual bases of agency in a dualistic schema; and a notion of apperception which allowed us to explore in more detail the manner in which habits shape our perceptions and conceptions. Furthermore, I suggested that Merleau-Ponty's detailed critique of both mechanistic determinism and the (Sartrean) notion of absolute freedom allows us to put a considerable amount more meat upon Bourdieu's contention that the habitus transcends the problematic dichotomy which has formed between these two alternatives within social scientific thought. Merleau-Ponty lends some philosophical depth to Bourdieu's important sociological endeavours.

The substantive links that have emerged in our exploration of these two themes, dualism and the theory of practice, are, I hope, evident. Bourdieu quite clearly aims to offer an embodied sociology and the practical and habitual/dispositional conception of the agent which he arrives at in his attempt to steer a path through problematic sociological dualisms (for example, agency and structure) is very close to that which Ryle and Merleau-Ponty arrive at in their effort to forge a path between equally problematic philosophical dualisms (for example, mind–body, subject–object). These two lines of argument and inquiry are parallel without becoming identical, however, and it is for this reason that they can be mutually informing. In particular I believe that Bourdieu offers us a path for developing the insights of Merleau-Ponty and Ryle into the sociological domain, whilst Ryle and Merleau-Ponty afford us a basis from which to strengthen, deepen and clarify the philosophical nature of Bourdieu's approach. More particularly, Merleau-Ponty and Ryle afford us an opportunity to exorcise some of the problems we find in Bourdieu. Bourdieu's work owes much to Merleau-Ponty and to the anglophone philosophical tradition to which Ryle belonged but some of the loose threads that I have identified in his work, and yanked upon, indicate a failure to fully carry through the implications of their insights. This is a costly failure since it lands one back in the same kind of dilemmas that they were busy helping us out of. We see this clearly, for example, when Bourdieu claims that human beings are 'empirical in three-quarters of their being'. This claim raises the prospect of a return to such dualisms as the transcendental/empirical distinction, if not also mind–body dualism. By constructing a dialogue between the work of Bourdieu and that of both Merleau-Ponty and Ryle we can see how it is possible to avoid these problems without taking steps which violate the assumptions of Bourdieu's approach. Indeed, in many respects we are led to extend Bourdieu's basic insights about the habitus even further than he has done.

I hope that this book will be read both as a step towards a sociological solution to the problem of dualism and as a sympathetically critical reflection upon some of the basic assumptions and concepts in Bourdieu's theory of practice. More importantly, however, I hope it will be read as a study which reflects upon the mutual implications of these two problematics for each other and suggests an integrated way of dealing with both.

BIBLIOGRAPHY

Alexander, J. (1995) *Fin de Siécle Social Theory*, London, Verso, 128–17.

Austin, J. (1971) *How To Do Things With Words*, Oxford, Oxford University Press.

Bakhtin, M. (1984) *Rabelais and His World*, Bloomington, Indiana University Press.

Barthes, R. (1973) *Elements of Semiology*, New York, Hill and Wang.

Benjamin, J. (1991) *The Bonds of Love*, London, Virago.

Blumer, H. (1969) 'Collective Behaviour', in McClung-Lee, A. (1969) *Principles of Sociology*, New York, Barnes and Noble, 67–121.

Blumer, H. (1986) *Symbolic Interactionism*, Berkeley, University of California Press.

Bourdieu, P. (1977) *Outline of a Theory of Practice*, Cambridge, Cambridge University Press.

Bourdieu, P. (1978) 'Sport and Social Class', *Social Science Information*, 17, 819–40.

Bourdieu, P. (1984) *Distinction*, London, RKP.

Bourdieu, P. (1986a) *Homo Academicus*, Cambridge, Polity.

Bourdieu, P. (1986b) 'What Makes a Social Class?', *Berkeley Journal of Sociology*, 32, 1–18.

Bourdieu, P. (1990) *In Other Words*, Cambridge, Polity.

Bourdieu, P. (1992a) *The Logic of Practice*, Cambridge, Polity.

Bourdieu, P. (1992b) *Language and Symbolic Power*, Cambridge, Polity.

Bourdieu, P. (1993) *Sociology in Question*, London, Sage.

Bourdieu, P. (1996) *The State Nobility*, Cambridge, Polity.

Bourdieu, P. (1998a) *Practical Reason*, Cambridge, Polity.

Bourdieu, P. (1998b) *On Television and Journalism*, London, Pluto.

Bourdieu, P. (2000) 'The Politics of Protest' (Interview), *Socialist Review* (June), 18–20.

Bourdieu, P., Darbel, A. and Schnapper, D. (1990) *The Love of Art*, Cambridge, Polity.

Bourdieu, P. and Haakce, H. (1995) *Free Exchange*, Cambridge, Polity.

Bourdieu, P. and Passeron, J. (1996) *Reproduction*, London, Sage.

Bourdieu, P. and Wacquant, L. (1992) *An Invitation to Reflexive Sociology*, Cambridge, Polity.

Brett, N. (1981) 'Human Habits', *Canadian Journal of Philosophy*, XI (3), 357–76.

Burkitt, I. (1999) *Bodies of Thought*, London, Sage.

Busfield, J. (1986) *Managing Madness*, London, Unwin Hyman.

Button, G., Coulter, J., Lee, J. and Sharrock, W. (1995) *Computers, Mind and Conduct*, Cambridge, Polity.

Buytendijk, F. (1974) *Prolegomena to an Anthropological Physiology*, Pittsburg, Duquesne University Press.

Camic, C. (1986) 'The Matter of Habit', *American Journal of Sociology*, 91, 1039–87.

Carruthers, P. (1986) *Introducing Persons*, London, Routledge.

Cooley, C. (1902) *Human Nature and the Social Order*, New York, Charles Scribner's Sons.

Coulter, J. (1979) *The Social Construction of Mind*, London, Macmillan.

Coulter, J. (1982) 'Remarks of the Conceptualisation of Social Structure', *Philosophy of the Social Sciences*, 12, 33–46.

Coulter, J. (1983) *Re-thinking Cognitive Theory*, London, Macmillan.

Crane, M. (ed.) (1996) *Dispositions: A Debate*, London, Routledge.

Crossley, N. (1994) *The Politics of Subjectivity: Between Foucault and Merleau-Ponty*, Aldershot, Avebury.

Crossley, N. (1995a) 'Merleau-Ponty, the Elusive Body and Carnal Sociology', *Body and Society*, 1 (1), 43–66.

Crossley, N. (1995b) 'Body Techniques, Agency and Intercorporeality', *Sociology*, 29 (1), 133–50.

Crossley, N. (1996a) *Intersubjectivity: the fabric of social becoming*, London, Sage.

Crossley, N. (1996b) 'Body-Subject/Body-Power', *Body and Society*, 2 (2), 91–116.

Crossley, N. (1998a) 'Emotion and Communicative Action', in Bendelow, G. and Williams, S. (1998) *Emotions in Social Life*, London, Routledge, 16–38.

Crossley, N. (1998b) 'R.D. Laing and the British Anti-Psychiatry Movement: A Socio-Historical Analaysis', *Social Science and Medicine*, 47, 877–89.

Crossley, N. (1999a) 'Fish, Field, Habitus and Madness: On the First Wave Mental Health Users in Britain', *British Journal of Sociology*, 50 (4), 647–70.

Crossley, N. (1999b) 'Working Utopias and Social Movements: An Investigation using Case Study Materials from Radical Mental Health Movements in Britain', *Sociology*, 33 (4), 809–30.

Crossley, N. (2000a) 'Emotions, Psychiatry and Social Order', in Williams, S., Gabe, J. and Calnan, M. (2000) *Health, Medicine and Society*, London, Routledge, 277–95.

Crossley, N. (2000b) 'Radical and Egological Intersubjectivity', *The Journal of Existential Analysis*, 11 (2).

Crossley, N. (2001 – forthcoming) 'Merleau-Ponty', in Elliot, A. and Turner, B. (2001) *Profiles in Contemporary Social Theory*, London, Sage.

Dawkins, R. (1976) *The Selfish Gene*, Oxford, Oxford University Press.

Descartes, R. (1968) *Discourse on Method and The Meditations*, Harmondsworth, Penguin.

Dewey, J. (1988) *Human Nature and Conduct*, Carbondale, Southern Illinois University Press.

Dreyfus, H. (1993) *Being-in-the-World*, Cambridge, MIT Press.

Dreyfus, H. and Rabinow, P. (1993) 'Can There Be a Science of Existential Structure and Social Meaning?' in Calhoun, C., LiPuma, E. and Postone, M. (1993) *Bourdieu: Critical Perspectives*, Cambridge, Polity, 35–45.

Durkheim, E. (1915) *The Elementary Forms of Religious Life*, New York, Free Press.

Durkheim, E. (1974) *Sociology and Philosophy*, New York, Free Press.

Durkheim, E. (1982) *The Rules of Sociological Method*, New York, Free Press.

Elias, N. (1978) *What is Sociology?* London, Hutchinson.

Elias, N. (1984) *The Civilising Process*, Oxford, Blackwell.

Elster, J. (1989) *Nuts and Bolts for the Social Sciences*, Cambridge, Cambridge University Press.

Evans, F. (1993) *Psychology and Nihilism*, New York, SUNY.

Fanon, F. (1986) *Black Skin, White Masks*, London, Pluto.

Fodor, G. (1968) *Psychological Explanation*, New York, Random House.

Freud, S. (1973) *Introductory Lectures on Psychoanalysis*, (Pelican Freud Library Vol. 1) Harmondsworth, Penguin.

Freud, S. (1985) *Civilisation, Society and Religion*, (Pelican Freud Library Vol. 12) Harmondsworth, Penguin.

Gagnon, J. and Simon, W. (1973) *Sexual Conduct*, London, Hutchinson.

Gallagher, S. and Cole, J. (1998) 'Body Image and Body Schema', in Welton, D. (1998) *Body and Flesh*, Oxford, Blackwell, 131–48.

Garfinkel, H. (1967) *Studies in Ethnomethodology*, New Jersey, Prentice-Hall.

Gibson, J. (1979) *The Ecological Approach to Visual Perception*, Boston, Houghton Mifflin.

Giddens, A. (1984) *The Constitution of Society*, Cambridge, Polity.

Giddens, A. (1991) *Modernity and Self-Identity*, Cambridge, Polity.

Giddens, A. (1992) *The Transformation of Intimacy*, Cambridge, Polity.

Goffman, E. (1959) *Presentation of Self in Everyday Life*, Harmondsworth, Penguin.

Goffman, E. (1972) *Relations in Public*, Harmondsworth, Penguin.

Goldstein, K. (2000) *The Organism*, New York, Zone.

Grosz, E. (1994) *Volatile Bodies*, Bloomington and Indianapolis, Indiana University Press.

Habermas, J. (1987) *The Theory of Communicative Action Vol. II*, Cambridge, Polity.

Habermas, J. (1988) *Legitimation Crisis*, Cambridge, Polity.

Habermas, J. (1989) *Structural Transformation of the Public Sphere*, Cambridge, Polity.

Hegel, G. (1979) *The Phenomenology of Spirit*, Oxford University Press, Oxford.

Heidegger, M. (1962) *Being and Time*, Oxford, Blackwell.

Heritage, J. (1984) *Garfinkel and Ethnomethodology*, Cambridge, Polity.

Hobbes, T. (1968) *Leviathan*, Harmondsworth, Penguin.

Hochschild, A. (1983) *The Managed Heart*, Berkeley, University of California Press.

Hollis, M. (1994) *The Philosophy of Social Science*, Cambridge, Cambridge University Press.

Homans, G. (1961) *Social Behaviour*, London, RKP.

Honneth, A. (1995) *The Struggle For Recognition*, Cambridge, Polity.

Hughes, A. and Witz, A. (1997) 'Feminism and the Matter of Bodies: From de Beauvoir to Butler', *Body and Society*, 3 (1), 47–61.

Huizinga, J. (1950) *Homo Ludens*, Boston, Beacon.

Husserl, E. (1970) *The Crisis of the European Sciences and Transcendental Phenomenology*, Evanston, Northwestern University Press.

Husserl, E. (1973) *Experience and Judgement*, Evanston, Northwestern University Press.

Husserl, E. (1989) *Ideas Pertaining to a Pure Phenomenology and to a Phenomenological Philosophy; Second Book*, Dordrecht, Kluwer.

Husserl, E. (1991) *Cartesian Meditations*, Dordrecht, Kluwer.

Jenkins, R. (1982) 'Pierre Bourdieu and the Reproduction of Determinism', *Sociology*, 16 (2), 270–81.

Joas, H. (1985) *G.H. Mead*, Cambridge, Polity.

Joas, H. (1996) *The Creativity of Action*, Cambridge, Polity.

Kant, I. (1933) *Critique of Pure Reason*, London, Macmillan.

Kant, I. (1948) *The Moral Law: Groundwork of a Metaphysic of Morals*, London, Routledge.

Kant, I. (1993) *Critique of Practical Reason*, New Jersey, Prentice Hall.

Kogler, H-H. (1997) 'Alienation as an Epistemological Source', in *Social Epistemology*, 11 (2), 141–64.

Kojéve, A. (1969) *Introduction to the Reading of Hegel*, New York, Basic Books.

Kuhn, T. (1970) *The Structure of Scientific Revolutions*, Chicago, Chicago University Press.

Lacan, J. (1989) *Ecrits*, London, Routledge.

Leder, D. (1998) 'A Tale of Two Bodies', in Welton, D. (1998) *Body and Flesh*, Oxford, Blackwell, 117–30.

Lemert, E. (1951) *Social Pathology*, New York, McGraw-Hill.

Levins, R. and Lewontin, R. (1985) *The Dialectical Biologist*, Cambridge MA, Harvard University Press.

Lewontin, R. (1993) *The Doctrine of DNA*, Harmondsworth, Penguin.

Mauss, M. (1979) *Sociology and Psychology*, London, RKP.

McNay, L. (1999) 'Gender, Habitus and the Field', *Theory, Culture and Society*, 16 (1), 95–117.

Mead, G. (1967) *Mind, Self and Society*, Chicago, Chicago University Press.

Merleau-Ponty, M. (1962) *The Phenomenology of Perception*, London, RKP.

Merleau-Ponty, M. (1964) *Signs*, Evanston, Northwestern University Press.

Merleau-Ponty, M. (1965) *The Structure of Behaviour*, London, Methuen.

Merleau-Ponty, M. (1968a) *The Visible and the Invisible*, Evanston, Northwestern University Press.

Merleau-Ponty, M. (1968b) *The Primacy of Perception and Other Essays*, Evanston, Northwestern University Press.

Merleau-Ponty, M. (1969) *Human and Terror*, Beacon, Boston.

Merleau-Ponty, M. (1971) *Sense and Non-Sense*, Evanston, Northwestern University Press.

Merleau-Ponty, M. (1973) *Adventures of the Dialectic*, Evanston, Northwestern University Press.

Merleau-Ponty, M. (1974) *The Prose of the World*, London, Heinemann.

Merleau-Ponty, M. (1988) *In Praise of Philosophy* and *Themes From the Lectures at the College De France*, Evanston, Northwestern University Press.

Merleau-Ponty, M. (1992) *Texts and Dialogues*, New Jersey, Humanities Press.

Mills, C. (1974) *Power, Politics and People: the Collected Essays of C.W. Mills*, London, Oxford University Press.

Nyiri, J. and Smith, B. (1988) *Practical Knowledge*, London, Croom Held.

Oakley, A. (1972) *Sex, Gender and Society*, London, Temple Smith.

O'Neill, J. (1989) *The Communicative Body*, Evanston, Northwestern University Press.

Orwell, G. (1962) *The Road to Wigan Pier*, Harmondsworth, Penguin.

Ostrow, J. (1981) Culture as a Fundamental Dimension of Experience, *Human Studies*, 4, 279–97.

Ostrow, J. (1990) *Social Sensitivity: A Study of Habit and Experience*, New York, SUNY.

Parsons, T. (1951) *The Social System*, New York, Free Press.

Parsons, T. (1966) *Societies*, New Jersey, Prentice Hall.

Parsons, T. (1968) *The Structure of Social Action* (2 Vols), New York, Free Press.

Pavlov, I. (1911) *Conditioned Reflexes*, Oxford, Oxford University Press.

Polanyi, M. (1966) *The Tacit Dimension*, Garden City, Doubleday.

Popper, K. (1969) *Conjectures and Refutations*, London, RKP.

Popper, K. (1972) *Objective Knowledge*, Oxford, Oxford University Press.

Porter, R. (1987) *Mind Forg'd Manacles*, Harmondsworth, Penguin.

Romanyshyn, R. (1982) *Psychological Life*, Milton Keynes, Open University Press.

Rose, N. (1989) *Governing the Soul*, London, Routledge.

Rose, S., Lewontin, R. and Kamin, L. (1984) *Not in Our Genes*, Harmondsworth, Penguin.

Ryle, G. (1949) *The Concept of Mind*, Harmondsworth, Penguin.

Ryle, G. (1969) *Dilemmas*, Cambridge, Cambridge University Press.

Sacks, O. (1984) *A Leg to Stand On*, London, Picador.

Sacks, O. (1985) *The Man Who Mistook His Wife For a Hat*, London, Picador.

Sahlins, M. (1977) *The Use and Abuse of Biology*, London, Tavistock.

Sartre, J-P. (1969) *Being and Nothingness*, London, Routledge.

Sartre, J-P. (1972) *The Psychology of Imagination*, London, Methuen.

Sartre, J-P. (1993) *The Emotions: Outline of A Theory*, New York, Citadel.

Sayer, A. (1999) 'Bourdieu, Smith and Disinterested Judgement', *The Sociological Review*, 47 (3), 403–31.

Schutz, A. (1970) *Reflections on the Problem of Relevance*, New Haven, Yale University Press.

Schutz, A. (1972) *The Phenomenology of the Social World*, Evanston, Northwestern University Press.

Scull, A. (1993) *The Most Solitary of Afflictions*, New Haven, Yale University Press.

Searle, J. (1969) *Speech Acts*, Cambridge, Cambridge University Press.

Searle, J. (1983) *Intentionality*, Cambridge, Cambridge University Press.

Searle, J. (1991) *Minds, Brains and Science*, Harmondsworth, Penguin.

Sharpe, S. (1976) *Just Like a Girl*, Harmondsworth, Penguin.

Shaw, G. (1957) *Pygmalion*, London, Longman.

Shilling, C. (1991) 'Educating the Body', *Sociology*, 25, 653–72.

Shilling, C. (1992) 'Schooling and the Production of Physical Capital', *Discourse*, 13 (1), 1–19.

Shilling, C. (1993) *The Body and Social Theory*, London, Sage.

Skinner, B. (1971) *Beyond Freedom and Dignity*, Harmondsworth, Penguin.

Stratton, G. (1896) 'Some Preliminary Experiments on Vision Without the Inversion of the Retinal Image', *Psychological Review*, 3, 611–17.

Stratton, G. (1897) 'Vision Without Inversion of the Retinal Image', *Psychological Review*, 4, 341–60 and 463–81.

Sudnow, D. (1993) *Ways of the Hand*, Cambridge, MIT.

Synnott, A. (1993) *The Body Social*, London, Routledge.

Taylor, C. (1993) 'To Follow a Rule', in Calhoun, C., LiPuma, E. and Postone, M. (1998) *Bourdieu: Critical Perspectives*, Cambridge, Polity, 45–60.

Turner, B. (1984) *Body and Society*, Oxford, Blackwell.

Turner, B. (1992) *Regulating Bodies*, London, Routledge.

Wacquant, L. (1993) 'Bourdieu in America', in Calhoun, C., LiPuma, E. and Postone, M. (1993) *Bourdieu: Critical Perspectives*, Cambridge, Polity, 235–62.

Wacquant, L. (1995) 'Pugs at Work', *Body and Society*, 1 (1), 65–94.

Watson, J. (1930) *Behaviourism*, Chicago, University of Chicago Press.

Weber, M. (1978) *Economy and Society*, New York, Bedminster Press.

Williams, S. and Bendelow, G. (1998) *The Lived Body*, London, Routledge.

Winch, P. (1958) *The Idea of a Social Science*, London, RKP.

Wittgenstein, L. (1953) *Philosophical Investigations*, Oxford, Blackwell.

Wittgenstein, L. (1969) *On Certainty*, Oxford, Blackwell.

Witz, A. (2000) 'Whose Body Matters?', *Body and Society*, 5.

Wrong, D. (1961) 'The Oversocialised Conception of Man in Modern Sociology', *American Sociological Review*, 26, 183–93.

Young, I. (1980) 'Throwing Like a Girl', *Human Studies*, 3, 137–56.

INDEX

action/practice
  Bourdieu's theory of, 91, 93–6
    criticisms of, 110–14, 115–18
  language as, 41–2
  Merleau-Ponty on habit and,
    120–1, 136–7
  and mind–body interaction, 20
  structuralist concept of, 92–3
  theme of embodied practice,
    3–5, 161–2
  see also agency; behaviour
aesthetic dispositions, 95
agency
  and behaviourism, 65–70, 74
  and Bourdieu's work, 94, 95–6,
    115, 116–17
  habit, freedom and, 133–5, 136
  and mind–brain identity
    theory, 23–4
  see also action/practice;
    emotion; perception;
    reflection and reflexivity
agitations, 45
Alexander, J., 110, 111
apperception, 130–2
art, consumption of, 105
Austin, J., 105

Bakhtin, M., 156
behaviour
  emotion as, 84
  and perception, 74–9
  and understanding, 49
behaviourism, 63–70, 74,
    121, 125–7
'black holes' in brain, 13, 30–2
body
  being and having, 140
  Descartes' concept of, 10–11,
    34–5
  problems of doubting, 15–17
  machine myth of see
    machine myth
  see also embodiment;
    mind–body dualism
body modification, 107–9
Bourdieu, Pierre
  concept of capital, 96–9
  and concept of desire, 102–4
  concept of field, 99–101
  concept of habitus, 4, 92–5
  criticisms of, 109–18, 136, 149
  and embodiment of
    difference, 153–4, 155
  games metaphor, 78, 88,
    100–1, 103–4, 110–11
  invisible dynamics of fields,
    104–6

Bourdieu, Pierre, *cont.*
  and phenomenology, 118–19
  physical and embodied
    cultural capital, 106–9
  theory of practice, 91, 93–6
    criticisms of, 110–14,
    115–18
  and work of Merleau-Ponty,
    78, 91, 120, 136–8, 162
boxing, 107–9, 151–2
brain see mind–brain identity
  theory

capital
  Bourdieu's concept of, 96–9
  embodiment of cultural,
    106–9
  embodiment of symbolic,
    151–2
  relationship with field,
    97, 101
Carruthers, P., 23, 35
category error, dualism as,
    39–41
choice, 117, 118, 134, 136
  see also decision-making
class, 96–9, 153–4
cognitive science, 33–4, 50–1
competence, 52, 94–5, 106–7
computational model of mind,
    33, 50–1
consciousness
  and agency, 23–4
  and meanings, 31, 32
  and perception, 46–8, 73–4
  problem of self-
    consciousness, 141–4
  Ryle's concept of, 46–8
  see also reflection and
    reflexivity; unconscious
constitutive rules, 92
Cooley, C., 143, 144
corporeal schema, 121–5
  and habit, 125–8
creation see innovation
critical perspective, in
  Bourdieu's work, 113–15
cultural capital, 96–7, 106–9
cultural transmission, 24, 33
  see also learning
culture, and nature, 128–30

Dawkins, R., 24, 33
decision-making, 28–30, 130
Descartes, René
  dualism of, 8–11
    as category error, 39–41
    context, 8, 11, 39

Descartes, René
  dualism of, *cont.*
    as ghost in machine, 10–11
    philosophical problems of,
      12–17
    sociological critique of,
      19–20
    sociological implications of,
      17–19
  and self-consciousness, 141
desire
  Bourdieu and concept of,
    102–4
  Merleau-Ponty's concept
    of, 86
  for recognition, 87–8, 102–3
  theme of, 6–7
determinism, in Bourdieu's
  work, 111–12, 115, 116
dialogue with self see reflection
  and reflexivity
difference (embodiment of),
    150–5
  gender, 155–9
  dispositions, 44–5, 49–50,
    53–5, 94–5, 99
  domination, and capital, 97,
    98–9
doxa, 99, 112–13
dreams, 47
dualism see mind–body dualism
Durkheim, E., 4–5, 22, 147

economic capital, 96, 97
education, and cultural capital,
    96–7
embodied cultural capital,
    106–9
embodied meaning, 30–2
embodied practice, theme of,
    3–5, 161–2
embodiment
  of difference, 150–5
    gender, 155–9
  of language, 80
  of perception, 71–4
  see also corporeal schema;
    reflexive embodiment
emotion, 42–5, 84–6
esprit de corps, 124
ethnomethodology, 104–5, 133
expectation, and habit, 130–3

Fanon, F., 158
feeling, and emotions, 42–4
field
  Bourdieu's concept of,
    99–101

field, *cont.*
  of boxing, 107–9
  and capital, 97, 101
  criticisms of habitus and,
    110–11, 115–16
  and desire for recognition,
    102–3
  games metaphor, 78, 88,
    100–1, 103–4, 110–11
  invisible dynamics of, 104–6
folk psychology, 26–7
football, action and perception,
  74–9
freedom, and habit, 133–5, 136
Freud, S., 86

Galileo, 39
games
  and corporeal schema, 124–5
  football action and
    perception, 74–9
  as metaphor for fields, 78, 88,
    100–1, 103–4, 110–11
  norms, laws and, 146
  see also play
gender, embodiment of, 155–9
ghost in the machine, 10–11,
  60–1
  see also mind–body dualism
Giddens, A., 147
goals, and mind–brain identity
  theory, 29–30
Goldstein, K., 86
grotesque realism, 156
groups
  and construction of self, 146
  and corporeal schema, 124
  and habitus, 94, 133

Habermas, J., 99
habit
  behaviourist concept of,
    125–7
  compared with disposition,
    53, 54
  and expectation, 130–3
  and freedom, 133–5, 136
  Merleau-Ponty's concept of
    action and, 120–1, 136–7
  corporeal schema and,
    125–8
  reflection, reflexivity and,
    137–8, 149–50, 159
  theme of, 3–4
habitual schemas, 72–3
habituation
  and innovation, 129–30, 137
  meaning, purpose and, 133
  Merleau-Ponty's theory of,
    128–30
  play, reflection and, 145
habitus
  Bourdieu's concept of, 4, 92–5
  capital, class and, 98
  criticisms of, 110–11,
    115–17, 118
  field and, 101, 108
  individual and group, 94, 133
  judgement and, 130

habitus, *cont.*
  reflection, reflexivity and,
    137–8
  structures and practice, 95–6,
    115–16
Hegel, G., 102
hexis, 154–5, 156–7
Honneth, Axel, 102
Huizinga, J., 88
Husserl, E., 14, 16, 35,
  130–3, 149

'I'
  Mead's concept of 'me' and,
    146–8
  systematic elusiveness of,
    59–60
illusio, 103, 108, 109
imagination
  and emergence of self, 144–6
  external basis of, 47
inclinations, 44–5
individual
  corporeal schema of, 124
  habitus of, 94, 133
individualism, and dualism, 18
innovation, and habituation,
  129–30, 137
intellectualism, 14–15, 33–4,
  51–3, 127–8
intention, and concept of will,
  55–6
intentionality of
  consciousness, 46
interaction, of mind and body,
  12–14, 20
interactionist sociology, 104–5
introspection
  external basis of, 58–9
  as retrospection, 59
  and systematic elusiveness of
    I, 59–60
  see also reflection and
    reflexivity

Jenkins, R., 111–12, 113–14

know-how, 52–3, 94–5
knowledge
  corporeal, 122–5
  see also know-how;
    propositional thought;
    understanding
Kogler, H-H., 113, 149
Kojéve, A., 87–8
Kuhn, T., 13

language
  as action, 41–2
  and consciousness, 47–8
  external basis of internal,
    58–9
  innovation and habituation,
    129
  mental terms, 26–7, 40, 41–5
  and problems of dualism, 18
  and shared habitus, 133
  speech, reflection and
    dialogue, 79–84, 137–8
laws, games and norms, 146

learning
  perceptions, habits and,
    72–3, 128
  see also behaviourism;
    cultural transmission
Lemert, E., 153
Levi-Strauss, C., 92–3
libido, 102
logic and reason, Descartes
  doubt of, 9
'looking glass' concept of self,
  143, 144

machine myth, 11
  in behaviourism, 63–5
  Merleau-Ponty's critique
    of, 65–70, 121
  see also mechanism
market, as metaphor for field,
  100, 104
masculinity, embodiment of,
  155–6
materialism, of mind–brain
  identity theory, 34–6
matter, body in terms of, 10,
  16, 35
'me', Mead's concept of 'I'
  and, 146–8
Mead, George Herbert
  concepts of 'I' and 'me',
    146–8
  and desire for recognition,
    87, 102
  on games, norms and
    laws, 146
  on play and self, 82–3, 144–6
  on reflexivity, 148–50
meaning
  and behaviourism, 66,
    67–8, 74
  and habituation, 133
  and mind–brain identity
    theory, 25–7, 30–2
  see also mental concepts
mechanism
  Ryle's objection to, 57–8
  see also machine myth
memes, 24, 33
mental concepts, 26–7, 40, 41–5
Merleau-Ponty, M.
  challenge to dualism, 62, 89
  challenge to machine model,
    65–70, 121
  on corporeal schema, 121–8
  and habit, 125–8
  critique of behaviourism,
    65–70, 121, 125–7
  critique of Descartes, 14,
    16–17
  on desire for recognition,
    87–8
  on emotion, sexuality and
    desire, 84–6
  on habit and action, 120–1,
    136–7
  on habit and freedom,
    133–5, 136
  on nature and culture, 128–30
  overview of work, 89

Merleau-Ponty, M., *cont.*
 on perception, 71–4
 and symbolic behaviour, 74–9
 on self-consciousness, 142–3
 on speech, reflection and
  dialogue, 79–84
 on understanding, 51
 and work of Bourdieu, 78, 91,
  120, 136–8, 162
mind
 Descartes' concept of, 10
 as ghost in machine, 10, 60–1
mind–body dualism
 as category error, 39–41
 of Descartes, 8–11
 Merleau-Ponty's challenge to,
  62, 89
 and mind–brain identity
  theory, 32–4
 philosophical problems of,
  12–17
 sociological critique of, 19–20
 sociological implications of,
  17–19
 theme of, 1–3, 161–2
mind–brain identity theory,
  23–5
 criticisms of, 22–3, 24–5, 37
 Cartesian framework, 32–4
 common sense meanings, 25–7
 reductionism, 27–30
 social meanings, 30–2
 vulgar materialism, 34–6
moods, Ryle's concept of, 45

natural attitude, 114
nature, and culture, 128–30
neuroscience, and mind–brain
  identity theory, 24, 25–7
normative rules, 92–3
norms, games and laws, 146

objective conditions, and
  subjective expectation,
  112–13

pairings, 132
Parsons, T., 92
Pavlov, I., 64
perception
 consciousness and, 46–8
 Descartes' consideration of,
  9, 14–15
 habit and expectation, 130–3
 Merleau-Ponty's theory
  of, 71–9
 and mind–body interaction, 12
 and social meaning, 31
 subjective perception and
  behaviourism, 66, 67
 symbolic behaviour and, 74–9
phenomenology
 approach to consciousness,
  46, 47
 and Bourdieu, 118–19
 critique of social
  phenomenology, 95
 and reflexivity, 138
philosophical problems of
 dualism, 12–17

physical cultural capital, 106–9
play
 and emergence of self, 83,
  144–6
 Huizinga's work on, 88
 see also games
political legitimation and
  domination, 98–9
Popper, K., 13
power, symbolic, 105–6
practice *see* action/practice
propositional thought, 14–15,
  51–2, 54–5
proprioception, 122
psychology
 folk psychology, 26–7
 see also behaviourism
public sphere, Bourdieu's
  concept of, 98–9
purpose, 69–70, 74, 133

race, and embodiment of
  difference, 158
reasons, propositional nature
  of, 54–5
recognition, desire for, 87–8,
  102–3
reductionism, in mind–brain
  identity theory, 27–30
reflection and reflexivity
 and Bourdieu's work, 113–15,
  117, 118, 137, 138, 149
 external basis of, 52, 58
 and habit, 137–8, 149–50, 159
 and Mead's work, 148–50
 in sociology, 113–15, 138, 149
 speech, dialogue and, 79–84
 theme of, 6
 see also introspection
reflexive embodiment, 140–1
 games, norms and laws, 146
 Mead's concept of 'I' and
  'me', 146–8
 role of imagination and play,
  144–6
 self-consciousness, 141–4
 see also embodiment, of
  difference
response, in behaviourism,
  68–70
retrospection, introspection
  as, 59
reversibility, 35
rules, structuralist concept of,
  92–3
Ryle, Gilbert
 on consciousness, 46–8
 critique of intellectualism, 15,
  51–2, 53
 on dispositions, 53–5
 on dualism as category error,
  39–41
 on dualism as ghost in the
  machine, 10–11
 on emotion, 42–5
 on 'I' and introspection,
  58–60
 on know-how, 51–2
 on language as action, 41–2

Ryle, Gilbert, *cont.*
 objection to mechanism, 57–8
 significance of work, 38,
  60–1, 162
 on social world, 17, 18
 on understanding, 48–51
 on will and volition, 55–6

Sartre, J–P., 85, 134, 135, 157–8
Schutz, A., 133
Searle, J., 50
self *see* 'I'; reflection and
  reflexivity; reflexive
  embodiment
self-consciousness
 problem of, 141–4
 see also consciousness
self-inspection *see* introspection;
  reflection and reflexivity
sensations, Ryle's analysis of, 46
sense *see* perception
sexuality, 86, 156
Shilling, C., 107
skill, and habitus, 94–5
social capital, 97
social class, 96–9, 153–4
social phenomenology, 95
social physics, 92
social world, as problem
  for dualism, 17–19
sociological critique of dualism,
  19–20
sociological implications of
  dualism, 17–19
sociology, reflexivity in, 113–15,
  138, 149
speech, and reflection and
  dialogue, 79–84
stimuli, in behaviourism, 66–8
stimulus-response, in
  behaviourism, 63–4, 66–70
Stratton, G., 74
structuralism, critique of, 92–3
structure, Bourdieu's theory of,
  95–6, 111–13, 115–16
sub-vocalisation, 58, 59
subjective expectation, and
  objective conditions, 112–13
symbolic behaviour, and
  perception, 74–9
symbolic capital, 97, 151–2
symbolic power, 105–6

thought *see* propositional
  thought; reflection and
  reflexivity
typification, 132–3

unconscious, 148
understanding, 48–51

volition, 55–6

Wacquant, L., 78, 107–8, 109
walking, and embodiment of
  difference, 155
will, 55–6
Wittgenstein, L., 44

Young, Iris, 157–8